Evolution and Design of Institutions

While the evolution of informal institutions is quite well understood in economic thinking, the development of consciously designed institutions has not been rigorously explored. In the New Institutional Economics, Public Choice, and Law and Economics literature the dynamic interplay between changing preferences and spontaneously evolving institutions on the one hand and the evolution of designed institutions on the other hand has been largely ignored.

Evolution and Design of Institutions assembles contributions by economists, legal scholars and psychologists in order to shed new light on these issues. The contributors analyze how designed norms influence preference behavior, examine the emergence and evolution of designed institutions and address normative approaches.

Christian Schubert is Research Associate at the Max-Planck-Institute of Economics, Jena, Germany.

Georg von Wangenheim is Professor of Law and Economics at the University of Kassel, Germany.

Studies in Global Competition

A series of books edited by John Cantwell, The University of Reading, UK and David Mowery, University of California, Berkeley, USA

Evolution and Design of Institutions

Edited by Christian Schubert and
Georg von Wangenheim

Routledge
Taylor & Francis Group

LONDON AND NEW YORK

First published 2006
by Routledge
2 Park Square, Milton Park, Abingdon, Oxon OX14 4RN

Simultaneously published in the USA and Canada
by Routledge
711 Third Ave, New York, NY 10017

Routledge is an imprint of the Taylor & Francis Group

First issued in paperback 2012

Typeset in Times New Roman by
Keyword Group Ltd

British Library Cataloguing in Publication Data
A catalogue record for this book is available from the British Library

Library of Congress Cataloging in Publication Data
Evolution and design of institutions / edited by Christian Schubert and
Georg von Wangenheim.
    p. cm.
"Contributions to an inter-disciplinary workshop that has taken place at
the Max-Planck-Institute of Economics (the former Max-Planck-Institute
for Research into Economic Systems) in Jena, Germany, in February
2004"—P.
Includes bibliographical references and index.
    1. Institutional economics—Congresses. 2. Evolutionary
economics—Congresses. 3. Economics—Psychological
aspects—Congresses. I. Schubert, Christian, 1971– II. Wangenheim,
Georg von. III. Title.
HB99.5.E957 2006   330.15′52—dc22

ISBN10: 0-415-37531-2
ISBN13: 9-78-0-415-64766-3

Contents

10   Human intentionality and design in cultural evolution   197
VIKTOR J. VANBERG

List of Figures

xii *List of Figures*

List of Tables

List of Contributors

Bruno S. Frey is Professor of Economics at the University of Zurich, Switzerland and Guest Professor at the University of St. Gallen, Switzerland.

Uta-Maria Niederle is Research Associate at the Max-Planck-Institute of Economics, Jena, Germany.

Elinor Ostrom is Arthur F. Bentley Professor of Political Science at Indiana University, Bloomington, Indiana, USA. She is also Co-Director of the Workshop in Political Theory and Policy Analysis and Co-Director of the Center for the Study of Institutions, Population, and Environmental Change, both at Indiana University.

Francesco Parisi is Professor of Law at George Mason University, Fairfax, Virginia, USA, Director of the Law and Economics Program at GMU and Co-Director of Program in Economics and the Law at the J.M. Buchanan Center for Political Economy at GMU. He is also Distinguished Professor of Law and Economics at the University of Milan, Italy.

Jan Schnellenbach is Research Associate at the University of Marburg, Germany.

Christian Schubert is Research Associate at the Max-Planck-Institute of Economics, Jena, Germany.

Tom Tyler is Professor of Psychology at New York University, USA.

Viktor J. Vanberg is Professor of Economics at the University of Freiburg and Director of the Walter-Eucken-Institute in Freiburg, Germany.

Georg von Wangenheim is Professor of Law and Economics at the University of Kassel, Germany.

Gerhard Wegner is Professor of Economics at the University of Erfurt, Germany.

Introduction

1 Institutional design, social norms and preferences in an evolving economy

Christian Schubert and Georg von Wangenheim

This book assembles contributions to an inter-disciplinary workshop that took place at the Max-Planck-Institute of Economics (the former Max-Planck-Institute for Research into Economic Systems) in Jena, Germany, in February 2004. It aimed at discussing the question how to fill a great lacuna within the research program of modern economics: How do consciously designed (or, synonymously, formal) institutions change over historical time? While the change of informal institutions has been a key concern throughout the last two centuries of economic theorizing, particularly for evolutionary economists, designed institutions, i.e., institutions that are enforced by a specialized agent or group of agents, have received much less attention. To be sure, research strands such as *Public Choice* and *Law & Economics* have analyzed legislative and judicial institutions – for the most part, however, this has been done within a methodological framework of comparative statics, based on behavioral assumptions that have been borrowed from orthodox Rational Choice theory. Hence, the puzzle of how designed institutions emerge and diffuse over time and what this implies in terms of public policy advise has still been left largely unsolved. What is clear, though, is that the mechanisms of change that are relevant here differ in a fundamental way from those that can be identified in the realm of informal institutions.

Three main avenues may be taken to approach this question. All three can be studied in this book and start from a very intuitive idea: To understand how formal institutions change, it is worth studying the dynamic interplay between designed institutions on the one hand and informal institutions (as a key determinant of individual behavior) on the other hand.

In order to examine this interplay, we have to understand, first, how designed institutions influence individual preferences. In Chapter 2, Bruno S. Frey (University of Zürich) dwells on insights from economic psychology to describe how changes of very broad designed institutions like the general structure of the state – in particular the rise and fall of dictatorships – affects people's apprehension of less formal institutions like markets. Following well established insights in psychology, he argues that individuals either align their preferences with the current environment to reduce cognitive dissonance or strengthen opposing preferences when state activities are felt to be controlling. For the case of dictatorships this means either that individuals tend to glorify the past after the dictatorship has decayed, or that they will revolt against a dictatorship once its suppressive power increases beyond a rather high threshold. When markets are newly introduced, again both reactions are possible: opposition to markets may prevail or an extreme pro-market creed may break its path.

In Chapter 3, Francesco Parisi (George Mason University) and Georg von Wangenheim (University of Kassel) deal with more specific rules when they discuss how legal norms may fail to influence people's norms and actions due to countervailing social norms. They develop a model which reflects how social norms form in the interaction of individuals complying with, and violating what other individuals think to be the social norm in a particular field of behavior. By allowing for several alternative social norms for one field of behavior, e.g., consumption of various drugs from cigarettes and alcohol to heroin and crack, they are able to study how legal norms may interfere with the process of social norms formation. They are particularly interested in countervailing effects of legal norms on social norms. By these countervailing effects, social norms may evolve in the opposite direction than intend by new law when the latter is too distant from the former. To overcome these effects, Parisi and Wangenheim propose piecemeal legislation in which the law only slightly deviates from the social norms of most people at the beginning, thus influences them in the desired direction, and may eventually become more extreme in a stepwise manner always remaining close enough to the current state of social norms. Since they describe social norms only in the dimension of which actions are allowed and which are not, an alternative way to circumvent countervailing effects seem to be large enough sanctions to enforce the law. If one includes the appropriate sanction to enforce social or legal norms as a second dimension, this alternative is likely to lose its viability.

Chapter 4 by Tom Tyler (New York University) offers a comparison of incentives and sanctions ("instrumental motivation") on the one hand and preferences for general or specific rule following ("social motivation") on the other hand as alternative ways of enforcing designed institutions. He compares the two motivations in four respects: (1) legitimacy of rule makers or enforcers is an important determinant of efficacy of rules; (2) closely linked to, and underlying legitimacy is fairness in the procedures of making and enforcing rules; procedural fairness seems to be more important than outcome-oriented distributive justice or similar concepts; (3) trust in officials enforcing (or making) rules promotes acceptance of these rules far more if such trust refers to the motives of the officials rather than to the predictability of their actions; (4) identification with the group supports following those rules which are to the benefit of the group. Tyler shows and concludes that "social motivations" outperform "instrumental motivations" (i.e., traditional incentive and sanction based models) in inducing cooperation necessary to overcome social dilemmas. The argument is based on a wide overview of relevant social psychological literature.

In its second part, the book turns to questions concerning the emergence and evolution of designed institutions. Chapter 5, by Uta-Maria Niederle (Max-Planck-Institute of Economics at Jena), discusses how preferences change in the course of time as a consequence of technological progress, learning and habituation.

Based on the distinction between, on the one hand, preferences for consumption goods and, on the other hand, preferences that are related to social interaction, she shows that in order to understand how formal, designed institutions change we need to know how preferences, or rather attitudes, related to social interaction (i.e., to institutions) evolve over time. Only if one understands the latter and their basis in the genetic endowment of man, is it possible to study how newly designed and formal institutions receive the necessary support they need for their implementation and their enforcement.

Based on a thorough description of how the institutions of Indian irrigation systems change, Elinor Ostrom (University of Indiana at Bloomington) classifies the huge number of rules that may guide behavior in common dilemmas into rules on participation, rules on allocating positions among participants, rules on allowable actions, payoff rules, and a last category comprising such diverse rules as rules on information, rules on the scope of exploitation of the resource, and requirements to harvest in teams. In her view, the rules governing a common pool resource (and any other social interaction) are too complex to be optimized by one-step design. Designing institutions is thus always experimenting by tinkering on a small sub-set of all relevant rules. Perfect prediction of the results is impossible. This problem becomes aggravated by the ever-changing natural (and economic and social) environment of all societies. Complexity not only affects outside observers of rule systems but also any in-group authority that is engaged in the purposeful design of rules. Emergence of rules, be they spontaneous or designed, should thus be conceptualized as an evolutionary process whose understanding requires knowledge of the system's environment, its adaptation mechanisms, and a measure of performance which feeds back into the adaptation mechanisms.

In Chapter 7, Jan Schnellenbach (University of Marburg) further elaborates on the incremental quality of institutional change. He shows that newly designed institutions are necessarily always a blend of already existing institutions and some new aspects. In particular, the evolution of consciously designed formal institutions is likely to be constrained by informal institutions (i.e., reliable modes of cooperation) that in turn are assumed to be stable in the short term. On this basis, Schnellenbach conceptualizes formal institutional change as *syncretic* change, i.e., as the voluntary path-dependent integration of new rules into a given institutional structure. Formal institutions are not phrased from scratch. Due to, for example, cognitive limitations and attempts to cope with uncertainty, we can normally only expect gradual change to take place in the realm of institutions. Finally, Schnellenbach compares the necessarily cautious, defensive institutional "entrepreneurship" with the much more offensive form of Schumpeterian economic entrepreneurship *strictu sensu*.

The third and last part of the book addresses normative questions. Chapter 8 by Christian Schubert (Max-Planck-Institute of Economics at Jena) examines the potential of a normative branch within Evolutionary Economics, i.e., he aims at developing a normative theory that helps to develop criteria in order to evaluate designed institutions from a perspective informed by insights from Evolutionary Economics. After briefly discussing the pitfalls of orthodox welfare theory,

Schubert proposes to use the contractarian approach within Constitutional Economics as a basic blueprint for this normative branch. Contractarian theories are compatible with an evolutionary world-view if they can pass both Hume's general anti-contractarian critique and Hayek's epistemological skepticism against "constructivist rationalism." Schubert argues that John Rawls' concept of "justice as fairness," if interpreted in a conventionalist way (i.e., with a focus on the idea of a reflective equilibrium), can indeed overcome these hurdles, because it can be seen as a way to anchor the contractarian model (in particular, the "original position") in the moral common sense and, more generally, the informal institutional context of a given society.

Since normative criteria are hard to define in a world of evolving preferences, Gerhard Wegner (University of Erfurt) pleads for legal competition as a way allowing the finding of best institutions just like the market for goods finds the best goods. He examines the question how institutional safeguards can be devised that make sure that legal norms which regulate market activities remain largely consistent with individual preferences. Legal competition is considered a potential remedy. Although the mere idea of replacing the legislative monopoly of the state by a market-like competition among legal rules suggests a radical redefinition of the idea of a state, Wegner shows that the concept is not a purely fictitious idea. It has rather emerged, if in an unintended way, as a practical result of the EU treaty and its interpretation by the European Court. Hence, legal competition is already in place as a key factor in the evolution of designed (regulatory) institutions in the European Union. By choosing among different goods, consumers can effectively choose among different regulatory rules without ever having to leave their country. Wegner critically discusses objections against the workability of legal competition and concludes that its welfare implications are largely positive.

Finally, Viktor Vanberg (University of Freiburg) discusses two methodological issues, one positive and one normative, that have been repeatedly raised in the Evolutionary Economics camp. First, he examines the relationship between biological and cultural evolution. What are their commonalities and their differences? According to Vanberg, the fact that human intentionality and deliberate institutional design play a key role in cultural evolution does *not* necessarily force us to reject a "Universal Darwinism" approach within economics. He argues that the Darwinian concepts of variation, selection and retention are compatible with the recognition of particulars in the sphere of cultural processes. Second, Vanberg explores a proposal made by Ulrich Witt according to which the fact that cultural evolution is (at least partly) man-made suggests that man should also be able to evaluate the results of cultural evolution. Vanberg agrees and proposes to use a contractarian approach to guide the human attempt to deliberately impose constitutional constraints on socio-economic evolution.

Hopefully, this book will deliver many inspiring ideas about how the complex methodological, theoretical and normative problems raised by the phenomenon of evolving formal institutions might be successfully tackled in future research.

We gratefully acknowledge the stimulating comments of all anonymous referees whose cooperation helped to improve the book substantially. The entire workshop could not have taken place without generous support by the Max-Planck-Society and the Max-Planck-Institute of Economics. We thank Ulrich Witt as head of the Evolutionary Economics Group within the Max-Planck-Institute for having initiated and greatly supported the workshop. Finally, we should stress Karin Serfling's assistance in organizing this get-together of experts in the field of evolution and institutions.

Part I

Designed institutions, preferences and behavior

2 Institutions shape preferences: The approach of "Psychology & Economics"

Bruno S. Frey

2.1 How to deal with preference changes

Why do so many people get used to, or even start to believe in, a dictator's ideology though they previously thought it to be ridiculous? Why do others actively oppose it while still others withdraw themselves, resorting to purely private values? Or why do some people upon the introduction of a market economy adopt a pro-market ideology while others become more adverse to commercialization? And why does the higher income produced by markets often not increase people's happiness, in particular of those materialistically inclined?

These are some of the issues this chapter addresses. It is, of course, not claimed that these questions are answered here in a satisfactory way. But it is suggested that new developments in the newly emerging field of "Psychology & Economics" offer a fruitful avenue for approaching these issues.

Everyone knows: human preferences are variable. They develop and change over time. Part of what we liked when we were younger is no longer cherished when we grow older, and vice versa. What individuals may have rejected in the past (e.g., abstract painting) may be greatly valued by the same individuals today. Everybody is also aware that to some extent preferences differ between cultures.[1]

Yet economics traditionally assumes that preferences are constant. This "unrealistic" assumption allowed economists to make great progress in explaining human behavior and in deducing relevant policy consequences. Taking preferences to be immutable focuses the analysis on the effect of (generalized) relative price changes (or changes in the opportunity set) on behavior. This approach has been most clearly visible in the work by Gary Becker (1962, 1976). To the surprise, and also the dismay, of many social scientists (including some economists), he demonstrated that the approach holding preferences constant provides valuable insights not only in the area of the economy, but far beyond. This success led to the claim of economics being the "Queen of the Social Sciences" (most prominently Stigler 1984, Lazear 2000).

At the same time, there were always economists who wanted to deal with changing preferences. There is a long intellectual history of attempts to explain changes in human preferences. But this approach has met with little success. Changing preferences play a minor role in economics. While quite a number of such efforts were undertaken in the 1970s and 1980s,[2] today there are but a few publications addressing this issue, at least in the leading journals. Economics, as revealed in advanced level textbooks, has essentially disregarded these attempts.

A different, and more successful, route explains changes in tastes by assuming the utility function to be time invariant and equal between individuals, but that individuals accumulate human capital based on their past experiences (Stigler and Becker 1977, Becker 1996). A particular consumption bundle leads to a different evaluation by individuals, depending on the amounts of such human capital accumulated. Most people would consider such a process to be a change in preference. This avenue produced noteworthy and empirically testable insights into human behavior (e.g., Becker and Murphy 1988 on addiction). It also yielded important policy results, for instance that drug addicts can only get rid of their dependence if they decide to abstain abruptly and completely ("cold turkey"). The approach, however, found relatively few followers, perhaps because such redefinition in terms of a change in human capital is considered to be somewhat artificial.

This chapter proposes that the situation has been changing quite considerably. "Psychology and Economics"[3] has emerged as an academic discipline combining the traditional, but so far separated, fields of psychology and economics in order to develop a more satisfactory science of human behavior (see, more fully, Frey 2001). It has, in particular, been demonstrated that it is possible and useful to introduce aspects from psychology into economics. The elements imported range from motivational psychology to social neuroscience (e.g., Cacioppo 2002, Glimcher 2003). In particular, "Psychology & Economics" has resulted in two important developments:

1   The psychological theories allow economists to fill preference changes with content and life; they serve as a basis for formally modeling preference changes.
2   Research on the economics of happiness[4] shows that reported subjective well-being or satisfaction are good approximations to individual utility. This allows economists to empirically address the phenomenon of preference change, a possibility so far lacking. Approximating utility by measurable data on reported subjective satisfaction makes it possible to directly test theories on preference changes. Empirical research has been greatly boosted by data on individual satisfaction being available in a panel form spanning many years.

This chapter pursues the avenue proposed by "Psychology & Economics". The goal is to indicate in as concrete a way as possible, and in an empirically testable way, how institutions affect individual preferences. A change in institutions affects the constraints faced by the individuals or, in other words, produces changes in (generalized) relative prices. To analyze the effect of such changes on individual preferences, specific psychological theories are employed and integrated into institutional economics, thus performing a bridging function. In contrast, this chapter does not intend to provide an in-depth discussion of the concept of preference as used in the various disciplines. This has been done elsewhere (see, for instance, Niederle, in this volume). For the purpose here pursued it suffices to state that the term "preference change" refers to all changes in the behavior of individuals *not* accounted for by the changes in generalized relative prices (see Becker 1976).

The outline of the basic relationships linking institutions and preferences is given in Section 2.2. In order to be as concrete and empirically orientated as possible, the framework is applied to two specific cases: Section 2.3 discusses the effects on individual preferences when a dictator with a particular ideology comes to power; Section 2.4 traces the effects on individual preferences when a market economy is introduced. Section 2.5 offers concluding remarks.

2.2   Relating institutions and individual preferences

2.2.1   *Two types of processes*

In order to analyze the effects of institutions, it is useful to distinguish between two kinds of processes affecting individual preferences.

The first type of process is based on a *conscious* process. Individuals react in a *cognitive* and *strategic* way to the changes in constraints that they face. Their aim is to maintain their overall or (meta-) utility in the case of restraining changes in their opportunity set, and to raise their utility as much as possible in the case of enlarging changes in their opportunity set. It is thus assumed that individuals adjust their preferences in order to maximize their meta-utility. In contrast to standard economic theory, individuals not only adjust their behavior to a change in (generalized) relative prices, but also adjust their beliefs of what they like, and therefore their preferences.

A case in point is "cognitive dissonance theory" (see Festinger 1967, Aranson 1984: 113–79, or the survey in Reeve 2001: 291–8). Individuals can raise their utility if, after having made a choice, they adjust their preferences to the decision taken. They adopt a different self-image because they must explain to themselves why they have made that choice of their own free will. For example, after having bought a particular brand of car, they make an effort not to have their preferences influenced in an adverse way. They therefore seek advertisements validating their choice, and try to disregard advertisements praising other brands. This theory has been used in a path-breaking contribution to "Psychology and Economics" (Akerlof and Dickens 1982, see also Akerlof and Kranston 2003), which explains why workers who chose to work in a dangerous job fail to take all the precautionary measures deemed reasonable to outsiders. The reason is that doing so continually reminds them that they have chosen a dangerous job. This thought reduces their utility. Therefore they "rationally"[5] decide to discount the danger to which they expose themselves.

As will be argued below, cognitive dissonance is only one particular case of the more general phenomenon of systematically adjusting one's preferences to changes in constraints.[6]

The second type of process is *unconscious*. It happens more or less automatically. It is not willingly controlled, nor strategically used, by the individuals. Preferences are formed within the individuals by motivational and non-rational forces. These changes are thus psychological in a more narrowly defined sense.

An example is *coping* behavior in the face of an unfortunate event. Most persons show a considerable amount of resilience when, for instance, they lose their long-term partner. After suffering intense grief over some period of time, they recover and subsequently attain a similar level of well-being to before the event (see Stroebe and Stroebe 1987 for losing one's partner, and Fredrickson *et al.* 2003 for the general processes). While this adjustment is unforeseen and unplanned, it is nevertheless real.

2.2.2   *Consciously changing preferences*

Individuals adjust their preferences in reaction to a change in relative prices in order to raise their meta-utility to a higher level than it would otherwise be. This can be done in two ways:

An *active* form is to strengthen those preferences in line with the changing constraints. Take, for example, the case of public transport being less expensive than private transport. One's meta-utility is increased by raising one's preference in favor of public transport. Similarly, when an individual is unable to attain a certain position (e.g., to become a full professor at a reputable university), he or she does well to emphasize the pleasures gained from engaging more fully in leisure-time activities. Such adjustments serve to increase the utility of the persons concerned. Indeed, people unable to adjust in this way lead miserable lives. It is difficult to imagine a world in which individuals would not cope in this way when they realize that they are unable to achieve a particular goal, even if it was initially very important. Many young people dream about becoming famous sportspeople or music superstars. But most of them find it quite easy to adjust their preferences when they see that they cannot reach their original goals.

A *passive* form of preference adaptation is to weaken those preferences incompatible with the change in relative prices. In the cases just given, an individual raises his or her utility by discounting a preference for private transport, e.g., by pointing out to him- or herself that private transport involves higher risk of accident. The person not attaining the desired professorial rank increases his or her utility, for instance, by persuading him- or herself that the "publish or perish" process involved is not worth the effort and does not really contribute to scientific advance. And those giving up their dreams of becoming a sports or music star can focus on the disadvantages of being famous.

These preference adaptations are familiar from everyday life and have also been discussed in the literature (for example Elster 1983). The "sour grapes" story describes how people adjust their preferences when they realize that they cannot attain a particular goal. In contrast, the "grass is always greener on the other side" story describes the utility decreasing inclination of focusing on unattainable goods and positions.

2.2.3   *Unconsciously changing preferences*

There are two different processes guiding the adjustment of preferences to relative price changes which are unconscious.

The first process works through the *perceptions* persons have of the outside intervention experienced by the relative price change. If the intervention is taken to be *supportive* for the existing preferences, the individuals have a tendency to strengthen them further. A pertinent example is receiving a commendation for doing an activity for intrinsic reasons (for example to work as a volunteer). This fosters the preferences for engaging in this kind of activity. If, in contrast, the individuals concerned take the external intervention via the change in relative prices to be *controlling,* the preference for the respective good or activity decreases. Individuals respond by going into inner withdrawal or by reactance, i.e., by finding unrelated or opposing activities more attractive.

These adjustments of preferences to changes in relative prices, and the causal relationship between extrinsic and intrinsic preferences implied, have in economics been discussed in crowding theory (Frey 1997). It is based on the psychological theories of "hidden costs of rewards" (Lepper and Greene 1978) and "cognitive evaluation theory" (Deci and Ryan 1985, Deci *et al.* 1999). Bénabou and Tirole (2003) and Gneezy (2003) have recently analyzed the systematic effect of outside interventions on intrinsic preferences by integrating them into standard economics. Crowding effects have been supported by a large number of experiments, as well as by field observations (see the evidence in Frey and Jegen 2001). The social experiments by Gneezy and Rustichini (2000a, 2000b) and by Frey and Oberholzer-Gee (1997) have received considerable attention in economics.

An important question is *under what conditions* people perceive an outside intervention to be controlling or supportive. An outside intervention is rarely considered to be fully controlling or fully supportive. Rather, the perceptions can be arranged on a scale including these conceptions as extremes. Accordingly the crowding-out effect is the *stronger*, the *more controlling* an outside intervention is felt to be. Three psychological processes have been used to account for crowding-out intrinsic preferences.[7] An outside intervention is perceived to be the more controlling (see, more fully, Deci and Ryan 1985, Frey 1997):

1   *The more self-determination is impaired.* When individuals perceive an external intervention to reduce their self-determination, they substitute their intrinsic preference by the intrinsic control imposed. Following Rotter (1966), the locus of control has shifted from the inside to the outside of the person affected. The persons concerned no longer feel themselves to be responsible,

but rather the person or institution undertaking the interference from outside. As a result, the intrinsic preference is partly or wholly given up.

2   *The more self-esteem is impaired.* When an outside intervention carries the notion that the actor's intrinsic preference is not acknowledged or esteemed,[8] his or her intrinsic preference is effectively rejected. The person affected feels that his or her involvement and competence is not appreciated by other people debasing its value. A person with intrinsic preferences is denied the chance to display his or her interest and involvement in an activity when someone else offers a monetary reward (or imposes a command) to undertake it.

3   *The more the possibility to express one's intrinsic preferences is impaired.* Persons subjected to an outside intervention is deprived the possibility of acting on the basis of her or his intrinsic preferences. They exhibit "altruistic anger" and tend to respond by relinquishing their intrinsic preferences and by adopting the external preferences imposed.

The crowding effects are not mechanistic in the sense that it is possible to a priori state for a specific case whether an outside intervention raises or lowers intrinsic preferences. Rather, it is necessary to carefully analyze to what extent the three psychological conditions just mentioned apply. But crowding theory *is* empirically testable (and refutable) as evidenced by the studies mentioned above and collected in Frey and Jegen (2001), as well as by so far unpublished research (see, e.g., Irlenbusch and Sliwka 2004).

The second process guiding the adjustment of preferences to relative price changes depends on *visceral* reactions,[9] which may be the result of an evolutionary quest for survival (see, e.g., Tooby and Cosmides 1990, Barkow, Cosmides and Tooby 1992). The basic idea is that those people who like to do what is being imposed by the environment (i.e., the relative prices) function better and are therefore fitter than those who cling to preferences at odds with their environment.

An important instance is how people react to greater opportunities reflected by higher disposable per capita income. Individuals with given preferences would quickly run into decreasing marginal utility of higher income. As a result, having a higher income would not provide any incentive to pursue hard work. They would be satisfied with the income reached and would use all further opportunities to work less and to enjoy leisure. What we observe, however, is quite different. People in rich countries, and the high-income recipients in rich countries, work more hours, and work more intensively, than those with lower income. A striking example is that of managers with often huge incomes. These are the people who work hardest in our societies. It would be difficult to explain why they work so hard if their preferences were constant. It might be argued that high-income recipients are not interested in their absolute income level but rather in their relative income compared to others. But this leaves the question open who the "others" are. It seems to be a hard-wired human trait that most people tend to compare themselves to people who are *better* off than they are. The reference group is not constant, but also moves upwards with increasing income, i.e., it is endogenous. This is again a preference change, this time with respect to the reference group.

Happiness research has dealt with these issues in an empirical way. People are shown to adjust to increases in income, or more generally to material possessions (Easterlin 1974, 2003, van Praag 1993, Diener *et al.* 1993, Stutzer 2003). An increase in income or consumption yields increasingly less utility because people become used to the higher level. After a year has passed, about two thirds of the utility increase due to higher income has evaporated. At the same time, individuals compare what they receive with what others receive. The income considered "necessary" for a decent standard of living shifts upwards due to both reasons. Over time, an increase in income produces only a very small increase in self-reported subjective well-being. This is "the basic paradox at the heart of modern civilization" (Layard 2005: 1): Real per capita income has increased considerably in developed economies, but life satisfaction or reported subjective well-being has stayed level (see, e.g., Frey and Stutzer 2002a, 2002b, 2003a, 2003b). The adjustment process discussed in, and empirically supported by, happiness research is consistent with a preference change induced by the higher income or consumption: the *same* collection of goods provides less utility than before.

Negative economic life events have also been shown to be subject to preference adjustments. Thus people to some extent get used to being unemployed, especially if surrounded by other people with the same fate. Also, when the social environment is more tolerant towards unemployment, the utility loss is smaller and tends to evaporate more quickly (see Stutzer and Lalive 2004). Again, the same event is evaluated differently over time, which suggests a preference change.[10]

Psychologists have collected extensive experimental evidence supporting these preference changes. In the case of negative life events, they point to resilience as a basic determinant of the extent of preference change. Resilience in turn is raised by positive affect (see Donaldson 2000, Fredrickson and Tugade 2003, Fredrickson and Joiner 2002, Fredrickson *et al.* 2003).

These general considerations on the relationship between the effects on changing preferences by changes in relative prices, in turn induced by institutions, is now applied to two specific cases. The next section looks at the effects of a change in government.

2.3   Effects on preferences of a change in government

Consider the case of a dictator with a particular ideology coming to power. This may be a dictator with fascist, communist or any other orientation. How are the population's preferences likely to be affected?

The individuals living in such a country seek to maintain their meta-utility by adjusting their preferences. They are confronted with a change in relative prices in the sense that they have to possibly carry considerable costs if they maintain their previous preferences (these are not identical to those of the dictator, because if they were, he would not have to be a dictator but could be democratically elected). The people may be economically sanctioned, incarcerated or even killed. In many cases, the dictator and the groups supporting him (often the army, police and secret service) do not only want to see a behavior consonant with official ideology. They also check whether the subjects also *believe* in it. In both cases, the individuals are *actively* or *strategically* able to reduce the utility loss by changing their preferences in such a way that they conform to the official ideology: the people start to believe in it. A more passive preference change is that the importance attached to other preferences, such as valuing family, friends and other associates, is decreased compared to following the dictator's ideology.

The effect on preferences is mediated through perceptions. If the government's interventions in individual private lives are taken to be *supportive* of the preferences previously held, there is an enhancing preference change. For instance, if people have a skeptical or inimical attitude towards foreigners, a dictator with a nationalistic ideology supports the skepticism and strengthens the corresponding preferences. In other cases, however, the individuals perceive the government's interventions to be *controlling*. Preferences inimical to official ideology will then be strengthened. The people's ideology will move away from that of the dictator. This does not necessarily result in an increased visible opposition, because the expected cost of doing so may be so high that the individuals are deterred. But if these costs are perceived to fall, there may be a very large swing to overt opposition. This is the typical pattern seen in many revolutionary uprisings. Most recently, it occurred when people sensed that the communist states were no longer able to impose heavy costs when overt opposition was shown (see Kuran 1995). Such a development was clearly visible in the German Democratic Republic (see Opp *et al.* 1995). Whether a dictator's ideology is considered to be supportive or controlling can, of course, not be determined without empirically analyzing the underlying psychological processes, in particular how people's perceived self-determination and self-esteem are affected. Depend on the content of an ideology, and the way it is projected, the persons living in the respective state may feel that their self-determination is reduced, and their self-esteem lowered in which case preferences contrary to those of the dictator are enhanced.

Intrinsic preferences may also be influenced by visceral reactions. People get used to the oppression imposed by a dictatorial regime. Their preferences adapt to some extent as it facilitates survival. After some time has passed, the individuals do not feel the oppression any more because they have adjusted their preferences to the dictator's ideology. In that case, a dictator's fall does not lead to a quick reversal of preferences. Rather, many individuals tend to glorify the past and think that everything was better when the dictator was still in power. This seems to have happened in parts of the former Soviet Union, where the population appears to have so strongly shaped their preferences according to the dictatorship of Communism that they find it preferable to what seems to them the anarchy of the market and democracy.

2.4   Effects on preferences of the introduction of a market

Consider the case of a country switching to a market economy, or which allocates new and important sectors of the economy to the price system.

Many individuals faced with this new situation seek to maintain or increase their meta-utility by *consciously* adopting *pro-market preferences.*[11] They actively internalize the "market creed," for instance that people should be paid solely according to their performance, or that income correctly reflects one's social worth. Stronger pro-market individualistic preferences allow them to engage in the competitive struggle induced by the price system without any moral qualms or reservations.

A more passive way to deal with the introduction of markets is to *downgrade non-market values,* such as the value attributed to family life, friendship and social connectedness, as well as civic virtues such as tax morale. This preference change makes it easier for individuals to engage in market activities as they have less need to be concerned with competing demands. There is, for instance, no need to care for the interests of family members or friends when a lucrative job can be filled. It is simply given to the best-suited job applicant, irrespective of personal connections.

The effect of the market, or of *commercialization*, on individual preferences has been commented on in a substantial literature (see Hirschman 1977, 1982; Lane 1991). Earlier Montesquieu (1749) thought that the market induces people to become more honest: "Commerce (...) polishes and softens barbaric ways" (see LeGrand 2003). This idea is known as "doux commerce" and has been proposed by philosophers and economists, such as Immanuel Kant, Georg Wilhelm Friedrich Hegel and Adam Smith. The preference change induced by the introduction of the market has thus been considered desirable. But there is an even larger literature stating that pro-market preferences are undesirable: commercialization makes people more selfish and egoistic. The most famous proponent of that view is Karl Marx (1867), but more recently also Hirsch (1976).

The introduction of markets also affects preferences by an *unconscious* process. People to some extent get used to markets, even if they at first mentally reject them. For example, most people did not like privatization of telecommunication, but now their preferences have adjusted to the use of the price system in this area.

But even when the market is introduced, the individuals concerned may from the very beginning perceive it to be *supportive* of their own preferences. They experience, for instance, that good performance is reflected in the form of higher income. In that case, people's preferences tend to move in an individualistic direction, away from more social concerns.

The intrusion of the market is, however, often perceived to be *controlling*. People often feel that their self-determination and their self-esteem is reduced when the market takes over (for empirical evidence see Kahneman *et al.* 1986; Frey and Pommerehne 1993). People's aversion to the market is then strengthened and an anti-market ideology is fostered. Ideologies inimical to the market, such as fundamentalist religions prohibiting taking interest (see Kuran 2004 for Islam), flourish. The environmentalist movement comprises many people who are convinced that markets destroy the natural environment. At the same time, styles of beliefs completely disconnected to market ideas gain more prominence, Buddhist or esoteric beliefs being examples.

These reactions inimical to market thinking on fundamental grounds can be well observed at present. Globalization, which is essentially the extension of capitalist or market ideas to the whole world, has been met with suspicion, if not great opposition, by a large number of people. This is manifested by the anti-globalization movement, which not only cherishes anti-market beliefs (see, e.g., Klein 2002), but also uses violence.

2.5   Concluding remarks

This chapter proposes some highly speculative notions and ideas. It relies on two important new developments in the newly emerging discipline of "Psychology and Economics":

1 *Psychological theories* help economists to *identify* important processes leading to preference changes. This allows us to fill the formerly often totally vacuous concept of preference change with content.
2 *Happiness research* enables us to approximate the concept of utility in a satisfactory way. This allows us to empirically test preference changes.

The discussion intends to show that the preference changes identified as a result of changes in relative prices and institutions can be empirically analyzed. Some of the conditions governing preference changes, especially those relating to the crowding effects, are well identified. Others have still to be more fully explored. It has also been argued that a considerable body of empirical knowledge exists about preference changes in happiness research, though it has so far not been looked at in terms of preference change. The research on happiness has econometrically identified important areas in which individual preferences change.

Notes

1 See the extensive survey by Bowles (1998).
2 See, e.g., Pollak (1976), Winston (1980), v. Weizsäcker (1971).
3 See the early survey by Rabin (1998), and the more recent surveys by Mullainathan and Thaler (2000), Frey and Stutzer (2001) and Frey and Benz (2002). Path-breaking contributions are, e.g., by Easterlin (1974), Scitovsky (1976), Thaler (1992) or Frank (1999).
4 For surveys see Kahneman *et al.* (1999), Lane (2000), Frey and Stutzer (2002a, 2002b, 2003a), van Praag and Ferrer-I-Carbonell (2004) and Layard (2003, 2005).
5 Such behavior appears non-rational to outsiders and over the long term is non-rational also for the individuals subject to cognitive dissonance.
6 See also the earlier studies by Gintis (1971, 1972) and Elster (1983).
7 Many economists do not like to use psychological theories as explanations. They make great efforts to account for the phenomena in question by standard economic theory. In the case of crowding effects this has been done, for instance, by Bénabou and Tirole (2003) who provide an explanation in terms of economic signalling theory. The present author is prepared to take psychological theories seriously and to rely on them on par with economic theories. For a discussion of this position see Frey (1999, 2001).
8 Self-esteem has so far not been a category used in economics but it is of central importance in many other disciplines. See, for instance, Rawls (1971: 86) who considers

self-esteem to be the most valuable of the goods he designates as "primary". Most recently, a joint team of an economist and a philosopher (Brennan and Pettit 2004) have analyzed the determinants and consequences of "esteem" (though not of self-esteem).

9 For visceral reactions and the role of emotions in this context, see Bowles and Gintis (2002).

10 It is interesting to note that these preference changes are partially, and sometimes totally unforeseen by the persons involved. Individuals underestimate how much their utility from income and consumption evaporates over time, and overestimate how much they suffer from negative life events. As a result, individuals make systematically distorted decisions according to their *own evaluation,* but they are unable to adequately correct this bias (see Frey and Stutzer 2003b).

11 Whether this strategy is successful in the long term is another matter. The evidence collected by Kasser (2003) indeed suggests that materialistic values do not make for happiness.

References

Akerlof, G. and Dickens, W.T. (1982) 'The Economic Consequences of Cognitive Dissonance', *American Economic Review*, 72: 307–19.

Akerlof, G. and Kranston, R.E. (2003) 'Identity and the Economics of Organizations', *Journal of Economic Perspectives*, 19: 9–32.

Aranson, E.D. (1984) *The Social Animal*, New York: Freeman.

Barkow, H., Cosmides, L. and Tooby, J. (eds) (1992) *The Adaptive Mind: Evolutionary Psychology and the Generation of Culture*, Oxford: Oxford University Press.

Becker, G.S. (1962) 'Irrational Behavior and Economic Theory', *Journal of Political Economy*, 70: 1–13.

Becker, G.S. (1976) *The Economic Approach to Human Behavior*, Chicago: University of Chicago Press.

Becker, G.S. (1996) *Accounting for Tastes*, Cambridge, MA: Harvard University Press.

Becker, G.S. and Murphy, K.M. (1988) 'A Theory of Rational Addiction', *Journal of Political Economy*, 96: 675–700.

Bénabou, R. and Tirole, J. (2003) 'Intrinsic and Extrinsic Motivation', *Review of Economic Studies*, 70: 489–520.

Bowles, S. (1998) 'Endogenous Preferences: The Cultural Consequences of Markets and Other Economic Institutions', *Journal of Economic Literature*, 36: 75–111.

Bowles, S. and Gintis, H. (2002) 'Prosocial Emotions', mimeo, Santa Fe Institute.

Brennan, G. and Pettit, P. (2004) *The Economy of Esteem. An Essay on Civil and Political Society*, Oxford: Oxford University Press.

Cacioppo, J.T. (2002) 'Social Neuroscience: Understanding the Pieces Fosters Understanding the Whole and Vice Versa', *American Psychologist*, 57: 819–31.

Deci, E.L. and Ryan, R.M. (1985) *Intrinsic Motivation and Self-Determination in Human Behavior*, New York: Plenum Press.

Deci, E.L., Koestner, R. and Ryan, R.M. (1999) 'A Meta-Analytic Review of Experiments Examining the Effects of Extrinsic Rewards on Intrinsic Motivation', *Psychological Bulletin*, 125: 627–68.

Diener, E., Sandvik, E., Seidlitz, L. and Diener, M. (1993) 'The Relationship between Income and Subjective Well-Being: Relative or Absolute?', *Social Indicators Research*, 28: 195–223.

Diener, E., Suh, E.M., Lucas, R.E. and Smith, H.L. (1999) 'Subjective Well-Being: Three Decades of Progress', *Psychological Bulletin*, 125: 276–303.

Donaldson, R.J. (2000) 'Affective Style, Psychopathology, and Resilience: Brain Mechanism and Plasticity', *American Psychologist* 55: 1196–214.

Easterlin, R.A. (1974) 'Does Economic Growth Improve the Human Lot? Some Empirical Evidence', in P.A. David and M.W. Reder (eds) *Nations and Households in Economic Growth: Essays in Honor of Moses Abramowitz*, New York: Academic Press, pp. 89–125.

Easterlin, R.A. (2003) 'Building a Better Theory of Well-Being', *IZA Discussion Paper* No. 742.

Elster, J. (1983) *Sour Grapes*, Cambridge, MA: Cambridge University Press.

Festinger, L. (1967) *A Theory of Cognitive Dissonance*, Stanford, CA: Stanford University Press.

Frank, R.H. (1999) *Luxury Fever. Why Money Fails to Satisfy in an Era of Excess*, New York: Free Press.

Fredrickson, B.L. and Joiner, T. (2002) 'Positive Emotions Trigger Upward Spiral on Well-Being', *Psychological Science*, 13: 172–5.

Fredrickson, B.L. and Tugade, M.M. (2003) 'Resilient Individuals Use Positive Emotions to Bounce Back from Negative Emotional Experiences', *Journal of Personality and Social Psychology*, 86: 320–33.

Fredrickson, B.L., Tugade, M.M., Waugh, C.E. and Larkin, G. (2003) 'What Good are Positive Emotions in Crises? A Prospective Study of Resilience and Emotions Following the Terrorist Attacks on the United States on September 11th, 2001', *Journal of Personality and Social Psychology*, 84: 365–376.

Frey, B.S. (1997) *Not Just for The Money. An Economic Theory of Personal Motivation*, Cheltenham, UK and Brookfield, USA: Edward Elgar.

Frey, B.S. (1999) *Economics as a Science of Human Behaviour. Towards a New Social Science Paradigm,* 2nd edn, Boston, Dordrecht and London: Kluwer.

Frey, B.S. (2001) *Inspiring Economics. Human Motivation in Political Economy*, Cheltenham, UK and Brookfield: E. Elgar.

Frey, B.S. and Benz, M. (2002) 'From Imperialism to Inspiration: A Survey of Economics and Psychology', *Institute for Empirical Research in Economics Working Paper* No. 118.

Frey, B.S. and Jegen, R. (2001) 'Motivation Crowding Theory: A Survey of Empirical Evidence', *Journal of Economic Surveys*, 15: 589–611.

Frey, B.S. and Oberholzer-Gee, F. (1997) 'The Cost of Price Incentives', *American Economic Review*, 87: 746–55.

Frey, B.S. and Pommerehne, W.W. (1993) 'On the Fairness of Pricing – An Empirical Survey among the General Population', *Journal of Economic Behaviour and Organization*, 20: 295–307.

Frey, B.S. and Stutzer, A. (2001) 'Economics and Psychology: From Imperialism to Inspired Economics', *Philosophie Economique*, 4: 5–22.

Frey, B.S. and Stutzer, A. (2002a) 'What Can Economists Learn from Happiness Research?', *Journal of Economic Literature*, 40: 402–35.

Frey, B.S. and Stutzer, A. (2002b) *Happiness and Economics*, Princeton: Princeton University Press.

Frey, B.S. and Stutzer, A. (2003a) 'Testing Theories of Happiness', in L. Bruni and P. Porta (eds) *Economics and Happiness. Framing the Analysis*, Oxford: Oxford University Press.

Frey, B.S. and Stutzer, A. (2003b) 'Economic Consequences of Mispredicting Utility', *Working Paper*, Institute for Research in Empirical Economics, University of Zurich.

Gintis, H. (1971) 'Education, Technology, and the Characteristics of Worker Productivity', *American Economic Review*, 61: 266–79.

Gintis, H. (1972) 'A Radical Analysis of Welfare Economics and Individual Development', *Quarterly Journal of Economics*, 86: 572–99.

Glimcher, P.W. (2003) *Decisions, Uncertainty, and the Brain. The Science of Neuroeconomics*, Cambridge, MA, and London: MIT Press.

Gneezy, U. (2003) 'The W Effect of Incentives', mimeo, University of Chicago Graduate School of Business.

Gneezy, U. and Rustichini, A. (2000a) 'A Fine is a Price', *Journal of Legal Studies*, 29: 1–17.

Gneezy, U. and Rustichini, A. (2000b) 'Pay Enough or Don't Pay at All', *Quarterly Journal of Economics*, 115: 791–810.

Hirsch, F. (1976) *The Social Limits to Growth*, Cambridge, MA: Harvard University Press.

Hirschman, A.O. (1977) *The Passions and the Interests: Political Arguments for Capitalism before its Triumph*, Princeton: Princeton University Press.

Hirschman, A.O. (1982) 'Rival Interpretations of Market Society: Civilizing, Destructive or Feeble?', *Journal of Economic Literature*, 20: 1463–84.

Irlenbusch, B. and Sliwka, D. (2004) 'Incentives, Decision Frames, and Motivation Crowding Out – An Experimental Investigation', *mimeo*, London School of Economics, August.

Kahneman, D., Knetsch, J.L. and Thaler, R.H. (1986) 'Fairness as a Constraint on Profit Seeking: Entitlements in the Market', *American Economic Review*, 76: 728–41.

Kahneman, D., Diener, E. and Schwarz, N. (eds) (1999) *Well-Being: The Foundation of Hedonic Psychology*, New York: Russel Sage Foundation.

Kasser, T. (2003) *The High Price of Materialism*, Cambridge, MA: MIT Press.

Klein, N. (2002) *No Logo: No Space, No Choices, No Jobs*, New York: Picador.

Kuran, T. (1995) *Private Truths, Public Lies: The Social Costs of Preference Falsification*, Cambridge, MA: Harvard University Press.

Kuran, T. (2004) *Islam and Mammon: The Economic Predicament of Islamism*, Princeton: Princeton University Press.

Lane, R.E. (1991) *The Market Experience*, New York and Cambridge, MA: Cambridge University Press.

Lane, R.E. (2000) *The Loss of Happiness in Market Economies*, New Haven and London: Yale University Press.

Layard, R. (2003) 'Happiness: Has Social Science a Clue?', Lionel Robins Memorial Lectures 2002/3 (http://cep.lse.ac.uk/events/lectures/layard/RL030303. pdf)

Layard, R. (2005) *Happiness: Lessons from a New Science*, London: Allen Lane.

Lazear, E. (2000) 'Performance Pay and Productivity', *American Economic Review*, 90: 1346–61.

LeGrand, J. (2003) *Motivation, Agency and Public Policy: of knights, and knaves, pawns and queens*, Oxford: Oxford University Press.

Lepper, M.R. and Greene, D. (1978) *The Hidden Cost of Rewards*, Hillsdale, NJ: Erlbaum.

Marx, K. (1867) *Das Kapital. Kritik der politischen Ökonomie*, Hamburg: Verlag von Otto Meissner.

Montesquieu, C.L. (1749) *De l'esprit des lois*, vol. XX, Paris: Garnier.

Mullainathan, S., and Thaler, R. (2000) 'Behavioral Economics', mimeo, MIT, Cambridge, MA.

Niederle, U.-M. 'Preferences in Social Interaction and their Influence on Formal Institutions', this volume.

Opp, K.-D., Voss, P. and Gern, C. (1995) *The Origins of a Spontaneous Revolution. East Germany 1989*, Ann Arbor: Michigan University Press.

Pollak, R.A. (1976) 'Interdependent Preferences', *American Economic Review*, 66: 309–20.

Rabin, M. (1998) 'Psychology and Economics', *Journal of Economic Literature*, 36: 11–46.

Rawls, J. (1971) *A Theory of Justice*, Cambridge, MA: Harvard University Press.

Reeve, J. (2001) *Understanding Motivation and Emotion*, New York: Wiley.

Rotter, J. (1966) 'Generalized Expectancies for Internal versus External Control of Reinforcement', *Psychological Monographs*, 80: No. 609.

Scitovsky, T. (1976) *The Joyless Economy: An Inquiry into Human Satisfaction and Consumer Dissatisfaction*, New York: Oxford University Press.

Stigler, G.J. (1984) 'Economics – The Imperial Science?' *Scandinavian Journal of Economics*, 86: 301–13.

Stigler, G.J. and Becker, G.S. (1977) 'De Gustibus Non Est Disputandum', *American Economic Review*, 67: 76–90.

Stroebe, W. and Stroebe, M.S. (1987) *Bereavement and Health: The Psychological and Physical Consequences of Partner Loss*, New York: Cambridge University Press.

Stutzer, A. (2003) 'The Role of Income Aspirations in Individual Happiness', *Journal of Economic Behavior and Organization,* forthcoming.

Stutzer, A. and Lalive, R. (2004) 'The Role of Social Work Norms in Job Searching and Subjective Well-Being', *Journal of the European Economic Association*, 2: 696–712.

Thaler, R.H. (1992) *The Winner's Curse. Paradoxes and Anomalies of Economic Life*, New York: Free Press.

Tooby, J. and Cosmides, L. (1990) 'The past explains the present: Emotional adaptation and the structure of ancestral environment', *Ethology and Sociobiology*, 11: 375–424.

Van Praag, B.M.S. (1993) 'The Relativity of the Welfare Concept', in M. Nussbaum and A.K. Sen (eds) *The Quality of Life*, Oxford: Clarendon Press, pp. 362–416.

Van Praag, B.M.S. and Ferrer-i-Carbonell, A. (2004) *Happiness Quantified. A Satisfaction Calculus Approach*, Oxford: Oxford University Press.

Von Weizsäcker, C.C. (1971) 'Notes on Endogeneous Change of Tastes', *Journal of Economic Theory*, 3: 345–72.

Winston, G.C. (1980) 'Addiction and Backsliding: A Theory of Compulsive Consumption', *Journal of Economic Behavior and Organization*, 1: 295–324.

3 Legislation and countervailing effects from social norms

Francesco Parisi and Georg von Wangenheim

3.1 Introduction[1]

Henry David Thoreau reportedly said, "if a man does not keep pace with his companions, perhaps it is because he hears a different drummer."[2] In this chapter we recognize the fact that human behavior is influenced by personal values, social norms of conduct and exogenous restrictions such as legal sanctions. We study the interaction between these legal and extralegal forces in affecting human conduct and we highlight the possibility of countervailing effects of social norms in the face of changes in the legal environment. Building on the stylized fact that individual values and social norms are partly static and partly subject to change over time, we consider the direct and indirect effects of law in the evolution of both individual values and social norms. We consider the effect of law in the formation of opinions and the countervailing effect of "civil disobedience", where individuals ostensibly violate a command of the law, justifying such departure on the grounds of individual freedom or unfairness of the law. By engaging in civil disobedience, individuals reveal their personal values to others. Through an opinion-formation process, this may result in a reinforcement of other individuals' dislike of the law. As a result, legal innovation may occasion a shift in equilibrium behavior that goes in the opposite direction from that intended by the law.

The expressions "personal" or "individual values", "social norms" and related terms fail to follow a general usage between and within legal science, social science and economics.[3] We therefore feel compelled to state clearly how we use these expressions. Personal or, equivalently, individual values in our diction are opinions of an individual person on what should and should not be allowed or, conversely, on what one ought and ought not do. We sometimes also call these opinions value judgments. An individual who holds the opinion that a certain action should not be allowed may be, and frequently is, willing to behave according to this opinion and to impose sanctions on others who violate this norm by their actions or their expressed values even if this is costly to him- or herself. We then say the personal values have turned into a "personal", "individual" or "internalized norm".

"Social values" and "social norms" are frequency distributions of individual values and norms, respectively, which concentrate much of their probability masses on one or few very similar individual values and norms, respectively. Note that this statistical concept of social norms differs from other definitions, but allows for situations in which a certain degree of an action is required by social norms. With these definitions, a social norm may effectively guide individual behavior even if not all individuals have internalized the norm or share the underlying values.

Legal rules are based on, and express, values in as much as they forbid certain actions and allow others. They may coincide with, or conflict with, social values and norms. Conflict and coincidence of legal rules and social norms is at the center of our interest.

To model evolution of individual and social norms[4] as they are now defined, we contemplate a process where individual values are formed in a manner similar to the opinion-formation process studied by Bikhchandani *et al.* (1992). Individuals have imperfect confidence in their value judgments and are influenced by other players' opinions whenever observable.

Building on these basic assumptions, we analyze the effect of new statutes on individual norms and behavior of individuals. New statutes that reflect current opinions may trigger public support, which in turn reinforce the underlying opinions. In this case, law plays an expressive role of pre-existing opinions similar to that studied by Cooter (1998, 2000). When values expressed by the law are consistent with one of two or several values competing to become a social norm, legal rules may also serve as focal points facilitating coordination and the emergence of a social norm (McAdams 2000, Wax 2000). On the other hand, legal rules that depart from current social values and norms may trigger opposition (Robinson 2000, Stuntz 2000).

Opposition to a new legal rule may take the form of protest or ostensible civil disobedience. We shall refer to these forms of opposition as "countervailing norms." Not every legal innovation that departs from current opinions triggers opposition. For example, laws that depart only slightly from the current mode of a social norm may occasion a gradual adaptation of the underlying individual values towards the new law. Here, the law drives the evolution of values and norms in the same direction as the law intends to. In other cases, new laws that differ substantially from the current mode of a social norm may lead to opposition. Some individuals will manifest their dissent by expressing their opposition to others (protest), while some people will oppose the law by ostensibly violating it (civil disobedience). Protest and civil disobedience signal dissent and may lead to reinforcing contrary social values and norms.

In all these cases we study the dynamic attributes of the interaction between individual values and laws, considering the countervailing effects of social norms. We identify a number of practical implications from this model. First, statutes intending to induce substantial shifts of social norms may have to proceed in a gradual fashion. Moving the statute in the desired direction in small consecutive steps that allow for the gradual adaptation of the individual values to the values expressed in the statutes, will avoid the countervailing effect of social norms – the opposition rate will be small in every step. Second, when gradual adjustments are not possible (e.g., due to the discrete nature of legal change) or not viable on political grounds, legislative change should be accompanied by higher enforcement in the initial phase. This is done in order to avoid public disobedience of a substantial frequency, which would undermine the authority and acceptance of the enacted law.

The chapter is structured as follows. In Section 3.2 we present the concept of countervailing norms, placing it in the context of the current norms literature. We further introduce the idea that individual value judgments are formed in a process similar to the opinion-formation and cascade process studied elsewhere in the literature. This argument will indicate the complexity underlying the dynamic interaction between law and social norms in influencing personal values and behavior. Therefore, we restrict the two models of this dynamics, which we present in Section 3.3, to those aspects which we think to be most relevant for understanding countervailing norms. In Section 3.4 we consider some relevant practical implications for lawmaking and formulate some testable predictions of this theory.

3.2   Unjust laws and illegal norms

Law and economics scholars have played an important role in integrating norms theory into legal analysis. Norms are undoubtedly very important both inside and outside regulated environments, and recent contributions to the law and economics of norms have illuminated the important interaction between formal and informal rules in influencing human behavior. We have reached a point of irreversibility in this interdisciplinary exercise, since it is probably no longer viable to think of a modern norm-free theory of the legal order, nor of a law-free understanding of social interactions. Attempts to construe grand theories ignoring either of the two determinants of human choice would be viewed as methodologically incomplete and would lack purchasing power for the understanding of human reality.

In this section we will elaborate on the terminological clarifications of the previous section and thereby set the stage for the study of the interesting relationship between formal and informal constraints on individual behavior.

3.2.1   Law, morality and the internalization of legal values

Laws may more effectively influence behavioral outcomes when legal norms are aligned with the existing social values. Studies of people's behavior in response to legal commands generally support the argument that the alignment of legal precepts and decisions of authorities with current social norms and values has a positive influence on whether people comply with law, even when it is not in their self-interest to do so (Tyler 1990, with respect to law, and Tyler and Huo 2002, with respect to the decisions of authorities). In the context of compliance with law, the notion of legitimacy (the belief that the lawmaking authority and the substantive content of the law are entitled to deference) is of critical importance. Using Tyler's (1990: 25) words, legitimacy represents an "acceptance by people of the need to bring their behavior into line with the dictates of an external authority." These conceptions of law differ from the purely instrumental idea of law relying on the enforcing authorities' use of rewards and sanctions. There are properties of the law that give it legitimacy and lead people to give it deference (Beetham 1991). Legitimacy is undermined when the content of the law departs from social norms, be they based on moral, ethical, or merely cultural values. Tyler (1990) and Sunshine and Tyler (2003) provide support for the argument that the public's perceptions of legitimacy impact on people's compliance with law and police orders.[5]

Absent such initial alignment between legal and social norms, then legislators can undertake the alternative paths of norm manipulation and coercion. In his foundational papers on expressive law, Cooter (1998, 2000) considers the three distinct ways in which law can influence behavior: deterrence, expression, and internalization. In order to effectively manipulate behavior, laws need to influence shared values and norms. Cooter develops a general theory of how legal rules can destroy or create social norms through the expression of social values. Our analysis can be viewed as complementary to Cooter's, as we consider the converse question of how social norms can react to law, undermining the effect of legal intervention. We show that this may require gradual and piecemeal intervention, to avoid public reaction and countervailing norms. A brief review of Cooter's analysis thus provides an important stepping stone for studying norm creation and the inducement of civil disobedience.

According to Cooter (1998), there are different ways in which the expression of legal rules can induce behavioral change. First, law can exert an external influence upon citizens by creating legal sanctions that impose costs; the law may modify the observed patterns of behavior while leaving individual preferences undisturbed. In turn, law may prompt citizens to adopt social norms without changing their preferences, or "tastes."[6] Second, citizens may internalize norms through changing their own tastes.

Cooter focuses on situations where the mere creation of legal rules may change social conduct even in the absence of enforced legal sanctions. Cooter refers to social psychological research that suggests the majority of citizens obey laws out of internal respect for the law in general and he aims to create an economic model to explain this phenomenon (Tyler 1990).[7] The way in which expressive laws influence behavior is very information-intensive. Expressive law is most effective when it aligns with pre-existing social values: it then may simply reduce the costs of private enforcement and thus facilitate the values' turning into norms. There is however a danger that unaligned law may crowd out moral norms rather than create them: individuals might feel it unnecessary to sanction violators of a norm if the government assumes this task.

Consequently, Cooter concludes that "lawmakers should proceed cautiously and skeptically with proposals for self-enforcing laws" (Cooter 1998: 597). The argument suggests that while law takes its notions of good and bad from citizens' pre-existing sense of justice, law can still create or destroy social norms. This idea was later restated by Cooter, observing that the state must rely on citizens to encourage civic virtue among one another, and "the primary way to prompt people to instill civic virtue in each other is by aligning law with morality" (Cooter 2000: 1597).

Following Cooter (1998, 2000), we consider the role of law in influencing human choice through internalization and gradual adaptation of citizens' taste.[8] Differently from Cooter, we consider the case of laws that do not align with pre-existing moral norms and social beliefs. Unlike Cooter's ideal scenario of non-paternalistic legal intervention, we allow for paternalistic intervention aimed at manipulating social beliefs and behavior.[9] In our world, law, values and existing social norms are not assumed to be aligned. In our setting, social norms could develop in opposition to law, inducing civil disobedience and reinforcing the social values contrary to law.

3.2.2   Civil disobedience and the emergence
of countervailing norms

Legal philosophers and political theorists have long debated the complex relationship between law and morality. Legal rules derive their legitimacy and acceptance because of their instrumental role for attaining a satisfactory common life. Political obligation is based on the recognition of the instrumental value of law. As Robinson (2000) observes as a matter of common sense, the law's moral credibility is not needed to tell a person that murder, rape, or robbery is wrong. Yet, the use of law is not limited to this. Even though in general it is morality that drives law,[10] in some situations law is utilized as an instrument of moral suasion, or in our terminology: value formation. To accomplish this task, the law cannot deviate too far from the community's current perceptions of justice.[11] The avoidance of a conflict between law and morality is important, inasmuch as "some citizens regard lawmakers as moral authorities, or citizens think that law as such deserves respect. For these citizens, obeying law is a requirement of morality (...) Instead of law aligning with morality, lawmakers can assume that some people will align their morality with new laws" (Cooter 2000: 20).

Under each of these views, the alignment of law to existing morality is critical for the preservation of legitimacy and the ability of law to effectively shape conduct. As laws begin to depart from social values, the influence of law on social norms becomes indeterminate. Laws that depart only slightly from the current mode may occasion a gradual adaptation of the opinions to the new statute. For example, the criminal law's influence as a moral authority has effect primarily at the borderline of criminal activity, where there may be some ambiguity as to whether the conduct really is wrong. Here the law drives the evolution of norms in the same direction of the law.

In other cases new statutes which differ substantially from the current opinion mode may lead to opposition. Dissent may result from a discrepancy between the present state of the law and the prevailing public attitude toward the regulated conduct. Some individuals will manifest their dissent by expressing their opposition to others (protest), while others will oppose the law by ostensibly violating it (civil disobedience). Protest and civil disobedience signal dissent and, through a process of hysteresis, may lead to reinforcing contrary social opinion.

Different types of disobedience have been identified in the literature. Civil disobedience may be a protest against laws that infringe against what individuals perceive to be their natural rights, or a protest against the failure of the law to recognize or fulfill individual rights and expectations. Zwiebach (1975: 169–96) provides examples of these two forms of civil disobedience. An example of the first form of disobedience in the United States is when someone disobeys a law on the grounds that it is unconstitutional. Through civil disobedience, individuals assert their (positive or natural) rights against an existing law. For example, an African American person that refuses to sit in a segregated section of a courtroom, or a student wearing a black armband as a symbol of political protest in violation of school regulations, or a doctor prescribing birth control in violation of a state law. In each of these instances violators assert that the law that they disobeyed violates their constitutional rights. The second form of disobedience is the assertion of a right that is not recognized in the existing system of law. In this case, a violator attempts to assert that a right which is not recognized by law today, ought to be recognized, or that the existing legal language must be interpreted to recognize such right. While the assertion of positive legal right is justified on legal grounds, the assertion of non-recognized law can be justified on moral grounds. Examples of such disobedience can be found in the various forms of protest in the area of human rights law. Historically, this form of civil disobedience has been very valuable to society, allowing acceptance and gradual discovery of new rights in ways that would not have been developed through traditional political or lawmaking processes.

Other examples of civil disobedience involve the assertion of private or conscious commitment against the legal system (Zwiebach 1975: 175). In this case violators justify their disobedience through private and subjective beliefs. For example, people who assert that religious commitment prevents them from saluting a flag. This form of disobedience supports the notion that a man is not merely a public creature but also a private one. This form of disobedience is generally met with an attitude of toleration. Toleration is instrumental to the expression of free thought, allowing others to weigh the significance and importance of a particular legal command against the cost imposed on members of the community. Law commands are counterbalanced by expressions of disapproval. Overtime consensus may be formed through the balancing of personal convictions against public purposes. An example in this category can be found in Hart's analysis of homosexuality and human sexual relationships, repressive laws generate moral outrage, and trigger the support of actions that are perceived as essential to the expression and free development of one's own personality.

Carried to its extreme, disobedience may be directed at the legal system as a whole, rather than at specific laws. This form of disobedience is what Zwiebach (1975: 192) calls revolution and is justified by the claim that the regime is illegitimate. Thus, the citizens disobey not laws, but rather the source of these laws. Such disobedience is observed in circumstances where the contested laws touch many aspects of life and where the rebelling members of society perceive that the regime cannot be easily corrected through the political process.

Stuntz (2000) provides other interesting illustrations of civil disobedience and the law's impact on social norms. Stuntz considers how criminal law can defeat itself due to the lack of alignment between criminal laws and laypeople's values and norms, generating disobedience rather than obedience:

> In a legal system structured as ours is, criminalization can work against the very norms on which it rests, meaning that popular norms may tend to move in the opposite direction from the law. Criminal law's relationship with popular norms

may sometimes be perverse – not the relationship of car to driver or driver to car, but rather the relationship of one side of a seesaw to the other. To put the point simply, some crimes may be self-defeating (...) Sometimes, the best way for the legal system to advance or reinforce norms may be to ignore them.

(Stuntz 2000: 1872–3)

Stuntz considers the examples of vice crimes (e.g., drinking during Prohibition, gambling) and highly divisive "moral" crimes (e.g., sodomy, slavery), noting that vice crime enforcement has historically been concentrated upon poor and urban neighborhoods, both because of the theory that in such neighborhoods, the incidence of a given vice will be correlated with the incidence of several others, and because detection has been easier since poor people have a harder time concealing vice activities.[12] Such enforcement led to the perception that these policies were driven by racial or class bias rather than moral justice, corroding the authority of the law for a larger portion of the public.[13] These examples are good illustrations of how law can positively or negatively influence social norms. Morals crimes, involving issues over which public opinion is widely split, tend to have a set of people "on the fence," highly susceptible to persuasion. Consequently, effective media coverage of criminalized activities can positively influence individual beliefs, creating a critical mass necessary to create a self-reinforcing norm. On the contrary, other persecutory laws may have generated sympathy for the targeted class of violators generating dominant social support for tolerance or repeal of the criminalizing law.

3.3 Two models of legislation with countervailing norms

3.3.1 Introduction

In Section 3.2, we discussed various ways in which law may influence individual values and social norms. In this section we will proffer two models which allow deeper insights into how countervailing social norms may reduce or even reverse the intended effect of legislation on actual behavior. We choose these two models for two reasons. First, because the countervailing norms effect has not yet been studied in the Law-and-Economics literature and second, because we think that these models may provide valuable insights for policy makers.

Both models are based on the observation that individual values and norms evolve in a process of communication and opinion formation in which the frequency of an opinion influences the probability that more individuals adopt this opinion. To keep the argument simple, we ignore the conceptual difference between values and norms, i.e., we assume that each individual is willing to act according to his or her values and to sanction violations of this norm. The role of the law in this process is twofold. On the one hand, law can be analogized to one big player in the opinion formation process. In a democratic system, the enactment of a law requires political support. This shows that there is a large (or otherwise sufficiently powerful)[14] constituency, perhaps with particular (informal, mental) authority, who accord with the values expressed in the enacted law. On the other hand, the introduction of a new law triggers and publicizes individual behavior: a new law that is met with widespread support and compliance signals that most people concord to a large degree with the new legal standard. This strengthens the law's authority in the eyes of the observers. If the introduction of a new law is followed by disobedience, individual observers infer that the law is not aligned with the common sense of justice. There are many individuals whose ideas and internal values differ so much from the law that they are willing to incur the cost of protest and face the risk of a sanction rather than complying with the law. This undermines the law's authority for the observing public.

Based on these basic assumptions, we analyze the effect of new statutes when individual values and social norms are affected by legal innovation. We differentiate between new statutes which differ slightly or strongly from the mode of the distribution of internal norms. In order to keep the formalism tractable, we discuss the two roles of law in separate models which, however, easily fit into the same framework of analysis.

The first of these models (Section 3.3.3) concentrates on direct communication as the driving force in the evolution of social norms. In this model, actual behavior depends both on legal and social norms, but does not influence their further evolution. We will discuss constellations in which a legal norm which substantially differs from the prevailing social norm may have very little influence on the social norm or drive the social norm away from the legal norm. In the same constellations, legal norms which are closer to the social norms may have a much stronger influence on the latter, and in the desired direction.

In the second model (Section 3.3.4), we assume away the effects of pure communication, and introduce actual behavior as a factor influencing the evolution of social norms. Behavior is itself being influenced by both social and legal norms. We again discuss constellations in which legal intervention may be self-defeating when laws are too distant from social norms. It will turn out, however, that legal norms which differ substantially from social norms may drive the latter further away from the legal norms only under very restrictive assumptions. This suggests that social norms may have a countervailing effect on laws only in a limited set of circumstances.

3.3.2   *General framework*

We consider a set A of actions a which is typically covered by one rule r dividing the set into two subsets: the set of permissible actions A^+ and the set of forbidden actions A^-. For simplicity, we assume that a natural order exists within the set of actions ($A = \{1, 2, 3, \ldots, N_A\}$) and that rule $r \in R = \{0, 1, 2, \ldots, N_A\}$ assigns all actions $a < r + 1/2$ to the set of permissible actions and all actions $a > r + 1/2$ to the set of forbidden actions, formally: $A^+ = \{a \in A|\ a < r + 1/2\}$ and $A^- = \{a \in A|\ a > r + 1/2\} = A \backslash A^+$.[15] This allows for $N_A + 1$ different possible rules. Rule $r = 0$ is most restrictive and forbids all actions in A while rule $r = N_A$ allows all actions in A.

As an example, one may think of norms on the consumption of drugs. The natural order is some mixture of how addictive the drugs are and how destructive their use or abuse is to the health and the productivity of their consumer. According to this order, consumption of heroin will be very high-numbered while the consumption of marihuana will be lower-numbered. Very low numbers will be assigned to the consumption of alcohol and tobacco. Obviously, one may well debate whether such order is actually natural. Many people would rather argue that this order is a consequence of the evolution of social norms itself or that one cannot reduce the many dimensions in which drugs differ from each other to one single order. However, we maintain this assumption in order to keep the model uni-dimensional and the analysis relatively simple. Given such "natural" order, a normative rule would state that one should not consume drugs numbered higher than some critical r, while the consumption of lower-numbered drugs is permissible. For example suppose the norm r_1 allows the consumption of alcohol, tobacco, caffeine etc. but forbids the consumption of marihuana, morphine, heroin etc. Then a norm $r_2 > r_1$ would be repressive on the same set of drugs as rule r_1 except for marihuana, the consumption of which rule r_2 permits.

Avoidance of negative externalities as production of a public good, for example littering or exhausting fumes from the automobile, may serve as a second example. Consider a situation in which all individuals privately benefit from performing all actions, but at the same time harm society – for some actions more than they benefit themselves. The natural order would then be the difference between the externalities and the private benefits, with those actions being high-numbered for which the negative externalities outweighs the private benefits by the largest difference. Note that in this example there may be an unambiguous objectively best rule from the social point of view (typically the action at which the difference turns zero). Still, this objectively best rule may be highly debated and subject to the opinion formation process which we introduce shortly when the evaluation of the externalities is subjective.

In such a setting, it is unlikely that all individuals share the same conviction about what rule r is best for society or what rule they internalize as norm. As we already mentioned, we abstract from the conceptual difference between values and norms. This implies that we assume that an individual who thinks that a certain action should be forbidden refrains from this action and is willing to impose sanctions on other individuals who perform this action. Indexing all individuals in a society by $i \in \{1, 2, 3, \ldots, I\}$, where I is the size of the population, we write r_i as the rule considered to be best for society by individual i. In addition to these individual norms, there may be a legal rule r_λ relevant for the society which forbids all actions $a > r_\lambda + 1/2$ and allows all actions $a < r_\lambda + 1/2$.

We do not take individual norms as exogenously given. Rather, we take into account that individual norms are a social phenomenon. Individuals form and revise their individual norms in interaction with other individuals.

There may be several explanations for why this happens. We propose the following. Let there be two levels of values guiding individual behavior. One is very general: to do what is good, to comply with God's will, to support the Nation, to do what is good for the more or less local or global community. These higher level norms are what Sen (1977) calls "meta-preferences".[16] The other, lower level is more specific and gives some basic rules on how the general goal may be achieved. While one can assume the upper level of beliefs to be stable, the lower level is subject to opinion formation for the following reason: if people use the lower level value judgments as guidelines for their behavior in order to reach the final goal, i.e., compliance with the upper value judgments, then they necessarily have to search for the "best" lower level norms. At least part of this search is by social interaction.

In order to understand the evolution of individual norms in reaction to legal change, we start from a model developed by Flieth and Wangenheim (1996),[17] which resembles information cascade models,[18] but differs in three important respects from the standard version of that approach. First, individuals always change their opinion on what behavior is best (i.e., their values) with a strictly positive probability. Second, individual learning is not Bayesian but follows a super-linear imitation pattern as frequently used in evolutionary game theory (cf. Ellison and Fudenberg 1993, 1995, who also go in this direction). Third, opinions are not about an action which directly influences the individual's well-being (such as choosing a restaurant, one of the standard examples in information cascade literature), but rather about policies which influence individual well-being only after a (political) opinion aggregation process. The model thus clearly differs from imitation models in evolutionary game theory where imitation not only depends on the frequencies of behavioral traits but also on their expected payoffs (for an overview see, e.g., Mailath 1998). The formal approach resembles a literature on opinion formation which developed independently of the information cascade literature, but was concentrated on cases of only two alternative opinions (e.g., Arthur 1988, 1989, Schnabl 1991, Weise 1992, von Wangenheim 1993, 1995).

Flieth and Wangenheim (1996) start from the simplifying assumption – which we will also adopt – that in every short time period, adjustment takes place by only one step. In other words, the probability that an individual norm changes from r_i to $r_i + \Delta r$ or $r_i - \Delta r$ is zero whenever $\Delta r > 1$. With this simplification, they denote the individual transition probabilities from r_i to $r_i + 1$ and $r_i - 1$ within a certain time period by $\pi^+(\cdot)$ and $\pi^-(\cdot)$, respectively. They further assume that all individuals adjust their opinions on what the just norm would be as the consequence of pairwise communication and other influences. In particular, they model the transition probabilities $\pi^+(\cdot)$ and $\pi^-(\cdot)$ as being given by a constant minimum term $\pi_o^+ > 0$ and, respectively, $\pi_o^- > 0$ plus a quadratic function of the number of all individuals with a higher or lower norm, respectively (i.e., a quadratic function of $\sum_{r=r_i+1}^{N_A} f(r,t)$ or $\sum_{r=0}^{r_i-1} f(r,t)$, respectively, where $f(r,t)$ is the frequency of individuals having r as norm at time t). They justify this assumption by a simple communication and discussion process: besides a base rate of random opinion changes, an individual may change his or her opinion in one direction only if he or she communicates with another individual whose opinion differs in this very direction. The probability of such communication is obviously proportional to the current frequencies with which such opinions are held. Within any such communication, individuals try to convince each other among other arguments by reference to a common acquaintance whose opinion deviates from the discussion partner's opinion in the same direction. Again, the probability that such a common acquaintance exists is proportional to the current frequencies with which such opinions are held. This accounts for the quadratic term form of the functions describing the transition probabilities.

By reducing the time period on which transition probabilities are defined towards zero and then reinterpreting the transition probabilities as transition rates, one can describe the evolution of norms held in society by the following differential equations system:

$$
\frac{\mathrm{d}f(r,t)}{\mathrm{d}t} = f(r-1,t)\pi^+(r-1; F(t)) + f(r+1,t)\pi^-(r+1; F(t))
$$
$$
- f(r,t)[\pi^+(r; F(t)) + \pi^-(r; F(t))]
$$

(1)

$\forall r \in A$ where $F(t) = f(1,t), \ldots, f(N_A, t)$ and $f(-1,t) = f(N_A+1,t) = \pi^+(-1;\cdot) = \pi^-(-1;\cdot) = \pi^-(N_A+1;\cdot) = \pi^+(N_A;\cdot) = 0$ control for border conditions.[19]

Inserting their simple transition rates (quadratic functions of $\sum_{r=r_i+1}^{N_A} f(r,t)$ and $\sum_{r=0}^{r_i-1} f(r,t)$,) Flieth and Wangenheim (1996) show that this system has an odd number of opinion distributions which form rest points. Among these, the number of stable rest points is larger than the number of unstable rest points by one. We follow Flieth and Wangenheim (1996) in calling the opinion (in our case: norm) distributions which form stable rest points "attracting distributions".[20]

3.3.3 Protest: Purely communicative norm formation

In our first model, we concentrate on the case of protest and treat social norm formation as a purely communicative process as Flieth and Wangenheim (1996) do it for opinions. However, we generalize their transition probabilities by allowing for a double influence of the distance of two individuals' opinions. First, this distance affects the probabilities that these two individuals communicate, and second, it affects the probability that reference to one of the two individuals' opinion convinces the other in a communication with a third individual. In addition, we treat a legal rule, if it exists, as affecting both the non-communication part of transition probabilities and as an explicit argument in discussions. We thus write for the individual transition probabilities from values r_i to r_i+1 and r_i-1

$$
\pi^+(r_i, r_\lambda; F(t)) = \pi_o^+ + \sigma_{r_\lambda - r_i}^0 + \sum_{\rho=r_i+1}^{N_A} \tau_{\rho-r_i}^1 f(\rho, t)
$$
$$
\left(\tau_o^+ + \sigma_{r_\lambda - r_i}^1 + \sum_{\rho=r_i+1}^{N_A} \tau_{\rho-r_i}^2 f(\rho, t) \right)
$$

(2)

and, respectively,

$$\pi^-(r_i, r_\lambda; F(t)) = \pi_o^- + \sigma_{r_i - r_\lambda}^0 + \sum_{\rho=0}^{r_i-1} \tau_{r_i-\rho}^1 f(\rho, t)$$

$$\left(\tau_o^- + \sigma_{r_i-r_\lambda}^1 + \sum_{\rho=0}^{r_i-1} \tau_{r_i-\rho}^2 f(\rho, t) \right) \tag{3}$$

where the variables are defined as follows: $\pi_o^+ > 0$, $\pi_o^- > 0$, $\pi_o^+ \geq 0$, $\pi_o^- \geq 0$ are constants denoting the unexplained part of the transition probabilities and of the power of an individual's arguments to convince another individual. For strictly positive Δ, σ_Δ^0 describes how the law affects the transition probabilities depending on the distance Δ between the individual and the legal norm. If $\Delta \leq 0$, $\sigma_\Delta^0 = 0$. Similarly, σ_Δ^1 describes how important an argument the legal norm may be in discussions depending on the distance Δ between the norm adopted by the individual to be convinced and the legal norm. Again, $\sigma_\Delta^1 = 0$ if $\Delta \leq 0$. Finally, τ_Δ^1 is the probability that two individuals whose norms differ by Δ communicate and τ_Δ^2 denotes the probability that reference to an individual whose norm differs by Δ convinces another individual to shift the norm one step towards this individual.

In general, one cannot solve a differential equations system as described in equation (1) with transition probabilities as defined in equations (2) and (3). For, $N_A > 3$, it is not even possible to determine the rest point distributions algebraically. We therefore rely on simulations of the differential equations system for the remainder of our chapter.

From a large number of simulations, we extrapolate the following:

> Proposition 1: Suppose the effect of legal norms on interactive individual norm formation is accurately described by the differential equations system (1) with transition probabilities as given in equations (2) and (3). Then

1   social norms may be self-reinforcing to the point of having a countervailing effect on legal norms;
2   the influence of legal norms on social norms may be smaller, if the distance between legal norms and social norms held by most individuals is larger;
3   legal norms may push social norms to the opposite side of the opinion space, if the distance between legal norms and social norms held by most individuals is too large and such large distance provokes open opposition.

Since this proposition only claims the possibility of a certain relationship, we can prove it by example. Consider the following set of parameters:[21]

$$N_A = 6; \pi_o^+ = \pi_o^- = 1/6; \tau_o^+ = \tau_o^- = 0; \tau^1 = \tau^2 = \left(\frac{10}{3}, \frac{5}{3}, 0, 0, 0, 0 \right). \tag{4}$$

We first simulate the situation without any law, i.e., we set $\sigma^0 = \sigma^1 = (0,0,0,0,0,0)$. Starting from various initial conditions, we find that there are seven different

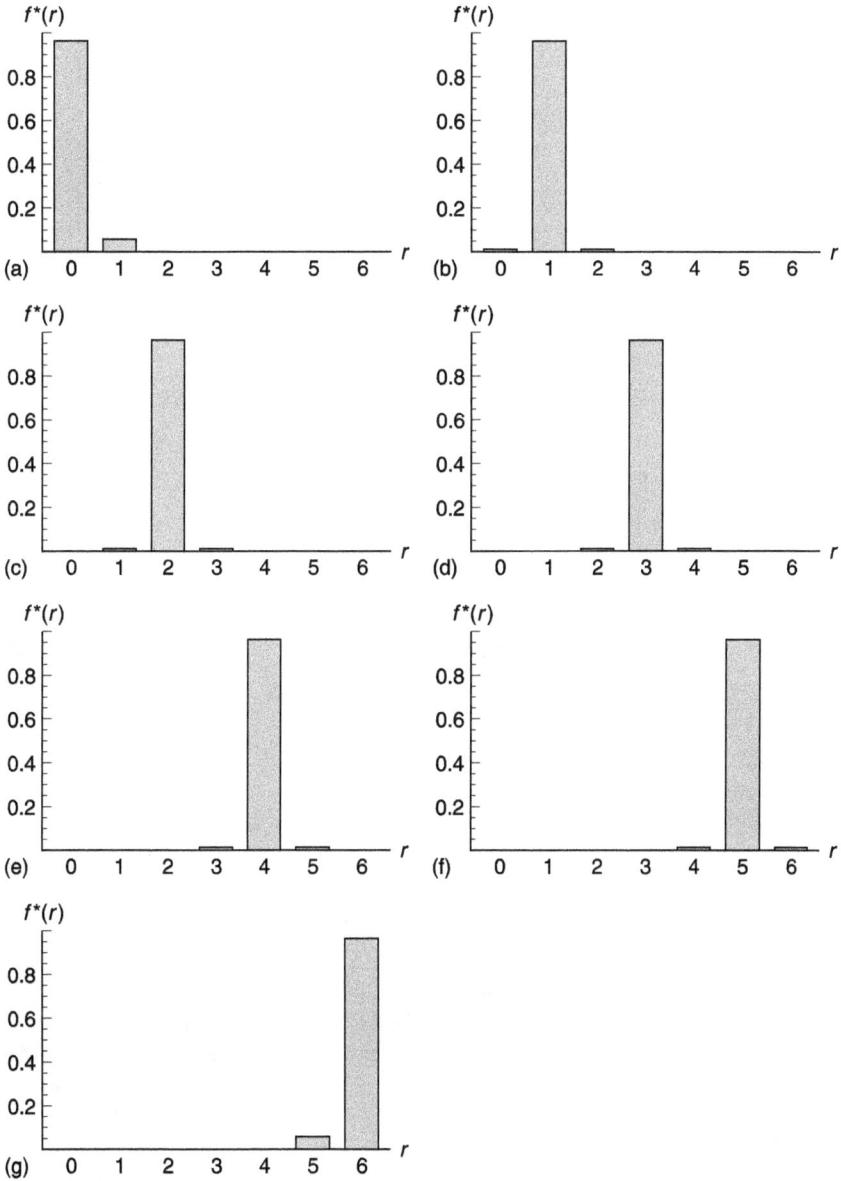

Figure 3.1 Attracting distributions without law for parameters given in equation (4).

attracting distributions, each possible opinion being the mode of one of them. Since the exact frequencies are of little relevance, we only present the attracting distributions graphically (Figure 3.1).

Now suppose social norms happen to be close to one of the attracting distribution with mode on $r = 5$ or on $r = 6$, i.e., close to a very permissive attracting

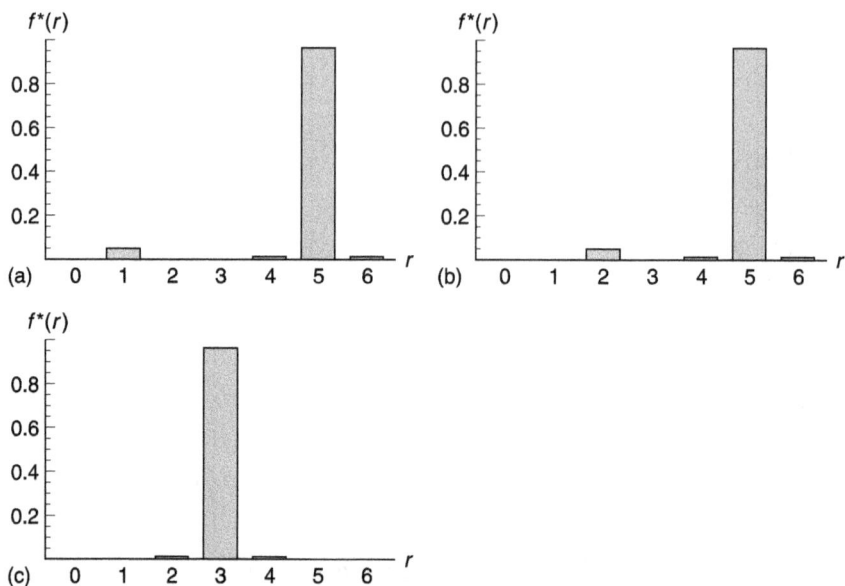

Figure 3.2 Attracting distributions for (a) $r_\lambda = 1$, (b) $r_\lambda = 2$, and (c) $r_\lambda = 3$, with the initial distribution given by most permissive attracting distribution without law as depicted in Figure 3.1(g).

distribution. To show that legal norms may fail to influence social norms substantially, we assume that legal rules influence individual norm revisions only for individuals whose norm is close enough to the legal rule. We use the explicit example: $\sigma^0 = (\frac{4}{3},\frac{2}{3},0,0,0,0)$ and $\sigma^1 = (\frac{2}{5},\frac{1}{5},0,0,0,0)$. We compare the legal rules $r_\lambda = 1$, $r_\lambda = 2$, and $r_\lambda = 3$. Figure 3.2 shows the attracting distributions to which social norms tend when starting at one of the very permissive distributions which were attracting without law.

One can see that the most restrictive of these legal rules fails to attract the majority of individuals (Figure 3.2a). Only a small number of individuals cluster around the legal norm, the vast majority remains close to the mode of the initial distribution or only moves one step. The attracting force of the law is not strong enough to draw enough individuals beyond the limits of the attraction basin of the second-most permissive attracting distribution. The same is true for a slightly less restrictive legal rule ($r_\lambda = 2$, see Figure 3.2b). Only if the legal norm is close enough to the initial distribution of norms ($r_\lambda = 3$), may it attract the social norms into its vicinity (see Figure 3.2c). This completes the proof of the first two parts of the proposition by example.

To prove the third part of the proposition by example, we change τ^2 to $\tau^2 = (\frac{1}{2},\frac{1}{4},0,0,0,0)$ and add outright opposition to the effect of distant legal norms by making σ_Δ^0 and σ_Δ^1 negative for large Δ. To avoid negative transition probabilities we require that $\sigma_\Delta^0 + \min(\pi_o^+, \pi_o^-) > 0$ and $\sigma_\Delta^1 + \min(\tau_o^+, \tau_o^-) > 0$

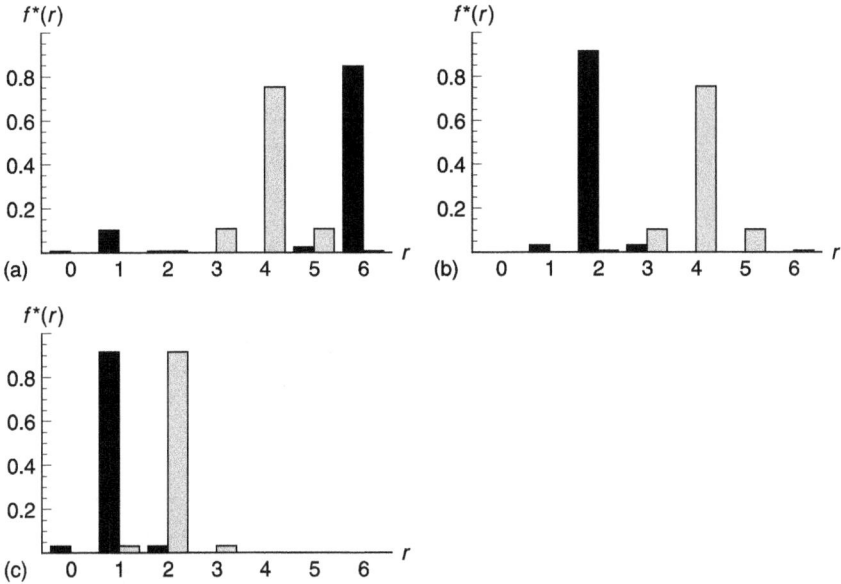

Figure 3.3 Attracting distributions to which social norms tend (black) when too distant legal norms trigger opposition and the dynamics start at initial distributions as depicted in gray: (a) initial distribution with mode on $r = 4$ as it may result from dynamics without law and with $r_\lambda = 1$; (b) same as (a) but with $r_\lambda = 2$; (c) initial distribution as it resulted in (b) and with $r_\lambda = 1$.

for all Δ. As particular example we choose $\sigma^0 = (\frac{4}{3}, \frac{2}{3}, 0, -\frac{1}{60}, -\frac{1}{15}, -\frac{1}{12})$ and $\sigma^1 = (\frac{2}{5}, \frac{1}{5}, 0, -\frac{1}{10}, -\frac{4}{5}, -\frac{4}{5})$. To guarantee non-negative transition probabilities we replace our assumptions on τ_o^+ and τ_o^- by $\tau_o^+ = \tau_o^- = 1$.

With these parameters, introducing a restrictive legal rule ($r_\lambda \leq 1$) when social norms have settled around a permissive mode of $r = 4$ or $r = 5$, opposition against the distant legal norm is strong enough to push social norms towards an attracting distribution with mode $r = 6$. (One should note that an initial distribution with mode $r = 6$ remains nearly unaffected by such a new legal rule.) Figure 3.3a shows this effect for $r_\lambda = 1$ and the distribution of social norms centered on a mode of $r = 4$ having resulted from the norm formation process without law. The initial distribution is plotted gray, the attracting distribution black. One should note that the legal norm is able to attract some individuals, but repels most of them. As soon as the law is closer to the social norms, however, it attracts nearly all individuals to its close vicinity (see Figure 3.3b).

Our numerical example thus provides a proof of the possibility stated in part 3 of the proposition.

For both parameter sets, more than one attracting distributions may exist for any given legal rule r_λ. The two bottom graphs of Figure 3.4 show in detail which

40 Francesco Parisi and Georg von Wangenheim

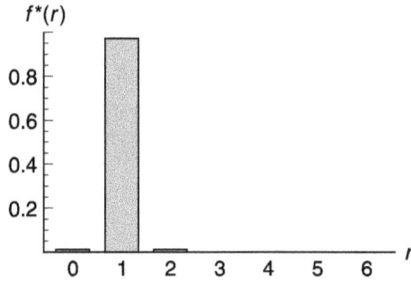

Figure 3.4 Top: Attracting distributions with $r_\lambda = 1$, when the initial distribution is given by the attracting distribution achieved by $r_\lambda = 3$ (Figure 3.2(c)); bottom: possible modes of attracting distributions resulting from various r_λ for the two exemplary parameter sets in proof of Proposition 1.

modes the attracting distributions may have for a given rule. One should note that at least for the extreme legal rules, the set of possible modes of the attracting distributions is not connected. One may thus speculate that reactions of social norms to legal change are path dependent.

In fact, it turns out for both parameter sets we used to prove proposition 1 that legal norms which are close to the social norms can induce a change of social norms in the desired direction even when legal norms more distant from the social norms are not. This leads us to:

Corollary 1: If legal norms are unable to induce a big change in social norms because of the law's large distance from social norms, the big change may be achieved by stepwise adaptation of the law.

For the proof we continue the examples. Running the simulation of the equation system of the example we used to prove parts (1) and (2) of the proposition with the attracting distribution induced by $r_\lambda = 3$ (Figure 3.2c) as initial distribution, yields attraction of social norms to the distribution depicted in Figure 3.4, if $r_\lambda = 1$. By introducing the legal rule $r_\lambda = 1$ in two steps (first step: $r_\lambda = 3$, second step: $r_\lambda = 1$), one can thus achieve a result which is blocked by the legal norm's lack of power to convince individuals holding distant norms if $r_\lambda = 1$ is introduced at once. Similarly, if we introduce the legal norm $r_\lambda = 1$ in two steps (first step: $r_\lambda = 3$, second step: $r_\lambda = 1$) in the example we used to prove part (3) of the proposition, we can again pull social norms towards an attracting distribution centered on $r = r_\lambda = 1$ as shown in Figure 3.3c. Again, stepwise introduction of a restrictive legal rule achieves a result which was impossible to achieve by introducing the strict legal rule in one big step.

The model based on pure communication presented in this section may explain those effects discussed in Section 3.2 which relied on protest. We have concentrated on the social norm formation process, but actual behavior will follow social norms rather than the legal norm, if their enforcement mechanism – social sanctions or internalization – is strong enough as compared to legal sanctions. Without opening a new discussion, we only hint at the possibility to model the strength of enforcement mechanisms of social norms in a similar model as the one presented here. What is missing in the model is disobedience as a driving force of norm formation. This is what we concentrate on in the model we will present in the following section.

3.3.4   *Observed behavior and norm formation*

Our second model concentrates on the case of the influence of observed behavior on the norm formation process. Again, we try to keep the model tractable by neglecting other aspects relevant for the evolution of social norms in the shadow of legal norms. We thus assume away the direct effects of the legal norm and reference to other individuals' values as an argument in communication. Instead, we assume that observation of other individuals' actual behavior is the only relevant argument in communication on norms or values.

We thus start this section with a very simple model of behavior within the general framework presented in Section 3.3.2. We assume that each and every individual enters into a situation in which he or she has to decide whether to perform action a with an average frequency of q_a within each standard time period.[22] To keep the model simple, we assume $q_a = q = 1$ for all a. Allowing for different q_a would expand the formalism but would not lead to additional insights.

Once an individual has entered into such a situation, he or she weighs his or her perceived benefits and costs of performing the action and opts for the action if the former outweigh the latter. For simplicity, we assume that each action a conveys the same[23] private benefits β to all individuals and induces only costs $c_\lambda(a)$ and $c_s(a)$, which result from sanctions associated to violating legal or social norms.[24] To allow for random influences, we assume that decision making is stochastic: the probability of opting for an action a is given by a reverse logit transformation $p(\text{NB}(a)) = \frac{1}{1+e^{-\alpha \text{NB}(a)}}$, where $\text{NB}(a) = \beta - (c_\lambda(a) + c_s(a))$ stands for the net benefit of action a and α is a non-negative constant which gives the degree to which the individual's action is determined by the sign of NB_a.[25]

We assume that violations of the legal rule are sanctioned (at least with a given probability) by the government, and violations of social norms are sanctioned (again at least with a certain probability) by all individuals who have adopted this or a more restrictive norm. For legal sanctions, we consider a fixed part of the sanction for any violation ($s_\lambda^o > 0$) and a variable part which depends on the distance of the action to the legal rule ($s_\lambda^1(a-r_\lambda-\frac{1}{2})$, where $s_\lambda^1 \geq 0$ is a constant and subtracting $\frac{1}{2}$ follows from the same arguments as in the previous section). We restrict social sanctions to a fixed term (with $s_s^o > 0$ as the sanction imposed by every individual who thinks an action to be forbidden). We neglect a corresponding marginal part – not because we think it to be empirically irrelevant but because it fails to provide additional insights despite the resulting complications of the formalism.

Given that the law leaves actions $a < r_\lambda + \frac{1}{2}$ unsanctioned and individuals only sanction actions $a < r_i + \frac{1}{2}$ we rewrite the net benefit of an action as

$$\text{NB}(a, r_\lambda, f) = \beta - \text{H}(a - r_\lambda)\left(s_\lambda^o + s_\lambda^1\left(a - r_\lambda - \frac{1}{2}\right)\right) - s_s^o \sum_{r=0}^{a-1} f(r) \quad (5)$$

where $\text{H}(x) = \begin{cases} 0 \text{ if } x \leq 0 \\ 1 \text{ if } x > 0 \end{cases}$ is the unit step function and f is a shortcut for the

entire distribution $(f(0), f(1), \ldots, f(N_A))$.

The norm formation part of our model is similar to the one presented in the previous section. Again, we assume that there is a base rate of opinion change in both directions. The probability that an individual communicates with some other individual who tries to convince the first one of a more restrictive or a more permissive norm remains proportional to $\sum_{r=0}^{r_i-1} f(r)$ and $\sum_{r=r_i+1}^{N_A} f(r)$, respectively.

What changes is the central argument in such communication. We assume that individuals may be convinced to become one step more permissive by reference to an observable action which the individual thinks to be forbidden – "look at Jim: he also does what you think is immoral." The striking argument for becoming more restrictive is reference to an observable omission of an action – "look at Jane: she also refrains from doing what you still think to be permissible." If all actions and omissions are equally observable, individual transition probabilities from value judgment r_i to r_i+1 and r_i-1 thus become:

$$\pi^+(r_i;\cdot) = \pi_o^+ + \tau_b \sum_{r=r_i+1}^{N_A} f(r) \sum_{a=r_i+1}^{N_A} p(NB(a, r_\lambda, f)) \quad (6)$$

and, respectively,

$$\pi^-(r_i;\cdot) = \pi_o^- + \tau_b \sum_{r=0}^{r_i} f(r) \sum_{a=1}^{r_i} (1 - p(NB(a, r_\lambda, f))) \quad (7)$$

However, identical observability of all actions neglects one important effect: reference to an action which is illegal but has been taken nevertheless is far more impressive an argument than reference to a legal action. We therefore add additional weight to such actions in equation (6) and rewrite:

$$\pi^+(r_i;\cdot) = \pi_o^+ + \sum_{r=r_i+1}^{N_A} f(r) \sum_{a=r_i+1}^{N_A} p(NB(a, r_\lambda, f))$$

$$\left[\tau_b + H(a - r_\lambda) \left(\tau_{v,0} + \tau_{v,1} \left(a - r_\lambda - \tfrac{1}{2} \right) \right) \right]$$

(8)

where $H(x) = \begin{cases} 0 \text{ if } x \leq 0 \\ 1 \text{ if } x > 0 \end{cases}$ is again the unit step function. In this transition

probability, $\tau_{v,0} \geq 0$ is the additional fixed weight which an illegal action gets irrespective of its distance from the legal rule. $\tau_{v,1} \geq 0$ corresponds to the variable term in the legal sanction's size: it puts the more weight on illegal actions the further they are from the legal rule. We suggest that $\tau_{v,1}$ tends to be strictly positive, at least if the variable term in legal sanctions is positive, since then it makes sense to distinguish between minor and major violations of the law, of which the latter are more impressive arguments than the former. We call the effects described by strictly positive $\tau_{v,0}$ or $\tau_{v,1}$ the "visibility effect" of a legal rule. We claim that a corresponding effect on the side of legal actions is negligible. One should note that completely permissive law ($r_\lambda = N_A$) is equivalent to no law at all: since $H(a - N_A) = 0$ for all a, the transition probabilities defined in equations (7) and (8) as well as the action probabilities defined in equation (5) become independent of the size of legal sanctions and of the power of the visibility effect.

Inserting these transition probabilities into equation (3) again results in a differential equations system which describes the evolution of individual norms in the course of time. Like the system in the previous section, it does not allow us to find general solutions. Again, we have to rely on numerical simulations. To discuss the various properties of the model, we leave the parameters

$$\alpha = 1, \beta = 4, s_s^o = 1/4, \pi_o^+ = \pi_o^- = 1/6, \tau_b = 8$$

(9)

unchanged throughout the discussion. Based on these parameters – and on many others, to check for sensitivity of our results – we ran a large number of simulations. From these simulations, we again deduce a number of insights which allow us to compare the current observed-behavior model with the protest model of the previous section.

In the following discussion, we concentrate on parameters for which behavior in the model differs from what one would expect when treating law as a simple incentive mechanism. In particular, we assume that (1) s_s^o and τ_b are large enough to induce substantial frequency dependencies in individual norm formation and that (2) the visibility effect is strong (i.e., $\tau_{v,0}$ or $\tau_{v,1}$ are large) as compared to the legal sanction (s_λ^0 and s_λ^1). The first of these assumptions allows multiple equilibria to

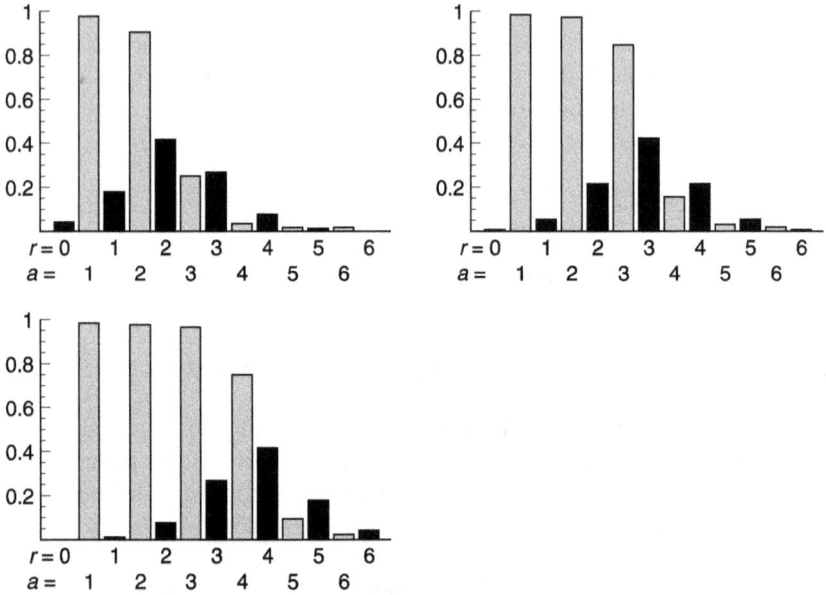

Figure 3.5 Attracting distributions without law with parameters as given in equation (9) and $r_\lambda = N_A$ (black) and consequential action frequencies (gray).

occur as in the protest model. By the second assumption we exclude cases in which the legal sanction is so strong that disobedience is effectively excluded by its very high costs.[26] These general assumptions leave room to separate two qualitatively different parameter combinations: the case in which the fixed parts of the legal sanction and the visibility effect predominate and the case in which the marginal parts predominate.

We start our discussion with the case of negligible marginal parts ($s_\lambda^1 = \tau_{v,1} = 0$), a severe fixed legal sanction ($s_\lambda^0 = 2$) for violating the law and an even stronger fixed visibility effect ($\tau_{v,0} = 4$). When the law is absent (or completely permissive), i.e., when $r_\lambda = N_A$, then the parameters we chose induce three attracting distributions of norms, which imply large action frequencies to the left of their mode and small ones to the right (cf. Figure 3.5).

Reducing permissiveness of the law has two effects. On the one hand, now illegal actions will become immediately less frequent, because of the legal sanctions associated to them. On the other hand, their being illegal will make them more recognizable and a stronger argument in favor of more permissiveness. As a consequence, the further evolution of social norms is not only guided by fewer of the now illegal actions but also by their stronger influence on norm formation. Which of the two effects prevails, depends on the exact parameters. If the latter effect prevails, more restrictive law may provoke the emergence of additional attracting distributions of social norms on the very permissive side, which may eventually replace all attracting distributions with intermediate modes. In our example,

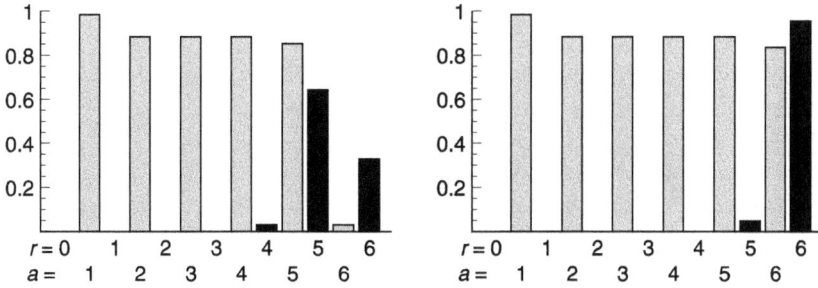

r_λ	Modes of attracting distributions						
	0	1	2	3	4	5	6
0						×	×
1						×	×
2							×
3							×
4				×			×
5				×	×		×
6			×	×	×		

Figure 3.6 (Extension of Figure 3.5) Attracting distributions for small r_λ (top), and effect of legal rule on possible modes of attracting distributions (bottom) for small s_λ^0 and large $\tau_{v,0}$

already the first step of additional restrictions in the law provokes the emergence of additional attracting distributions of social norms (similar to the distribution depicted in the top right graph of Figure 3.6). One should note that at the same time, the previously least permissive attracting distribution of social norms disappears (see the table in Figure 3.6).

When the law becomes more restrictive ($r_\lambda = 4$), no further extremely permissive attracting distribution of social norms emerges, but the original set of attracting distributions degenerates to a single one. Now suppose that social norms used to be close to one of the attracting distributions which exist without law. Then the first steps of additional restrictions by the law induce only minor changes in social norms: the mode will move by at most one position. As a consequence, actual behavior will also change only slightly.

However the next increase in restrictiveness of the law will induce major changes: it will erase the last attracting distribution with an intermediate mode and thus social norms will evolve quickly towards the now unique attracting distribution. This will radically increase the frequency of actions which the law intends to suppress. If the legislator tries to work against this change of behavior by forbidding ever more actions, this will have little or no effect: social norms, which effectively drive most of the individuals' behavior will remain extremely permissive. Only with extremely restrictive legal rules ($r_\lambda = 1$ or $r_\lambda = 0$), a second attracting distribution emerges, which is slightly less permissive.

From these observations and similar ones on many more simulations with other parameter sets, we extrapolate:

> Proposition 2a: Suppose social norm formation follows the differential equations system (1) with transition probabilities as given in equations (7) and (8). Further suppose that the fixed part of the visibility effect is large as compared to the fixed part of the legal sanction and that the marginal parts of the visibility effect and the legal sanction are negligible.
>
> Then the modes of the attracting distributions form

1   one connected set which need not include extremely high or low permissiveness, if the law is highly permissive;
2   one connected set which only concentrates on high permissiveness, if the law is highly restrictive;
3   two disjoint connected sets consisting of the two mentioned under 1 and 2, if the law's permissiveness is intermediate.

One should note that according to this proposition, the evolution of social norms is subject to a hysteresis effect for changing legal rules: for the same intermediate permissiveness of the law, social norms will be of intermediate permissiveness if the law had been very permissive before and they be extremely permissive if the law had been very restrictive before.

Varying r_λ in small steps between the two extreme values in the table of Figure 3.6 allows us to deduce:

> Corollary 2: Under the conditions of Proposition 2a, too restrictive legal norms induce a shift of social norms towards far more permissiveness. Actions which the new restrictive law makes illegal may become more frequent as a result of the introduction of the law and the consequential change in social norms. This countervailing effect cannot be avoided by piecemeal aggravation of the law's restrictiveness.

Hence, when the marginal parts of the visibility effect and of the legal sanction are negligible, we observe countervailing effects of social norms against restrictive legal norms in the observed-behavior model as we did in the protest model. These countervailing effects may again justify particular care with weakly enforced legal norms which are more restrictive than social norms. However, in contrast to the protest model, it is impossible to avoid these countervailing effects by piecemeal legislation.

We now turn to the case of predominant marginal parts of the visibility effect and of the legal sanction with the marginal effect of the visibility effect being substantially stronger. As a representative set of parameters we choose $s_\lambda^1 = 0.1$ and $\tau_{v,1} = \frac{3}{4}$ as well as $s_\lambda^0 + \frac{1}{2} s_\lambda^1 = 1.45$ and $\tau_{v,0} + \frac{1}{2}\tau_{v,1} = \frac{1}{24}$ from the set of our simulations.[27]

r_λ	Modes of attracting distributions						
	0	1	2	3	4	5	6
0	×					×	×
1	×					×	×
2			×			×	×
3			×	×		×	×
4			×	×			
5			×	×			
6			×	×	×		

Figure 3.7 Effect of legal rule on possible modes of attracting distributions for parameters as given in equation (9), $s_\lambda^0 = 1.4$, $s_\lambda^1 = 0.1$, $\tau_{v,0} = -\frac{1}{3}$, and large $\tau_{v,1} = \frac{3}{4}$.

In the absence of law and with highly permissive law, we of course get the same (connected) set of attracting distributions of social norms for this set of parameters as for the previous set. However, the effects of stepwise reductions of the law's permissiveness now differ in two important respects from what we observed for the previous set of parameters (see Figure 3.7). On the one hand, the connected set of rather restrictive modes of attracting distributions of social norms becomes smaller, but does not vanish, even for very restrictive legal rules. On the other hand, both the upper and the lower bound of this set become monotonously more restrictive when the law becomes more restrictive. As for the previous set of parameters, a second set of very permissive modes of attracting distributions emerges when the law is sufficiently restrictive. As before, this set is a connected set and disjoint from the first set. Figure 3.8 shows examples for the attracting distributions with modes other than those of Figure 3.5 which more restrictive law affects only to a minor degree as long as they persist. (In Figure 3.8 the top left graph is drawn for $r_\lambda = 0$ and the other two are drawn for $r_\lambda = 1$; hence the small step in action frequencies between actions 1 and 2.)[28]

In the following proposition we summarize and extrapolate these insights:

Proposition 2b: Suppose social norm formation follows the differential equations system (1) with transition probabilities as given in equations (7) and (8). Further suppose that the variable part of the visibility effect is large as compared to the variable part of the legal sanction and that the fixed parts of the visibility effect and the legal sanction are relatively small and follow the reverse order.

Then with restrictive law the modes of the attracting distributions form two disjoint connected sets, a permissive one, which includes a mode at $r = N_A$, and a restrictive one. With more permissive law, the lower and upper bounds of the two sets are not less permissive and may be more permissive. With very permissive law, the permissive set vanishes.

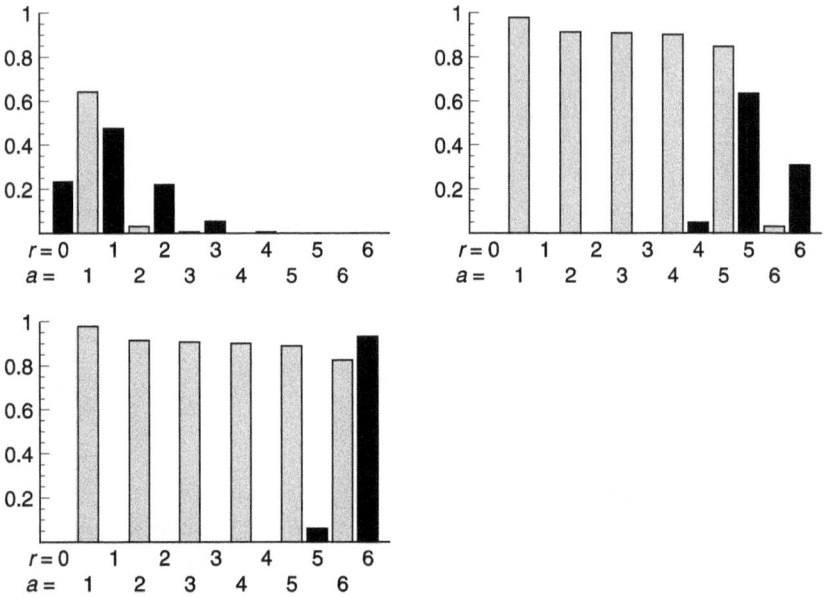

Figure 3.8 Additional attracting distributions with parameters as given in equation (9), $s_\lambda^0 = 1.4$, $s_\lambda^1 = 0.1$, $\tau_{v,0} = -\frac{1}{3}$, and $\tau_{v,1} = \frac{3}{4}$ (black) and consequential action frequencies (gray).

It is important to note that for $r_\lambda = 0$ and $r_\lambda = 1$ only attracting distributions with mode at $r = 1$, $r = 5$ and $r = 6$ occur (again see Figure 3.7). This implies that the attracting distribution to which the social norms evolve is highly path dependent. Suppose the legislator wants to overcome quite permissive social norms which have evolved in the absence of law. In particular, assume that social norms have been attracted to the distribution with mode $r = 4$. The legislator could either introduce highly restrictive legal norms – say $r_\lambda = 0$ or $r_\lambda = 1$ – in one big step. Or he could start with a rather permissive legal norm only slightly more restrictive than the mode of the social norms, and then make the law more restrictive step by step whenever the social norms have moved close enough to the legal norm. As one may expect from the proposition, simulations show that big leap legislation towards more restrictiveness will suffer from the full effect of countervailing social norms: the big leap will induce social norms to evolve towards the attracting distribution with mode $r = 5$. However, starting with the legal norm $r_\lambda = 3$, social norms will move towards the attracting distribution with mode $r = 3$. Once social norms are close enough to this distribution, reducing the permissiveness of the legal norm to $r_\lambda = 2$ induces a further shift of social norms towards the attracting distribution with mode $r = 2$. Proceeding further in small steps will eventually allow the legislator to choose $r_\lambda = 0$ or $r_\lambda = 1$ and thereby induce social norms to evolve towards the attracting distribution with mode $r = 1$ as depicted in Figure 3.8. Only then will actions labeled by $a > 1$ become very rare and the frequency of action $a = 1$ be reduced to somewhere close to 60 percent. With big leap legislation, all actions labeled by $a < 6$ will occur frequently.

We emphasize that we were unable to find superiority of piecemeal legislation within the framework of this model for any structurally different set of parameters, we postulate the following:

> Conjecture 2: Within the observed-behavior model, piecemeal legislation may achieve restrictive social norms and consequentially few undesired actions better than restrictive legislation in one big step if and only if (1) legal sanctions are large for minor violations of the law and only grow slightly for more severe violations and (2) the visibility effect is small for minor violations but grows quickly for more severe violations.

Formally equivalent to the conditions stated in the conjecture is the following: the visibility effect has to grow in the distance between action and legal norm in a convex way while the legal sanction must grow in a concave way. Since we do not believe such structures of costs and visibility effects to be convincing, we claim:

> Corollary 3: Piecemeal legislation may be justified by countervailing social norms only on the basis of communicative norm formation as described in the protest model of the previous section, in which communication is concentrated on individuals with similar values. Disobedience based on the visibility effect of making actions illegal presented in this section can hardly serve as a justification for piecemeal legislation.

This caveat on the superiority of piecemeal legislation may vanish if one models disobedience not only as the consequence of social norms conflicting with legal norms, but as an expression of protest. We leave such further modeling attempts to future research.

3.4 Conclusions

Our analysis explores the effect of legal rules that do not conform to current social values or are perceived as lacking legitimacy. When countervailing social norms are taken into consideration, the ability of legal rules to meet their goals depends upon the communication and behavior of the people subject to the laws and the possible ways in which such actions may influence the evolution of social norms in the shadow of the law.

Legal systems can motivate individuals through incentives and sanctions. In some instances, laws which differ from current social norms may necessitate a greater expenditure of resources for their enforcement.

We have developed two models of countervailing norms to identify the situations where creation of these additional incentives is necessary to ensure the desired effect of laws. Expenditures in law enforcement are shown to be required for the sustainability of law when social norms are likely to have a countervailing effect on law. Our models try to reflect in a rigorous way the general observations underlying protest and civil disobedience as we described them in Section 3.2. They show how the enactment of new laws whose values are close to the current opinion mode induces an adaptation of internal norms to what the new statute expresses as norms. We then turned to the case of new laws which depart more substantially from the current opinion mode. We have shown that the effect of such statutes on the evolution of internal norms may be counter-intuitive.

We modeled the two possible reasons for these countervailing effects of social norms – protest and visibility of disobedience – in two models, which are separate but based on a common foundation. From these models, we could derive a number of important implications. Both in the protest model (Section 3.3.3) and in the observed-behavior model (Section 3.3.4) we found that the countervailing effects of social norms may outweigh the effects of legislation: norms and behavior need not change in the direction intended by the legislator.

However, the two models differ with respect to a second counter-intuitive effect. Only in the protest model the effectiveness of law on influencing social norms in the direction of the law itself may depend on the distance between the values underlying the law and the values underlying the social norms. If they are too distant and social norm formation is sufficiently interactive, only a small number of individuals, whose internal norms are currently close to the new statute, will adopt the values expressed in the statute, while the social norms adopted by the majority of individuals will stabilize where they were or even move in the opposite direction. If this effect is strong enough, not only social norms may move in the undesired direction, but even behavior may evolve in a way contrary to what had been intended by the law. In the observed-behavior model a similar effect may only occur if one adopts extreme and hardly plausible assumptions on how more severe violations of the law make actions a more visible expression of obedience to social norms and on how legal sanctions rise when actions deviate more from what is legal.

As a consequence, only in the protest model gradual change of the law may be superior to big-leap legislation. Only in this model the legal norm may be able to pull the social norm in the desired direction in small consecutive steps but unable to achieve the same result in one big leap. In the observed-behavior model, gradual legislation may only slow down the change of social norms (again, except for extreme and hardly plausible assumptions).

This insight helps us to better understand the nature of civil disobedience. If disobedience to the law is merely triggered by existing social norms, gradualism in the change of law does not help to overcome the problem. However, if disobedience to the law is a way to express one's opinion, in particular one's protest against a too-immoral law, then disobedience like any other form of expression of protest may render big leaps in forming the society by legislation impossible. As we argued in the presentation of our protest model, gradualism then may be a promising way to overcome societies reluctance to adopt the new legal norms as social norms. We think that only this conscious case of disobedience should be named "civil disobedience".

If a legislator wants to shortcut the process of gradual change in cases of civil disobedience in this sense, he can overcome countervailing social norms by suppressing protest by disobedience: he can impose high sanctions in the initial enforcement of the new law. Without modeling the argument explicitly, we conjecture that in societies with civil disobedience, statutes which intend to change behavior in a way which radically differs from prevailing social beliefs will not be sustainable unless backed by very strong expected sanctions. Large scale (civil) disobedience erodes the authority of law in general. In turn, this renders future compliance with law harder to obtain. This argument provides a testable hypothesis. Authoritarian regimes aiming at introducing odious and sudden changes in the legal system ought to back up the enactment with strong enforcement. Particularly, the enforcement should be front-loaded in the initial periods to avoid public disobedience of a substantial frequency. This also explains why democratic regimes constrain the possibility of any such manipulative intervention by setting constitutional bounds on legal sanctions (e.g., legality and proportionality principles, etc.).

When protest and civil disobedience follows the enactment of a new law, the stability of the specific legislation is threatened. As a consequence, the legislator will either repeal the statute, or replace it by one which is closer to the majority's internal norms, or reinforce the expected sanctions backing the statute. The increase in sanctions would have to be stronger than the sanction that would have been sufficient when the law was first enacted, since protest and civil disobedience have reinforced the public's internal norms contrary to the values expressed in the law.

The protest model further reveals two possible alternative effects of social intervention. A more obvious possibility is where preexisting bimodal or multimodal social preferences may converge towards a unimodal distribution. That would be the case in which diversity and multiculturalism may be destroyed by legal intervention (e.g., rules prohibiting the use of signs of religious affiliation in public schools, etc.). But our model interestingly shows that the opposite may also be true. Unimodal distributions may become bimodal distributions as an effect of legal intervention. This means that previously unified social groups may split and drift apart as the result of their diverging reactions to legal intervention (e.g., laws may create or exacerbate differences between social groups).

Further research should consider the possible direct effect of social norms on the net benefits of actions, rather than treating norms as exogenously enforced as in the model we presented here. In this variation, the individual's private benefit from an action could be lowered (augmented) the more an action violates (conforms with) the values and norms that an individual has adopted. A substantial extension of the model might include the second (and possibly third) dimension of norms: the degree to which individuals are willing to support their values by costly imposition of sanctions and the degree to which they feel bound by their personal norms. With this extension, we could avoid the simplifying assumption of the model that all values are equivalent to norms. The costs of such an extension in terms of complexity of the model are obvious. Finally, one could extend the framework of the model to also include the effects of conflicts between social and legal norms on the process of (further) legislation.

Notes

1 We would like to thank the participants of the 2004 Workshop on the Evolution of Designed Institutions and an anonymous referee for helpful comments and Lee Istrail and David Lord for their valuable editorial and research assistance. All remaining errors are ours.
2 Cited by Coffin and Leibman (1972: Foreword).
3 For a brief overview on alternative usage of the term "social norms" see, for example, Cooter (1998: 585–7).
4 For economic approaches to the evolution of social norms not based on a distribution concept as ours see, e.g., Binmore and Samuelson (1994) and Ullmann-Margalit (1977).
5 The findings of Sunshine and Tyler (2003) extend prior research by the author (Tyler 1990) and support the arguments of Weber (1968) about the normative basis of public reactions to authority. Tyler (1994) evaluates the role of procedural justice in shaping reactions to legal rules and policies. People might comply with a law or a decision by an authority when it is obtained through deliberations that they view as procedurally just, even when the outcomes are not favorable to them. Often preference is accorded to procedural justice even over distributive fairness.
6 Cooter defines "taste" as "strength of individual commitment to the norm" (Cooter 1998: 589).
7 The model is restricted to the set of circumstances in which moral, cooperative behavior increases overall productivity (Cooter 1998: 587). For instance, "agents who faithfully serve their principals increase the productivity of principal-agent relationships by reducing monitoring costs" (Cooter, 1998: 587). As another example, "sellers who disclose the truth about their products promote commerce by providing buyers with valuable information at low costs" (Cooter 1998: 587). Cooter suggests that this is a very large set because substantial empirical evidence suggests cooperative behavior is prevalent in many game theoretic situations (Cooter 1998: 588).
8 In his discussion of internalization, Cooter shows the similarities with the deterrence model, but stresses that deterrence is designed to influence an actor who does not value civic virtue, while the internalization model targets those citizens who are willing to pay to promote civic virtue: "Law and economics scholars typically make the rational bad man into the decision-maker in their models, who treats the sanctions from breaking the law as a cost. The bad man does not have a "taste" for obeying the law. In reality, society includes bad people and good citizens, as well as many citizens who are in between (...) Officials should not proceed by making laws only for bad people, because the response of good people also determines the effects of the laws" (Cooter 2000: 18). In a previous paper Cooter (1998) discussed how this change could happen when the change in preferences confers a net benefit, resulting in what Cooter refers to as a "Pareto self-improvement." Cooter defines "Pareto self-improvement" as "a change made by the actor in his preferences that makes feasible an allocation preferred by original preferences and final preferences" (Cooter 1998: 18). By assumption, 1) "To reward good character, people must observe it", 2) "the actor can choose his character" and 3) "the choice of character influences the opportunities available him" (Cooter 1998: 17).
9 Cooter touts the advantages of expressive law: "Policies that create opportunities for Pareto self-improvements respect the judgments of individuals about their preferences, rather than imposing a judgment on them about the superiority of some preferences to others. Identifying Pareto self-improvements enables people with different values to agree about some policies to change preferences" (Cooter 1998: 21). In addition, "[i]nternalization of social norms decentralizes law and increases production through cooperation. By reducing the need for state coercion, voluntary obedience makes liberal government possible" (Cooter 1998: 28).

10 As Stuntz says of Robinson's view, "Ordinarily, his work shows, norms are in the driver's seat and criminal law is the car." (Stuntz 2000: 1871, 1872).

11 Robinson (2000: 1869): "Why does the criminal law care what the layperson thinks is just? Because it is only by heeding those views that the criminal law can provide effective crime control."

12 Morals crimes and vice crimes seem likely to generate active civil disobedience in the form of protests. Stuntz (2000) points out that moral crimes and vice crimes tend to involve civil rights issues such as racial or income discrimination, but rights at issue in morals crimes tend to be viewed as more basic, so morals crimes may cause more protest. The public opinion on these crimes is qualitatively very different from the public's perception on other crimes.

13 For example, poor ethnic neighborhoods, which produced cheap beer locally during Prohibition, were more often targeted than more affluent neighborhoods which served as conduits for imported and exported wine (Stuntz 2000: 1873–8).

14 Kuran (1989) explicitly discusses individuals with different power in the opinion formation process. However, this complication fails to provide additional insights in our model. We therefore simplify our approach by modeling the law as a large number of additional individuals having adopted the legal norm.

15 We add $\frac{1}{2}$ to the value denoting the rule in order to avoid problems of indifference and artificial asymmetries.

16 The standard model of *homo oeconomicus* usually fails to have any such values. However, casual observation shows that most real people do have such values. In addition, evolutionary arguments support the view that individual fitness increases when some personal norms guide individual behavior; see, e.g., Dufwenberg and Güth (1999), Güth and Kliemt (2000) and Bergstrom (2002: 82–4).

17 See Flieth and Foster (2002) for an application of the model to business cycle theory.

18 For an overview see, e.g., Bikhchandani *et al.* (1998).

19 Note that $\sum_{r \in A} (df(r,t)/dt) = 0$; hence $\sum_{r \in A} f(r,t) = 1$ always remains satisfied.

20 One should not confuse this concept with the stationary distribution, which is the distribution over all possible distributions of individual norms in the very long run. The concept of the stationary distribution takes into account that stochastic influences may always induce the system to leave the range of attraction of one attracting distribution and move it into the range of attraction of another. We here concentrate on a shorter time span in which such random influences are not relevant and thus attractors of a stochastic dynamic process are relevant to describe the direction of the evolution of norms.

21 We choose $N_A = 6$ here and in the following examples, because this allows us to discuss a large array of effects without having to deal with too many differential equations.

22 This may, for example, be justified by arguing that the time elapsing between two such situations is exponentially distributed with an expected value of $1/q_a$. The average frequency with which an individual enters into such situation then is q_a.

23 Private benefits which depend on a do not affect the substance of our results. In some variations of the model not presented here, we replaced the constant private benefit β by a linearly increasing function of the action number $\beta + \gamma a$, where $\beta \geq 0$ and $\gamma \geq 0$ and could not detect any systematic change of results.

24 We deliberately neglect internalized norms which could be included, e.g., by arguing that each violation of an individual's own norm induces costs to this very individual. This would complicate the model, but we do not see how it might provide additional insights relevant for the current chapter.

25 Note that if α is very large, stochasticity of the individuals' behavior nearly vanishes and if $\alpha = 0$, the individuals' decisions are purely random: each action is chosen with probability ½.

26 This restriction is necessary because our model does not include the possibility of effective support by other violators of the legal norm, e.g., in the form of concealing the fact of the violation or the identity of the violator from the enforcement authorities.

27 The second pair of parameters implies $s_\lambda^0 = 1.4$ and $\tau_{v,0} = -1/3$. This negative value does not constitute a problem since it only occurs jointly with at least one half times $\tau_{v,1} = -3/4$ which guarantees that all transition probabilities are strictly positive.

28 In the left figure, $r_\lambda = 1$ would induce a substantially higher frequency for action $a = 1$ and leave the rest essentially unaffected. We chose $r_\lambda = 0$ to show what restrictive law may achieve at most. With $r_\lambda = 0$ also in the two right figures, the small step between the frequencies of the first and the second action would vanish, all actions below action 5 would have essentially the same frequency.

References

Arthur, W.B. (1988) 'Competing Technologies: An Overview', in G. Dosi, C. Freeman, R. Nelson, G. Silverberg and L. Soete (eds) *Technical Change and Economic Theory*, London, New York: Pinter Publishers.

Arthur, W.B. (1989) 'Competing Technologies, Increasing Returns and Lock-in by Historical Events', *Economic Journal*, 99: 116–131.

Bergstrom, T.C. (2002) 'Evolution of Social Behavior: Individual and Group Selection', *Constitutional Political Economy*, 13: 149–72.

Beetham, D. (1991) *The Legitimation of Power*, Atlantic Highlands, N.J.: Humanities Press International.

Bikhchandani, S., Hirschleifer, D. and Welch, I. (1992) 'A Theory of Fads, Fashion, Custom and Cultural Change as Informational Cascades', *Journal of Political Economy*, 58: 211–21.

Bikhchandani, S., Hirschleifer, D. and Welch, I. (1998) 'Learning from the Behavior of Others: Conformity, Fads, and Informational Cascades', *Journal of Economic Perspectives*, 12: 151–70.

Binmore, K. and Samuelson, L. (1994) 'An Economist's Perspective on the Evolution of Norms', *Journal of Institutional and Theoretical Economics*, 150: 45–63.

Coffin, W.S. and Leibman, M.I. (1972) *Civil Disobedience: Aid or Hindrance to Justice?*, American Enterprise Institute for Public Policy Research.

Cooter, R. (1998) 'Expressive Law and Economics', *Journal of Legal Studies*, 27: 585 608.

Cooter, R. (2000) 'Do Good Laws Make Good Citizens? An Economic Analysis Of Internalized Norms', *Virginia Law Review*, 86: 1577–601.

Dufwenberg, M. and Güth, W. (1999) 'Indirect Evolution versus Strategic Delegation: A Comparison of Two Approaches to Explaining Economic Institutions', *European Journal of Political Economy*, 15: 281–95.

Ellison, G. and Fudenberg, D. (1993) 'Rules of Thumb for Social Learning', *Journal of Political Economy*, 101: 612–43.

Ellison, G. and Fudenberg, D. (1995) 'Word-of-Mouth Communication and Social Learning', *Quarterly Journal of Economics*, 110: 93–125.

Flieth, B. and Foster, J. (2002) 'Interactive Expectations', *Journal of Evolutionary Economics*, 12: 375–95.

Flieth, B. and von Wangenheim, G. (1996) 'Interactive Opinion Formation in a Multi-Opinion Model', *Papers on Economics and Evolution* # 9604, Max-Planck-Institute of Economics, Jena.

Güth, W. and Kliemt, H. (2000) 'Evolutionarily Stable Co-operative Commitments', *Theory and Decision*, 49: 197–221.

Kuran, T. (1989) 'Sparks and Prairie Fires: A Theory of Unanticipated Political Revolution', *Public Choice*, 61: 41–74.

McAdams, R.H. (2000) 'A Focal Point Theory of Expressive Law', *Virginia Law Review*, 86: 1649–729.

Mailath, G.J. (1998) 'Do People Play Nash Equilibrium? Lessons from Evolutionary Game Theory', *Journal of Economic Literature*, 36: 1347–74.

Rabe, B.G. (1994) *Beyond NIMBY: Hazardous Waste Siting in Canada and the United States*, Washington, DC: Brookings Institution.

Robinson, P.H. (2000) 'Why Does the Criminal Law Care What the Layperson Thinks Is Just – Coercive Versus Normative Crime Control', *Virginia Law Review*, 86: 1839–69.

Schnabl, H. (1991) 'Agenda-Diffusion and Innovation', *Journal of Evolutionary Economics*, 1: 65–85.

Sen, A.K. (1977) 'Rational Fools: A Critique of the Behavioral Foundations of Economic Theory', *Philosophy and Public Affairs*, 6: 317–45.

Stuntz, W.J. (2000) Self-Defeating Crimes, *Virginia Law Review*, 86: 1871–99.

Sunshine, J. and Tyler, T.R. (2003) 'The Role of Procedural Justice and Legitimacy in Shaping Public Support for Policing', *Law and Society Review*, 37: 555–89.

Tyler, T.R. (1990) *Why People Obey the Law*, New Haven: Yale University Press.

Tyler, T.R. (1994) 'Psychological Models of the Justice Motive', *Journal of Personality and Social Psychology*, 67: 850–63.

Tyler, T.R. and Huo, Y.J. (2002) *Trust in the Law*, New York: Russell-Sage.

Ullmann-Margalit, E. (1977) *The Emergence of Norms*, Oxford: Clarendon Press.

von Wangenheim, G. (1993) 'The Evolution of Judge-Made Law', *International Review of Law and Economics*, 13: 381–411.

von Wangenheim, G. (1995) *Die Evolution von Recht*, Tübingen: Mohr.

Wax, A. (2000) 'Expressive Law and Oppressive Norms: A Comment on Richard McAdam's "A Focal Point Theory Of Expressive Law"', *Virginia Law Review*, 86: 1731–79.

Weber, M. (1968) *Economy and Society*, ed. by G. Roth and C. Wittich, Berkeley: University of California Press.

Weise, P. (1992) 'Eine dynamische Analyse von Konsumtionseffekten', *Jahrbuch für Nationalökonomie und Statistik*, 211: 159–72.

Zwiebach, B. (1975) *Civility and Disobedience*, Cambridge, MA: Cambridge University Press.

4 Social motives and institutional design

Tom Tyler[1]

In the past several decades there have been tremendous advances in the connection between economics and psychology. Economists have drawn upon the research and insights of psychologists and have also conducted their own empirical research as part of the burgeoning field of behavioral economics. A major area of psychology upon which economists have drawn is judgment and decision making. This area, characterized by the work of psychologists such as Tversky and Kahneman, focuses upon the errors and biases that shape the individual judgments of people seeking to pursue their material self-interest during decision making (Brocas and Carrillo 2003, Dawes 1988, Hastie and Dawes 2001, Hogarth 1980, Nisbett and Ross 1980, Plous 1993, Thaler 1991).

The literature on judgment and decision making is not primarily focused on issues of motivation. It is based upon the assumption that people are motivated to maximize their own personal self-interest, a self-interest defined in terms of material gains and losses. No doubt most psychologists would acknowledge that people can be motivated by a broader range of motivations than material gains and losses, but these other motivations have not been the primary focus of this research. My goal is to join economists working in this area by arguing for the potential benefits to economists of considering a broader range of the motivations that can shape behavior in institutional settings.[2]

I will characterize the additional motivations I describe as "social" motivations to distinguish them from instrumental motivations. Instrumental motivations reflect people's desire to gain material resources and to avoid material losses. Social motives, as discussed by psychologists, differ in that they are motivations that flow from within the person.

There are four ways to distinguish between instrumental and social motivations. The first is by the content of the concerns that people express within each domain. Instrumental concerns focus on the potential for material gains and/or the possibility of material losses. Such gains and losses involve gains in terms of rewards, or losses in terms of costs or punishments. In contrast, social motivations are linked to gains and losses of a nonmaterial nature. Such gains and losses are linked to issues such as personal identity and consistency with ethical/moral values.

Second, indicators of social motivations should be found to be empirically distinct from indicators of material gain or loss. For example, in the literature on social justice, it is found that people distinguish between receiving a favorable outcome and receiving fair treatment (Tyler *et al.* 1997). Hence, judgments about justice are found to be distinct from the favorability of one's outcomes. This distinction is clear in the literature on distributive justice, a literature in which the fairness of outcomes is distinguished from their desirability (Walster *et al.* 1978). It is even clearer with the literature on procedural justice, which focuses on the fairness of the procedures by which allocation decisions are made (Lind and Tyler 1988). If people simply viewed a favorable outcome as fair, for example, social motivations would not be distinct from material judgments. However, this is not the case.

Third, social motivations should have a distinct influence on cooperative behavior. Again, the justice literature finds that the degree to which people are willing to accept an outcome from an authority is linked, first, to the favorability of that outcome. In addition, however, people are more willing to accept an outcome that they evaluate as being fair and fairly arrived at. Hence, their fairness judgments exercise an independent influence upon their acceptance behavior that cannot be explained by outcome favorability.

Fourth, social motivations should produce a consistency of behavior across situations and over time. If, for example, someone feels an obligation to obey rules, their behavior should consistently reflect higher levels of cooperation across settings that vary in their reward and cost characteristics. Further, they should show the same consistency in the same situation across time. This does not mean that situational forces will not influence behavior. But, it will be possible to see constancies in behavior that are not linked to those forces.

The best way to understand the value of this larger motivational framework is to consider it within the context of a particular type of socially important behavior. In this chapter I focus on motivating cooperative behavior. Cooperation is valuable for groups, and securing cooperation has been the focus of social science research across a variety of fields, including both economics and psychology.

4.1   Motivating cooperation as a goal for social science research

One way that psychologists, economists, and other social scientists are united is in their long-standing interest in understanding how to obtain cooperation in groups, institutions, and societies. Within social psychology this interest is reflected in a number of literatures, including the study of social dilemmas, regulation, institutional performance, helping and altruism, leadership and group dynamics.

A key aspect of this interest in motivating cooperation is a concern with institutional design. We all want to understand how to structure social situations so as to most effectively promote cooperative behavior among the people within those situations. As a result of this common interest, there are considerable mutual benefits to be gained by bridging among social psychology, economics, political science, sociology, law, and management.

Social scientists generally recognize that people have a mixed motivation when interacting with others. On the one hand, there are clear personal advantages to be gained by cooperation. On the other hand, people are often unable to maximize their pursuit of personal self-interest if they act in ways that simultaneously maximize the welfare of the group. So, to some extent people are motivated to cooperate, and to some extent to compete. People must balance between these two conflicting motivations when shaping their level of cooperative behavior.

Social psychologists examine how people manage these motivational conflicts in interpersonal situations ranging from dyadic bargaining to long-term relationships (Thibaut and Kelley 1959, Rusbult and Van Lange 2003). The problem of cooperation in mixed motive dyads also lies at the root of classical problems in economics, problems such as the prisoner's dilemma game and the ultimatum game. In the prisoner's dilemma game the pursuit of material self-interest without taking the interests of others leads people to act in ways that does not lead them to the best personal outcomes (Proudstone 1992).

While social psychology is generally focused upon dyads and small groups mixed motive conflicts within institutions and societies have been studied most directly by social psychologists within the literature on social dilemmas. This literature asks how people deal with situations in which the pursuit of short-term self-interest by all has negative implications. Social dilemmas have two characteristics: "(a) at any given decision point, individuals receive higher payoffs for making selfish choices than they do for making cooperative choices, regardless of the choices made by those with whom they interact and (b) everyone involved receives lower payoffs, if everyone makes selfish choices than if everyone makes cooperative choices" (Kopelman *et al.* 2002: 94).

4.1.1   Real world cooperation

The issue of cooperation is not confined to games and experiments. It is also central to many of the problems faced by real-world groups, institutions, and societies (Van Vugt *et al.* 2000). As a result, the fields of law, public policy, and management all seek to understand how to most effectively design institutions to best secure cooperation from the people within. Their efforts to address these issues are informed by the findings of social psychological and economic research on dyads and small groups.

Within law a central concern is with how to effectively regulate behavior so as to prevent people from engaging in actions that are personally rewarding, but destructive to others and to the group – actions ranging from illegally copying music and movies, to robbing banks (Tyler 1990, Tyler and Huo 2002). In addition, the police and courts need the active cooperation of members of the community to control crime and urban disorder by reporting crimes and cooperating in policing neighborhoods (Tyler and Huo 2002). Hence, an important aspect of the study of law involves seeking to understand the factors shaping cooperation with law and legal authorities.

Government also wants people to cooperate by participating in personally costly acts ranging from paying taxes to fighting in wars (Tyler 2000). Further, it is also important for people to actively participate in society by voting, working to maintain their communities by working together to deal with community problems, and otherwise help the polity to thrive. For these reasons, understanding how to motivate cooperation is central to political scientists.

Work institutions seek to prevent personally rewarding, but destructive acts such as sabotage and stealing office supplies by creating and encouraging deference to rules and policies. They also encourage positive forms of cooperation like working hard at one's job and contributing extra-role and creative efforts to one's work performance (Tyler and Blader 2000). For these reasons a central area of research in institutional behavior involves understanding how to motivate cooperation in work settings.

4.1.2 *Motivating cooperation*

This joint interest in understanding the motivation underlying cooperation suggests an important area for interface between social psychology and the other social sciences. Social psychologists can benefit from the findings of research from the disciplines of organizational psychology, law, political science, and management, all of which explore motivational issues in institutions and societies. Conversely, these other social sciences can benefit by drawing upon the empirical findings of social psychological and microeconomic studies of behavior in interpersonal interactions and small groups.

Drawing upon the literature on one shot and repeated play experimental games, economics begin by focusing upon the role of material incentive and sanctioning systems in shaping cooperative behavior (Fehr and Falk 2002, Nagin 1998). Social psychologists, of course, also recognize the important role of anticipated or experienced rewards and punishments in shaping behavior (Rusbult and Van Lange 2003). Both literatures suggest that one way of changing behavior is by altering the individuals short-term self-interest by providing incentives to promote desired behavior and/or by sanctioning undesirable behavior. In either case, the group is changing the person's calculation of their own short-term self-interest to bring behavior into line with the welfare of the group.

The motivating effect of incentives and sanctions is well known. I will refer to these as instrumental motivations, since they assume that people are motivated by their self-interest and have their influence by shaping the individual's assessments of which actions are in their personal self-interest.

The literature on cooperation suggests that the use of incentives and sanctions *can* effectively shape cooperative behavior. However, while effective, rewards and punishments are not always an efficient mechanism for shaping behavior. First, their general impact on behavior is marginal. In the area of drug use, for example, MacCoun (1993) estimates that sanctions account for about five percent of the variance in compliance with drug laws. A similar examination of incentives in work institutions suggests that they explain about 10 percent of the variance in performance (Tyler and Blader 2000). Of course, the magnitude of this influence is not constant and both experimental research (Fehr and Gächter 2002)

Table 4.1 The nature of the connection between the person and the group

	Values	Identity	Justice	Trust
Instrumental motivation	Incentives/ sanctions	Favorability of outcomes from group	Policy favorability, policy fairness	Trust that others will deliver promised outcomes
Social motivation	Social values; legitimacy	Merger of self with the group	Procedural justice	Trust that others are benevolent

and field studies (Tyler and Huo 2002) suggest that their impact varies across settings.

When they do occur incentive/sanction effects are costly to obtain, since institutions must commit considerable resources to the effective deployment of incentive and sanctioning systems. For these reasons, the adequacy of instrumental approaches to motivating cooperation has been questioned within law (Tyler 1990, Tyler and Huo 2002), political science (Green and Shapiro 1994), and management (Pfeffer 1994, Tyler and Blader 2000).

A key contribution of social psychology is the suggestion that there are *social motivations* that can supplement instrumental motivations in securing cooperation within institutions. This focus on social motivations coincides with the increasing focus by economists on interpersonal processes within groups and institutions.

There is already a large literature on incentives and sanctions. Social motivations represent a new approach to motivation that offers the possibility of moving beyond the use of incentives and sanctions when seeking to motivate cooperative behavior. In this chapter, I outline four types of social motivations. Each is contrasted with a corresponding instrumental model. These four motivations are shown in Table 4.1.

4.1.3   *Instrumental models of motivation*

Increasingly, social scientists have recognized the limits of an exclusive reliance on instrumental approaches to managing cooperation that are rooted in the use of incentives and sanctions. In political and legal settings, authorities have recognized that both social regulation (Tyler 1990, 2002) and the encouragement of voluntary civic behavior (Green and Shapiro 1994) are difficult when authorities can only rely upon their ability to reward and/or punish citizens. Similarly, institutional theorists are recognizing the difficulties of managing employees using command and control strategies (Pfeffer 1994).

The alternative to such instrumental strategies is to focus on approaches based upon appeals to social motivations. If people have social motivations that lead them to voluntarily defer to authorities and to act in prosocial ways that help the group, then authorities need not seek to compel such behavior through promises of reward or threats of punishment. They can instead rely upon people's willingness to engage in the behavior voluntarily.

4.1.4 Types of cooperation

Two types of cooperation are central to the viability of groups. The aspect of cooperation examined in social dilemma studies and in many experimental games is cooperation that occurs when people follow rules limiting their exercise of their self-interested motivations. People want to fish in a lake, but limit what they catch. They want to exploit others in bargaining, but follow rules dictating fairness. They want to steal from a bank, but defer to the law. In all of these situations, people are refraining from engaging in behavior that would benefit their self-interest, but is against the welfare of others and/or of their group. This area of research is referred to as regulation and involves limiting undesirable behavior.

The other aspect of cooperation involves proactive behavior on behalf of the group (the promotion of desired behavior). Groups also want their members to actively engage in tasks that effectively deal with group concerns. In work institutions these tasks include job performance issues. In communities they involve working with neighborhood groups, meeting about community problems, and otherwise helping the community to deal with its concerns. Governments rely upon their members to vote and participate in the political process. The performance of these behaviors encourages the viability of the group.

4.1.5 Voluntary cooperation

The focus on social motivations is especially relevant in situations in which our goal is to motivate voluntary cooperative behavior. Motivation is linked to the viability of a strategy of delivery. Employees motivated by incentives need a clear set of expected behaviors and a direct link between those behaviors and rewards. So, for example, coming to work on time and performing clearly specified tasks can be connected to rewards. Sanctions are similar, although they add the complexity that people try to hide their behavior, so there must be effective surveillance strategies in place to detect rule breaking. In either case, people are not motivated to act in the absence of a link between their actions and a reward/sanction.

In many settings, however, it is desirable for people to engage in cooperation even when incentives and sanctions are not being effectively deployed. The political case is illustrative of the problem with incentive-based approaches. One way to win political support is to provide people with benefits for themselves or their groups. However, it is usually difficult to give everyone all the benefits they want. Further, governments are least able to provide desired benefits during times of war or economic downturn, when they are most in need of public cooperation if they are to be viable. Hence, governments benefit when people will cooperate for noninstrumental reasons. We label such cooperation "voluntary" because it is shaped by social, rather than instrumental, motivations.[3]

With sanctions the value of voluntary cooperation becomes even clearer. Sanction based strategies are always costly to implement because they require the development and maintenance of credible sanctioning strategies. So, for example, it is clear that crimes can be deterred by sanctions, but only when the authorities deploy sufficient resources to establish credibility. In this context it is clear that the authorities benefit when people cooperate for social, rather than instrumental reasons. Again, such cooperation is "voluntary" in character.

4.2   The four types of social motivation

4.2.1   Social values

As I have noted, one reason that people do not break rules is that they fear being caught and punished for wrongdoing. This is the instrumentally based deterrence motive that is central to many efforts to manage rule following in institutions by creating a credible surveillance system that creates reasonable risks of detection when rules are broken.

It is also important to be able to activate the ethical motivations that lead people not to do things that undermine institutional policies. This involves motivating people to feel a sense of personal responsibility and obligation to support group decisions. People's rule following behavior is influenced by their internal motivation to uphold moral values relevant to the group. In particular, people feel a loyalty to the group and a sense of responsibility to support its decisions and policies.

Let us give one example, from a study of social dilemmas. Brann and Foddy (1988) studied a situation in which a common resource was being depleted. In this situation the self-interested response is to take more resources, something that, when undertaken by everyone, destroys the common resource pool. However, in this situation, those who were motivated by ethical feelings of obligation to the group took fewer resources, seeking to aid the group at the expense of their own immediate self-interest. Those not so motivated acted on their self-interest and took more resources when they saw the pool being depleted.

Hence, ethical motivations acted as a moderator in this situation. When people had such motivations, they were less likely to act on their self-interested motivations. Instead, their ethical values led them to take actions that opposed their own self-interest.

Studies of people's behavior in institutions also generally support the argument that internal motivations in the form of ethical values have a positive influence on whether people act to aid their groups and institutions, leading people to act in ways that support their institutions even when it is not in their self-interest to do so. This is true when we study people's adherence to laws (Tyler 1990); their acceptance of the decisions of authorities (Tyler and Huo 2002); and their deference to informal decisions and agreements in work settings (Tyler and Blader 2000).

In all of these situations, activating the ethical values of the people within an institution encourages greater levels of adherence to formal and informal agreements. One limit of such efforts is that ethical values are quite stable over time, and difficult to change. Hence, institutions must draw upon preexisting values to activate these motivations.

A second mechanism that might be used to enhance relational contracts is to activate people's feelings of responsibility and obligation to obey those contracts ("legitimacy"). Unlike moral values, the legitimacy of institutions and institutional practices is changeable in response to the actions of an institution, providing institutions with the possibility of shaping the motivations through changes in institutional practice. In legal studies the social value of key interest is legitimacy.

Legitimacy is a property of an authority or institution that leads people to feel that that authority or institution is entitled to be deferred to and obeyed. It represents an "acceptance by people of the need to bring their behavior into line with the dictates of an external authority" (Tyler 1990: 25). This feeling of obligation is not simply linked to the authorities' possession of instruments of reward or coercion, but also to properties of the authority that lead people to feel it is entitled to be obeyed (Beetham 1991). Since the classic writing of Weber (1968) social scientists have recognized that legitimacy is a property that is not simply instrumental, but reflects a social value orientation toward authority and institutions – i.e., a normative, moral, or ethical feeling of responsibility to defer (Beetham 1991, Kelman and Hamilton 1989, Sparks *et al.* 1996, Tyler 1990). This analysis will explore the importance of legitimacy, beyond the influence of instrumental factors shaping reactions to the police.

Consider two specific examples of the influence of legitimacy. Building on the work of Tyler (1990), Sunshine and Tyler (2003a) examined the antecedents of compliance and cooperation with the police among people living in New York City. The results of this analysis show that police legitimacy influences people's compliance with law and their willingness to cooperate with and assist the police. These findings also support the argument that legitimacy is a social value that is distinct from performance evaluations. They show that such values have both an important and a distinct influence of people's support for the police. This finding supports the arguments of Weber (1968) about the normative basis of public reactions to authority. It extends prior research findings (Tyler 1990) by showing that cooperation and empowerment, in addition to compliance, are influenced by legitimacy.

In addition to legitimacy, people are influenced by their judgments about the degree to which authorities share their moral values. Sunshine and Tyler (2003b) demonstrate that people are more willing to defer to the police when they believe that the police hold and act upon the moral values shared by members of the community. These moral values are a second aspect of people's ethical connection to law and legal authorities. In contrast to legitimacy, however, moral values are less open to change. To activate moral values, institutions must engage in practices congruent with the moral values people already have. Legitimacy is more open to being shaped by institutional practices.

Tyler and Blader (2004) examined the same social values in two studies of employees focusing on people's values in relationship to the institutions for which they work. Their findings support the argument that employee's ethical values – legitimacy and moral congruence – shape their rule-following behavior in work settings. They suggest that companies benefit by fostering ethical values in their employees that support rule-following. Those ethical values are a major motivation leading to employee compliance with company policies and rules.

They also lead to lower levels of rule-breaking behavior on the part of employees. These results suggest that one promising way to bring the behavior of corporate employees into line with corporate codes of conduct is to activate employee values.

In addition to the empirical support for the utility of the self-regulatory strategy reported here, such an approach has additional benefits over a strategy linked to incentives and sanctions. For instance, it prevents institutions from expending resources on creating and maintaining credible systems of surveillance to enforce rules. These problems are typical of any efforts to regulate conduct using incentive or sanction-based strategies. Exacerbating this problem, such strategies actually encourage people to hide their behavior and thus make it necessary to have especially comprehensive and costly surveillance systems.

Besides their actual costs, these strategies have the additional problem that they undermine employee's commitment to their company and enjoyment of their jobs. Employees whose focus is on avoiding sanctions have their intrinsic motivation and commitment to their company undermined (Frey 1997). They then contribute less to their workplaces. Hence, there is a downside to sanctions and the surveillance associated with them. They hurt company productivity by undermining the ethical values that encourage commitment to work (Tyler and Blader 2000).

The findings of Tyler and Blader (2004) point to the potential value of using a self-regulatory approach to employee motivation that is centered around the encouragement of social motivations. In recent decades, the recognition that self-regulation has value has been a widespread one within the law. Self-regulation is widely touted as a means of avoiding the problems that occur when government seeks to regulate business, and to lessen the costs of government agencies with a regulatory role (Rechtschaffen 1998, King and Lenox 2000, Gunningham and Rees 1997, Aalders and Wilthagen 1997). These same arguments can be applied within companies. Companies benefit when they can develop self-regulatory strategies that encourage their employees to take increased responsibility for rule following.

4.2.2   *Identity*

A second dispositional type of social motivation relevant to cooperation is identification with the group. There is a large literature within social psychology on social identity (Hogg and Abrams 1988) and a number of discussions of the influence of identity on conflict and cooperation within and between groups. In addition, economists have recently recognized the importance of identity (Akerlof and Kranton 2000).

Because identity matters, social identity theories argue that it is important where people draw group boundaries. When they are within a group, people often merge their own identities and the identities of the groups to which they belong (Hogg and Abrams 1988). When they do so, the boundary between self and group blurs, and the interests of the group become one's self-interest.

From the perspective of encouraging cooperation, we would like to have people merging their identities into the institutions to which they belong when we want them to act in terms of the interests of the group, and not in terms of their own self-interest. The social identity literature makes two key points: that the merger of self and group (1) is easily accomplished and (2) when people identify with a group, it changes how they think about cooperation. In fact, recent research shows that cooperation in public good dilemmas is reinforced when people exhibit strong identification with the group, because their motives are transformed from the personal to the group level, that is, people think of the interests of the group as being their own interests (De Cremer and van Dijk 2002) and become intrinsically motivated to pursue the group's interest.

Tyler and Degoey (1995) argue that this merger of self and group leads people to decide whether to cooperate by evaluating the quality of their *treatment* by others in the group – a relational issue – instead of focusing on the favorability of their outcomes, as do those low in identification. De Cremer and Tyler (2003) support this argument by demonstrating that when identity issues involving reputation or belongingness are more salient, people's cooperation decisions are more strongly shaped by how they are treated by others in the group.

It is also possible to directly test the influence of group identification on cooperation by looking at whether identification encourages loyalty to the group and cooperation. Abrams *et al.* (1998) demonstrate that employees who identify with their work institution are less likely to quit, while Tyler and Blader (2000) show that identification predicts job performance and rule following in work groups.

4.2.3 *Procedural justice*

Studies of procedural justice suggest that procedural justice is a social motivation that is distinct from the motivating influence of favorable, or even fair, policies or outcomes (Tyler and Lind 1992). People also react to the fairness of the procedures used to make decisions (Tyler *et al.* 1997, Tyler and Smith 1998).

Thibaut and Walker (1975) performed the first systematic set of experiments designed to show the impact of procedural justice. Their laboratory studies demonstrate that people's assessments of the fairness of third-party decision-making procedures shape their satisfaction with their outcomes. This finding has now been widely confirmed in subsequent laboratory studies of procedural justice (Lind and Tyler 1988). Subsequent field studies have also found that when third-party decisions are viewed by the disputants as being fairly made, people are more willing to voluntarily accept them (Tyler 2000). What is striking about these studies is that these procedural justice effects are found in studies of real disputes, in real settings, involving actual disputants.

Procedural justice judgments are found to have an especially important role in shaping adherence to agreements over time (Pruitt *et al.* 1993, Pruitt *et al.* 1990). Pruitt and his colleagues studied the factors that lead those involved in disputes to adhere to mediation agreements that end those disputes. They found that the procedural fairness of the initial mediation session was a central determinant of whether people were adhering to the agreement six months later.

One area in which procedural justice is found to be important is regulation. Two levels of regulation have been examined: general rule following (Tyler 1990, Sunshine and Tyler 2003a) and decision acceptance (Tyler and Huo 2002). These approaches are based on the idea of process based regulation, in which self-regulation occurs when people are motivated to follow rules and accept decisions based upon legitimacy. Legitimacy, in turn, is motivated by experiencing procedural justice. The key assumption upon which process based regulation is that evaluations of legitimacy are primarily based on procedural fairness. That assumption is supported by the findings of surveys, which identify procedural justice as a primary antecedent of legitimacy (Sunshine and Tyler 2003a).

Studies of the legitimacy of authority more broadly suggest that people decide how legitimate authorities are, and how much to defer to those authorities and to their decisions, primarily by assessing the fairness of their decision-making procedures (Kim and Mauborgne 1991, 1993, Sparks *et al.* 1996, Tyler 1990). Tyler and Huo (2002) refer to governance based on procedural justice as process based regulation. They demonstrate that procedural justice is a key antecedent of deference to the decisions made by police officers and judges. In other words, procedural justice also leads to deference in particular personal encounters with legal authorities.

The same conclusions are reached in the work of Tyler and Blader (2004) on the legitimacy of work institutions. The findings outlined suggest that one way that work institutions can motivate their employees is by exercising authority in ways that will be judged by those employees as fair. Those employees who feel that they work in a fair work environment are especially willing to view the rules as legitimate and take the responsibility to follow company policies upon themselves, with the obvious advantage the company does not then have to compel such behavior.

Interestingly, the procedural justice perspective is consistent with emerging trends in law and the legal regulation of business. As sanction based strategies of regulation have increasingly been questioned, government regulatory agencies have developed a variety of strategies for enlisting businesses and other "stakeholders" in the formulation and implementation of regulatory policy. These include negotiation to reach consensus on administrative regulations (Coglianese 1997), cooperative arrangements for delivering social services (Stewart 2003), and joint efforts to manage wildlife and wildlands (Karkkainen 2002, Lin 1996). These policies decentralize power to "enable citizens and other actors to utilize their local knowledge to fit solutions to their individual circumstances" (Dorf and Sabel 1998: 267). All of these efforts involve procedures for decision-making that embody the procedural justice values of voice, participation, neutrality, and acknowledging the rights, needs and concerns of people involved in the decision. This does not mean that they involve wide employee participation, but rather that they reflect the values inherent in procedural justice perspectives on management.

It has also been found that people who experience work organizations as procedurally just are more likely to help their groups by engaging in proactive behaviors. Within formal institutions such actions have been labeled "extra-role" behaviors, since they involve nonrequired actions not required by the group. Research suggests that people voluntarily cooperate with groups in these proactive ways when they judge that group decisions are being made fairly (Bies *et al.* 1993, Moorman 1991, Moorman *et al.* 1993, Niehoff and Moorman 1993).

4.2.4 Trust

Studies of cooperation indicate that people are more willing to cooperate when they trust others to also cooperate. One level of trust is the ability to trust that people will behave as expected, based upon their promises, or upon our knowledge of their past behavior. We will refer to this as instrumental trust because it is linked to the ability that we believe we have to predict what other people will do in the future. Trust as predictability due to a willingness to keep promises – instrumental trust – is one level on which trust is studied. For example, Burt and Knez (1996) define trust as "anticipated cooperation" (ibid.: 70).

Kramer (1999) labels approaches that link trust assessments to one's perceived ability to estimate others' future actions to be "cognitive" approaches to trust. Attention to such future actions illustrates a key element of social interaction – the element of risk. When people interact with others their outcomes become intertwined with the outcomes of others – they become interdependent. This creates the possibility that one person's failure to act as agreed will hurt the interests of another person within a relationship. On some level, each person must make estimates of the likelihood that others will keep their agreements and not act opportunistically (Bradach and Eccles 1989). Those estimates of likely future behavior are cognitive estimates of the trustworthiness of others.

This cognitive model of trust is consistent with the image of trust that emerges from the large literature on rational choice (Coleman 1990, Williamson 1993). In this literature, trust is based upon the view that people are rational actors, who judge the likely actions of others so that they can include those estimates into an overall model of likely costs and gain of possible future actions. From this perspective: "When we say we trust someone or that someone is trustworthy, we implicitly mean that the probability that he [or she] will perform an action that is beneficial or at least not detrimental to us is high enough for us to consider engaging in some form of cooperation" (Williamson 1993: 463). So, trust is linked to a heuristic judgment about "the likelihood that the trustee will undertake expected actions if trusted" (Scholz 1998: 137).

A calculative or instrumental view of trust can also be found within the social psychological literature on social dilemmas. That literature examines situations in which groups and communities are faced with scarcities in shared, communal resources. Much of the literature on social dilemmas explores people's willingness to trust others in their community who also consume these resources. One reason that people behave cooperatively in such settings is that they trust that other community members will reciprocate cooperation – i.e., if I cooperate, I expect that others will cooperate in return. I think I know how others will behave in the future, and can therefore shape my own behavior in response to my anticipation of the actions of others (Brewer and Kramer 1986).

An example of this type of trust in social dilemma contexts is the problem of a dwindling resource pool. If people are collectively drawing resources from a common pool, they might all limit their yield so as not to destroy the pool. Fishermen face this problem and sometimes cooperate not to over-fish certain areas. In such a setting people must estimate what others will do. When resources are dwindling, everyone has a desire to take as many of the few remaining resources as possible, and collectively, this can destroy the pool for the future. Each person must, therefore, base his own decision on whether to conserve or overuse resources on an estimate of the likelihood that others will overuse, leaving no long-term gain from the pool and no short-term gain from overuse. In such settings, one motivation shaping people's behavior is their trust, i.e., their expectations, about how others will behave.

Within social relations, people engage in a variety of approaches to make the future behavior of others more predictable. Laws are one example of a social device designed to regularize social interactions by attaching penalties to failures to keep promises. We have more confidence that others will not fail to live up to the terms of a contract, because society has established rules about such actions and assigned authorities to sanction those who engage in them. As a consequence, we can more willingly trust, in the instrumental sense that we think that others will do as they promise. More generally, people seek conditions that encourage "credible commitments" (Williamson 1993) – commitments that we can believe will be honored because those who make them would be harmed by failing to keep them.

However we define this instrumental model of trust, the underlying premise is that people want to know that the situation is one which will lead the other person to act in ways that will benefit them. They can create such a situation by adjusting their own level of risk taking to their estimates of the likelihood that the other person will reciprocate any cooperative efforts that they make. As a result, people feel that they are acting in their self-interest no matter how much they cooperate with others. They only cooperate as much as is reasonable given their estimate of the other person's likely behavior in response.

4.2.5   *Motive-based trust*

Motive-based trust involves social inferences beyond whether someone else will keep specific promises or commitments. Instead, motive-based trust involves inferences about intentions behind actions, intentions that flow from a person's unobservable traits and character.

Consider the example of a burglary. If the police respond when called, they have kept their commitment – they have behaved as expected, and earned trust in the instrumental sense. However, even when commitments are kept, the more complex issue of motive inferences plays a role. If the police take a report after a burglary, but the stolen items are never recovered, and the criminal never identified and arrested, the person who called the police to report the problem must consider whether the police "tried" to solve the problem; "did everything they could to try to find what was stolen"; "were concerned about the citizen's problem"; "tried to do what was right"; and "cared about whether the crime was solved." These are all inferences about the motivations of the police that the person gleans from what the police say and do in response to the problem.

In this sense motive-based trust is an estimate of the likely character and motives of others. It is based upon the assumption that knowing another's character and motives tells us whether they will act reasonably toward us in the future. Hence, our expectation is not that the person will engage in particular actions that they have agreed to perform. Instead, we expect that they will act out of "good will" and do those things that they think would benefit us.

The problem of motive-based trust has recently emerged in the context of racial profiling (Tyler and Wakslak 2004). When the police stop a person on the street, that person must make an inference about why they were stopped. The police seldom directly explain their actions as being due to race ("I stopped you because you are Black"), so people make inferences about whether or not they were actually stopped for that reason, and about the motives of the authorities who stopped them, based on more subtle cues.

Problems of motive-based trust are not confined to the police. When dealing with judges, for example, people receive a legal ruling determining the outcome of their case. However, the judge is in possession of legal knowledge, as well as knowledge about how other cases are typically resolved, that the litigants do not have. Litigants cannot very effectively determine if they have received an "appropriate" outcome. It is clear that repeat offenders, who spend time in jail or prison, are better able to do so, since they exchange information with others (Casper *et al.* 1988). Nonetheless, even such repeat offenders lack the knowledge held by an experienced judge or lawyer.

One reason that we might "trust" that legal authorities have acted in good faith in these various situations is that we tend to view as trustworthy those who occupy particular roles in society, e.g., police officers, judges, doctors. These authorities act as agents of society, fulfilling a particular social role (Barber 1983). Part of that role is a set of responsibilities and obligations mandating that the authority act in the interests of those whom they represent. These responsibilities are created and reinforced through training into a specialized role, and via various accounting mechanisms (Meyerson *et al.* 1996). One aspect of trust involves issues of technical competence. The other – the focus here – involves the expectation of moral responsibility, i.e., that authorities will act in the best interests of others.

The concept of a fiduciary relationship is central in all situations in which an authority has power over the lives or property of others. Key to such relationships is the expectation that the authority involved will act in the interests of those for whom they exercise authority. That person is trusted. Trust, in these cases, refers to a judgment about the intentions or motives of the fiduciary agent, i.e., a reliance on the "good will" of that person (Baier 1986).

This focus on the intentions or motives of the authority can be clearly distinguished from a focus on the "truth" or "correctness" of their decisions. Well-intentioned authorities can act in good faith and make mistakes – as we learn from weather forecasters every day. But such a failure to make a correct prediction or decision, does not destroy motive-based trust, if we believe that authorities have good intentions. Philosophers similarly recognize the distinction between intention and result (Bok 1978), with intention viewed as reflecting a person's motivations. The law makes this distinction as well. The "business judgment rule" used by the courts to evaluate corporate authorities recognizes that "decisions made by a board in good faith, with due care, and with regard to the best interests of the corporation" should not be evaluated by courts based upon whether they lead to good or bad results (Mitchell 1999).

People also make the distinction between intention and result. For example, Tyler and Degoey (1996) found that:

> Some people interviewed indicated that police officers and judges are acting in a non-neutral, biased way, yet nonetheless evaluated those authorities to be fair. People seemed willing to forgive surface features of racism and sexism, for example, if they felt that the authorities involved are basically motivated to act in a benevolent manner. It was the trustworthiness of the intentions of the authorities that shaped reactions to the procedures they employed, not surface features of those procedures (e.g., neutrality).
>
> (ibid.: 334)

People focus on their assessment of the motives of authorities for two reasons. First, because they lack enough information to directly determine what actions the authority has taken. People are usually not in the position to know all that has been done in response to their problem or to understand whether the police or courts are doing everything possible to try to solve the problem in a reasonable way. As a result, we cannot exercise control by constant monitoring of the authorities' behavior (Luhmann 1979).

Second, because they lack enough expertise to decide whether those actions are the most appropriate actions to have taken. Authorities are often in possession of special knowledge and training that allow them to make better professional decisions. Judges and police officers, like doctors, lawyers, and teachers, all spend significant time learning their roles and responsibilities which allow them to make decisions that cannot easily be explained to an untrained member of the public. We expect a doctor to know, for example, about the appropriate way to treat an illness and we must to some degree trust that the doctor is acting in good faith.

The problem for people is to distinguish between situations in which cooperation with authorities is reasonable, and situations in which exploitation is occurring. For example, we should cooperate with our doctor when that doctor is motivated by an interest in protecting our health. However, if our doctor is taking kickbacks from a drug company to prescribe ineffective or harmful drugs, our trust is being exploited, and we should not cooperate. The difficulty lies in determining which situation we are in, when we lack the expertise to independently evaluate the appropriateness of the drug, or lack the knowledge that the doctor prescribes that same drug to all patients, regardless of their illness.

Making a judgment about the trustworthiness of political authorities is particularly difficult because there is an inherent conflict of interest in the relationship between members of the public and legal and political authorities, in which the public must cooperate with the authorities while simultaneously protecting their own interests. Of course, to some degree, the conflict of interest in this relationship mirrors that in the relationship which people have with society and with others in their private lives. The key judgment that shapes the way that people balance the opposing factors in the context of their relationship with the police and courts is their trust in the motives of the authorities.

The alternative social regulatory model that we have proposed depends in part on the possibility that voluntary decision acceptance may be enhanced by trust in the motives of authorities, rather than in the outcomes they provide. Tyler and Degoey (1996) tested the argument that people's trust in the motives of particular authorities shapes the willingness to accept their decisions, by studying decision makers in three settings: management, politics, and the family. In each of these three settings, they found that people are more willing to voluntarily accept conflict resolution decisions made by third parties when they trust the motives of those authorized to make the decision. Trustworthiness also had an important influence on people's feelings of obligation to generally follow institutional rules.

4.2.6   *Do social motivations matter?*

The potential gains of a model that includes social motivations can be illustrated using a study of New York City based employees, interviewed about their motivations and workplace behaviors. The details of the sample and the operationalizations of the variables are provided in Tyler and Blader (2000). Two types of cooperation were targeted for the analysis: deference to rules and extra-role behavior.

Using regression the analysis first estimated the ability of instrumental judgments to predict cooperation above and beyond the influence of each of the four types of social motivation. The approach taken was to examine how much variance in each dependent variable was explained by one group of variables, beyond what was explained by the other. So, for example, the ability of instrumental motivations to explain rule following was first established. In a second equation social motivations were then included, and a larger percentage of variance explained by both groups. The addition in the amount of variance explained when the second group was added, beyond that explained by only the first group of variables is the unique variance explained by that second group of variables. The results are shown in Table 4.2.

Table 4.2 The influence of social motives on cooperative behavior

	Deference to rules					Extra-role behavior				
	Eq1	*Eq2*	*Eq3*	*Eq4*	*Ave.*	*Eq5*	*Eq6*	*Eq7*	*Eq8*	*Ave.*
Unique contribution	13%					8%				
Values (morality; legitimacy)										
Procedural justice		6%					6%			
Motive-based trust			4%					5%		
Identification				8%					22%	
Average					8%					14%
Unique contribution (policies yield favorable outcomes; incentives for performance; sanctions for deviance; job rewards are high)	4%	5%	6%	7%		9%	2%	1%	0%	
Average					6%					3%

Source: based on a sample of 404 employees in New York City. The sample is discussed in detail in Tyler and Blader (2000).

On average instrumental judgments explained six percent of the variance in voluntary limiting behavior (deference to rules) beyond what could be explained by social motivations, and three percent of the variance in voluntary proactive behavior (extra-role behavior). In contrast, social motivations explained an average of eight percent of the unique variance in deference to rules beyond that explained by instrumental judgments, and 14 percent of the unique variance in extra-role behavior. This suggests that, in each case, our ability to understand cooperation improves when we expand the motivational model to include consideration of social motivations. While instrumental motivations shape cooperation, they are an incomplete source of motivation.

4.3 Conclusions

Understanding motivation can help us suggest guidelines for managing groups, institutions and societies; i.e., for regulating undesirable and encouraging desirable cooperative behavior. Integrating the psychological and economic perspectives provides suggestions about how to use social motives to supplement traditional incentive and sanction based models, leading to less costly and more effective institutional management. Of course, as already noted, these perspectives are already becoming blurred as economists demonstrate the importance of social motivations in their own experiments.

The key point to both groups is that the limits of economic incentives and sanctions as strategies for motivating voluntary cooperation, due both to limits in resources and difficulties in implementation, have led to an increasing focus on the need to understand social motivations for cooperation. The changing nature of identity, of citizenship, and of work, are all leading to greater attention to the factors shaping voluntary engagement and cooperation with groups, institutions, and societies. A world in which people will work unceasingly on behalf of and even willingly die for causes they believe in must be understood through the lens that includes a focus on social motivations.

These recent findings of both social psychological and economic research on the nature of motivation in institutional settings have important implications for understanding how to promote cooperation in real-world settings. They point to the importance of encouraging social motivations, and as a result, broaden the framework within which motivation is understood. Approaching cooperation from this framework suggests new approaches to our understanding of how most effectively to design groups, institutions and societies.

Notes

1 This chapter is based on a paper presented at the workshop on the Evolution of Designed Institutions. Evolutionary Economics Group, Max-Planck-Institute of Economics, Jena.
2 Economists working to expand the range of motivations considered in institutions include Frey (1997); Fehr (Fehr and Rockenbach 2003, Fehr and Fischbacher 2004); Falk (Falk and Kosfeld 2004); Stutzer (Stutzer and Lalive 2001) and others.
3 Institutions can also be made more efficient by establishing markets and then relying on people's self-interest to direct behavior. The issue of whether such markets are a more efficient approach than seeking to activate social motivations is important, but is beyond the scope of this chapter.

References

Abrams, D., Ando, K. and Hinkle, S. (1998) 'Psychological attachment to the group', *Personality and Social Psychology Bulletin*, 24: 1027–39.
Akerlof, G.A. and Kranton, R.E. (2000) 'Economics and identity', *Quarterly Journal of Economics*, 115: 715–53.
Aalders, M. and Wilthagen, T. (1997) 'Moving beyond command and control: Reflexivity in the regulation of occupational safety and health and the environment', *Law and Policy*, 19: 415–43.
Baier, A. (1986) 'Trust and antitrust', *Ethics*, 96: 231–60.
Barber, B. (1983) *The Logic and Limits of Trust*, New Brunswick, NJ: Rutgers.
Beetham, D. (1991) *The Legitimation of Power*, Atlantic Highlands, NJ: Humanities Press International.
Bies, R.J., Martin, C.L. and Brockner, J. (1993) 'Just laid off, but still a "good citizen": Only if the process is fair', *Employee Responsibilities and Rights Journal*, 6: 227–48.
Bok, S. (1978) *Lying: Moral Choice in Public and Private Life*, New York: Vintage.
Bradach, J.L. and Eccles, R.G. (1989) 'Price, authority, and trust', *Annual Review of Sociology*, 15: 97–118.

Brann, P. and Foddy, M. (1988) 'Trust and the consumption of a deteriorating resource', *Journal of Conflict Resolution*, 31: 615–30.

Brewer, M.B. and Kramer, R.M. (1986) 'Choice behavior in social dilemmas', *Journal of Personality and Social Psychology*, 50: 543–9.

Brocas, I. and Carrillo, J.D. (2003) *The Psychology of Economic Decisions*, Oxford: Oxford University Press.

Burt, R.S. and Knez, M. (1996) 'Trust and third-party gossip', in R. Kramer and T.R. Tyler (eds) *Trust in Organizations*, Thousand Oaks: Sage.

Casper, J.D., Tyler, T.R. and Fisher, B. (1988) 'Procedural justice in felony cases', *Law and Society Review*, 22: 483–507.

Coglianese, C. (1997) 'Assessing consensus: The promise and performance of negotiated rulemaking', *Duke Law Journal*, 46: 1255–349.

Coleman, J. (1990) *Foundations of Social Theory*, Cambridge, MA: Harvard University Press.

Dawes, R.M. (1988) *Rational Choice in an Uncertain World*, San Diego: Harcourt Brace Jovanovich.

De Cremer, D. and Tyler, T.R. (2003) 'Am I respected or not? Inclusion and reputation as issues in group membership?' unpublished manuscript.

De Cremer, D. and van Dijk, E. (2002) 'Reactions to group success and failure as a function of identification level: a test of the goal-transformation hypothesis in social dilemmas', *Journal of Experimental Social Psychology*, 38: 435–42.

Dorf, M.C. and Sabel, C.F. (1998) 'A constitution of democratic experimentalism', *Columbia Law Review*, 98: 267–371.

Falk, F. and Kosfeld, M. (2004) 'Distrust – The hidden cost of control', *IZA Discussion Paper* No. 1203.

Fehr, E. and Falk, A. (2002) 'A psychological foundation of incentives', *European Economic Review*, 46: 687–724.

Fehr, E. and Fischbacher, U. (2004) 'Social norms and human cooperation', *Trends in Cognitive Sciences*, 8: 185–90.

Fehr, E. and Gächter, S. (2002) 'Do incentive contracts undermine voluntary cooperation?', *IZA Working Paper* No. 1424–59.

Fehr, E. and Rackenbach, B. (2003) 'Detrimental effects of sanctions on human altruism', *Nature*, 422: 137–40.

Frey, B. (1997) *Not Just for the Money*, Cheltenham: Edward Elgar.

Green, D.P. and Shapiro, I. (1994) *Pathologies of Rational Choice Theory*, New Haven: Yale.

Gunningham, N. and Rees, J. (1997) 'Industry self-regulation', *Law and Policy*, 19: 363–414.

Hastie, R. and Dawes, R.M. (2001) *Rational Choice in an Uncertain World*, Thousand Oaks, CA: Sage.

Hogarth, R. (1980) *Judgment and Choice*, New York: Wiley.

Hogg, M.A. and Abrams, D. (1988) *Social Identifications*, New York: Routledge.

Karkkainen, B.C. (2002) 'Collaborative ecosystem governance', *Virginia Environmental Law Journal*, 21: 190–243.

Kelman, H.C. and Hamilton, V.L. (1989) *Crimes of Obedience*, New Haven: Yale University Press.

Kim, W.C. and Mauborgne, R.A. (1991) 'Implementing global strategies: The role of procedural justice', *Strategic Management Journal*, 12: 125–43.

Kim, W.C. and Mauborgne, R.A. (1993) 'Procedural justice, attitudes, and subsidiary top management compliance with multinationals' corporate strategic decisions', *Academy of Management Journal*, 36: 502–26.

King, A. and Lenox, M. (2000) 'Industry self-regulation without sanctions', *Academy of Management Journal*, 43: 698–716.

Kopelman, S., Weber, J.M. and Messick, D.M. (2002) 'Factors influencing cooperation in commons dilemmas: A review of experimental psychological research', in E. Ostrom, T. Dietz, N. Dolsak, P.C. Stern, S. Stonich and E.U. Weber (eds) *The Drama of the Commons*, Washington, D.C.: National Academy Press, pp. 113–56.

Kramer, R.M. (1999) 'Trust and distrust in organizations', *Annual Review of Psychology*, 50: 569–98.

Lin, A.C. (1996) 'Participants' experiences with habitat conservation plans and suggestions for streamlining the process,' *Ecology Law Quarterly*, 23: 369–437.

Lind, E.A. and Tyler, T.R. (1988) *The Social Psychology of Procedural Justice*, New York: Plenum.

Luhmann, N. (1979) *Trust and Power*, New York: John Wiley.

MacCoun, R.J. (1993) 'Drugs and the law: A psychological analysis of drug prohibition', *Psychological Bulletin*, 113: 497–512.

Meyerson, D., Weick, K. and Kramer, R.M. (1996) 'Swift trust and temporary groups', in R.M. Kramer and T.R. Tyler (eds) *Trust in Organizations*, Thousand Oaks, CA: Sage.

Mitchell, L.E. (1999) 'Trust, contract, process', in L.E. Mitchell (ed.) *Progressive Corporate Law: New Perspectives on Law, Culture, Society*, Boulder, CO: Westview Press.

Moorman, R.H. (1991) 'Relationship between organizational justice and organizational citizenship behaviors: Do fairness perceptions influence employee citizenship?', *Journal of Applied Psychology*, 76: 845–55.

Moorman, R.H., Niehoff, B.P. and Organ, D.W. (1993) 'Treating employees fairly and organizational citizenship behavior', *Employee Responsibilities and Rights Journal*, 6: 209–25.

Nagin, D.S. (1998) 'Criminal deterrence: Research at the outset of the twenty-first century', *Crime and Justice: A Review of Research*, 23: 283–357.

Niehoff, B.P. and Moorman, R.H. (1993) 'Justice as a mediator of the relationship between methods of monitoring and organizational citizenship behavior', *Academy of Management Journal*, 36: 527–56.

Nisbett, R. and Ross, L. (1980) *Human Inference: Strategies and Shortcomings of Social Judgment*, Englewood Cliffs, N.J.: Prentice-Hall.

Pfeffer, J. (1994) *Competitive Advantage through People*, Cambridge, MA: Harvard.

Plous, S. (1993) *The Psychology of Judgment and Decision Making*, New York: McGraw-Hill.

Proudstone, W. (1992) *Prisoner's Dilemma*, New York: Doubleday.

Pruitt, D.G., Peirce, R.S., Zubek, J.M., Welton, G.L. and Nochajski, T.H. (1990) 'Goal achievement, procedural justice, and the success of mediation', *International Journal of Conflict Management,* 1: 33–45.

Pruitt, D.G., Peirce, R.S., McGillicuddy, N.B., Welton, G.L. and Castrianno, L.M. (1993) 'Long-term success in mediation', *Law and Human Behavior*, 17: 313–30.

Rechtschaffen, C. (1998) 'Deterrence vs. cooperation and the evolving theory of environmental enforcement', *Southern California Law Review*, 71: 1181–272.

Rusbult, C.E. and Van Lange, P.A.M. (2003) 'Interdependence, interaction, and relationships', *Annual Review of Psychology*, 54: 351–75.

Scholz, J.T. (1998) 'Trusting government', in V. Braithwaite and M. Levi (eds) *Trust and Governance*, New York: Russell-Sage Foundation.

Sparks, R., Bottoms, A. and Hay, W. (1996) *Prisons and the Problem of Order*, Oxford: Clarendon Press.

Stewart, R.B. (2003) 'Administrative law in the 21st century', Presentation at the New York University Law School, February 10.

Stutzer, A. and Lalive, R. (2001) 'The role of social work norms in job searching and subjective well-being', *IZA Discussion Paper* No. 300.

Sunshine, J. and Tyler, T.R. (2003a) 'The role of procedural justice and legitimacy in shaping public support for policing', *Law and Society Review*, 29: 747–58.

Sunshine, J. and Tyler, T.R. (2003b) 'Moral solidarity, identification with the community, and the importance of procedural justice', *Social Psychology Quarterly*, 66: 153–65.

Thaler, R.H. (1991) *Quasi-rational Economics*, New York: Russell Sage Foundation.

Thibaut, J. and Kelley, H.H. (1959) *The Social Psychology of Groups*, New York: Wiley.

Thibaut, J. and Walker, L. (1975) *Procedural Justice*, Hillsdale, NJ: Erlbaum.

Tyler, T.R. (1990) *Why People Obey the Law*, New Haven: Yale.

Tyler, T.R. (2000) 'Social justice: Outcome and procedure', *International Journal of Psychology*, 35: 117–25.

Tyler, T.R. (2002) 'Leadership and cooperation in groups', *American Behavioral Scientist*, 45: 769–82.

Tyler, T.R. and Blader, S.L. (2000) *Cooperation in Groups*, Philadelphia: Psychology Press.

Tyler, T.R. and Blader, S.L. (2004) 'Regulation in work settings', unpublished manuscript, New York University.

Tyler, T.R., Boeckmann, R., Smith, H.J. and Huo, Y.J. (1997) *Social Justice in a Diverse Society*, Denver, CO: Westview.

Tyler, T.R. and Degoey, P. (1995) 'Collective restraint in social dilemmas', *Journal of Personality and Social Psychology*, 69: 482–97.

Tyler, T.R. and Degoey, P. (1996) 'Trust in organizational authorities', in R. Kramer and T.R. Tyler (eds) *Trust in Organizations*, Thousand Oaks, CA: Sage, pp. 331–56.

Tyler, T.R. and Huo, Y.J. (2002) *Trust in the Law*, New York: Russell-Sage.

Tyler, T.R. and Lind, E.A. (1992) 'A relational model of authority in groups', *Advances in Experimental Social Psychology*, 25: 115–91.

Tyler, T.R. and Smith, H. (1998) 'Social justice and social movements', in D. Gilbert, S. Fiske and G. Lindzey (eds), *Handbook of Social Psychology*, 4th edn, vol. 2, New York: McGraw-Hill, pp. 595–629.

Tyler, T.R. and Wakslak, C. (2004) 'Profiling and the legitimacy of the police: Procedural justice, attributions of motive, and the acceptance of social authority', *Criminology*, 42: 13–42.

Van Vugt, M., Snyder, M., Tyler, T.R. and Biel, A. (2002) *Cooperation in Modern Society: Promoting the Welfare of Communities, States, and Organizations*, New York: Routledge.

Walster, E., Walster, G.W. and Berscheid, E. (1978) *Equity*, Boston: Allyn and Bacon.

Weber, M. (1968) *Economy and Society*, ed. by G. Roth and C. Wittich, New York: Bedminster Press.

Williamson, O. (1993) 'Calculativeness, trust, and economic regulation', *Journal of Law and Economics*, 34: 453–502.

Part II

Emergence and change of designed institutions

5 Preferences in social interaction and their influence on formal institutions

Uta-Maria Niederle

5.1 Introduction[1]

It is a well-established theory in economics since Demsetz' seminal paper (1967) that institutions, and especially the formal variant of property rights, have their origin in beneficial or harmful effects that human action can have on others and that they change in order to internalize these upcoming externalities over time. It is equally commonplace by now that the devices to internalize (positive and negative) external effects work more or less efficiently. External effects may be due to external shocks as is the case in Demsetz' paper with the colonial commercialization of fur trade in the case of the North American Labrador Indians. Another example from anthropology of an external shock is the introduction of the horse for hunting buffalo among the Blackfeet Indians (Nugent 1993). External effects can also arise from endogenous technological progress, however, a variant that is mentioned by Demsetz, but not further discussed. Nor in his (2002) article, where he broadly outlines the history of dissemination of private property along the line of technological revolutions furthering specialization, Demsetz is clear about the mechanisms of change.

Instead, he does seem to presuppose something like a human genetic predisposition or "preference" for private property (Demsetz 1967: 350). This is a very interesting assumption in that it draws attention back to the question of invariant human endowment and unchanging preferences. Part of this unchanging human genetic endowment are instincts in social interaction or, in short, social instincts, such as reciprocity or commitment.[2] These instincts in social interaction shape informal and formal institutions in a more fundamental way than economists seem to know or accept in their theories. The presumption can, of course, be challenged that innate characteristics explain behavior of different groups or societies (Anderson and Swimmer 1997), which are rather to be explained by constraints and incentives. Demsetz himself modified his implicit presumption of innate preferences for private property in his (2002) paper.[3]

Nonetheless, a system where the law were not respected to some extent "instinctively" would fail, since costs of control and sanctioning, i.e., enforcement of rules, would override gains from the rule itself. Here, innate characteristics or social instincts supporting the "rule of law" come in again. The *rule of first possession* is an example of a rule that is supported more or less universally and seems to have some instinctive acceptance. It has been the organizing principle of most social institutions, and it seems hard to displace it although other rules of acquiring title might have become more efficient in some cases (Epstein 1979). An alternative rule might be effective use or distributional equity. For instance, the exploitation of the ocean bed or the Antarctic regions need not rest upon the first possession rules, but most likely they will.

Hence, innate characteristics may not only influence institutions, but shape them in a unique and systematic fashion. Then, the design of institutions would have to deal much more with the human endowment of social instincts than is done so far. In this way, also puzzles of institutional inefficiency like the one mentioned above might be solved.

The present chapter attempts to provide the missing link between preferences in social interaction and formal institutional change. Advances have indeed been made to account for the influence of institutions like markets on endogenous preferences (Bowles 1998) and in the political sphere (Frey, in this volume) but not the other way round. What can we say about the reverse influence of preferences on institutions? This chapter traces the impact that innate human characteristics have on rules of ownership as one form of a formal institution. It also distinguishes endogenously changing bases of preferences. In that respect, Section 5.2 discusses differences between varying bases of preferences for certain rules or outcomes in a given situation, relating to attitude formation, and the underlying more invariant substantive bases of such preferences, i.e., social instincts. Section 5.3 looks at the impact of such instincts at the advent of institutional rules in first simple societies and then compares the findings with today's modern economies. The problem of mutual influence between the variant bases of preferences, i.e., attitudes, and institutions is also addressed here. Section 5.4 concludes.

5.2   Changing and unchanging bases of preferences in social interaction – some clarifications

There is an ongoing debate on the nature and endogeneity of preferences. As stated before, advances have been made to account for the framing of preferences by institutions. But still, what about the framing of institutions by more or less unchanging human characteristics? As an example, people immediately accept certain rules in interactions, like reciprocity. From there institutions spring as whole systems of rules, including mechanisms of control and sanctioning. People have, however, a bias as to what outcome of a rule or institution they judge to be "fair" and what process of origin of the rule they think legitimate. Most people seem to accept a rule in a certain context but not in others. Norms of reciprocity as well as fairness and legitimacy considerations also seem to diverge in different societies and have changed in the course of time (see Bowles 2001, Henrich *et al.* 2001).

Becker (1976) holds that there are stable, underlying preferences (or tastes), which are "defined over fundamental aspects of life, such as health, prestige, sensual pleasure, benevolence, or envy" (Becker 1976: 5, see also Stigler and

Becker 1977). In his theory, tastes themselves do not vary due to a new argument in the otherwise unchanging utility function. This argument is a function of time allocation and learning of human capital, where the latter changes according to Becker's (1996) "personal and social capital theory". His theory lacks, however, the naturalistic foundation that is the focus in this chapter to analyze institutions; it is still strongly oriented at decision theoretic formulations of methodological individualism. Contrary to Becker, who states "that basic needs for food, shelter, and rest have little to do with the average person's choice of consumption and other activities in modern economies" (Becker 1996: 3), in what follows it will be held that, in order to analyze institutional change, it is indeed necessary to look into the natural foundations and systematic, not arbitrary, change of preferences, following substantive (socio-)biological and (socio-)psychological insights.[4] The task of this section is to show how a naturalistic version of preference bases enhances our understanding of changing institutions and of their invariance.

This chapter distinguishes between two kinds or layers of preferences: the well-known "revealed" preferences in a given situation, dealt with in economic decision theory, and a more "substantive" version of preferences. Substantive preferences are grounded, on the one hand, on basic needs[5] and social instincts in the case of social interaction.[6] It is important to draw a sharp distinction between the rather unchanging substance of basic needs and social instincts and culturally changing tastes for satisfying these needs and living up to basic instincts. Hence, on the other hand, substantive preferences also emerge from a variant basis, which correlates to attitudes, and may change endogenously on this attitude basis. Drawing on the social psychological concept of attitudes and attitude formation based on beliefs and (emotional) evaluation, it is scrutinized how learning of attitudes and their repercussions may influence patterns of rules in interaction and institutions apart from their instinctive counterpart. Since human beings are a product both of biological and cultural evolution, a conflict may arise between biological underpinnings and cultural influences on preferences. This is the topic of the next section, but first, social instincts are discussed as the central basis of all preferences in social interaction and, second, attitudes are introduced as the main element of expressing and shaping endogenous preferences.

5.2.1 Social instincts

There seem to be clear biological underpinnings of behavioral expectations in social interaction, like a sense of reciprocity and fairness in cooperation (Jones 2001: 1182, see also Henrich *et al.* 2001). Such biological underpinnings of behavior are adaptive in the sense that they have responded to and have enhanced survival and reproductive chances in a selective environment – for the individual herself and in the social group. In this way "evolutionary processes inevitably and importantly contribute to the *common origins* and ordering of some preferences" (Jones 2001: 1166, emphasis added, U.-M.N.). In this sense, people are no *tabula rasa*.

This section focuses on substantive preferences in social interaction, i.e., biases in favor of specific rules but also of certain outcomes. If social interaction is interpreted in a strategic, i.e., game theoretic, context, then substantial preferences are directed towards certain payoffs and procedures in a game. Preferences can be interpreted as substantive in that deriving some ordering of preferences involves a calculus that is based on the sensation of real pleasure and pain springing from human needs and their satisfaction.

Here, the specific question is whether some rules may be adopted more easily than others and to what factors this might be due (Cosmides and Tooby 1994). Thus, one can start from the hypothesis that some decisional bias in a situation of social interaction is genetically based. In the social context one might speak of social instincts as innate impulses to act. These social instincts, in the end, support the satisfaction of individual (basic) needs.[7] For example, cooperating and reciprocating for gaining food ultimately serves satisfying not only bodily needs but also, by acting and being treated cooperatively, even serves social-psychological needs like social integrity.

A list of such bases of substantive preferences, or social instincts in social (or strategic) interaction, should at least comprise the following six elements: reciprocity (in cooperation and retaliation),[8] conformity,[9] commitment and loyalty,[10] readiness to help others[11] like giving and sharing, status[12] and prestige, possessiveness.[13] Since it is a tentative compilation, this list does not claim completeness. Single elements given in the list, however, are discussed in diverse contexts of social interaction in socio-biology and evolutionary psychology. Let us now discuss some of the list's elements and also why some features figuring prominently in the literature are not included here.

Altruism is an important, but difficult notion in the context of being ready to help, since it seems to stand for any behavior that is considered to be irrationally social. In evolutionary biological terms altruism is defined in terms of survival and reproduction: "A behavior is altruistic when it increases the fitness of others and decreases the fitness of the actor" (Sober and Wilson 1998: 17). In psychological terms altruism applies to motivational states. Therefore, altruism is an elusive concept in that it can be either some other-regarding *behavior* or it does rather belong to the realm of emotive *motivation* when it includes the well-being of others in one's own well-being. Since more concrete social instincts like reciprocity or sharing include part of what is globally termed as altruism, I stick to the more concrete terms here. Instincts of reciprocity and sharing immediately translate into rules and are the most basic concern of them. As an example, certain duties and obligations of preserving one's real estate for public interests exist in the law, modifying the general rule of proceed as you please.

A special position is taken by instinctive behavior like possessiveness and status seeking. It is clear that both have implications for accumulating material goods to satisfy human needs. Likewise, both social instincts have implications for substantive rule and outcome preferences: Since most rules mark some property rights in their core, their compliance ensures enduring possession of goods and immaterial things that are needed to survive and prosper. Hence, possessiveness, or rather abstaining from possessive behavior, also guides, e.g., rules of reciprocity or sharing. Status seeking (also in connection with possessiveness) seems to support foremost social-psychological needs of having one's place in a social group. Using one's status may be particularly relevant for legitimizing and diffusing rules, but also seeking status can be a motor for adhering to the rules and being considered to be faithful (loyal). This argument is used by Richerson and Boyd (2001: 196f.) to underline their co-evolutionary argument of prestigious mating, combined with pro-social prestige norms, e.g. commitment and conformity. Prestigious mating can even evolve as a genetic predisposition. This is the case when cultural fitness of prestige outweighs genetic fitness, meaning that culturally determined competition favors investments in pro-social prestigious behavior over not investing in conforming to such prestige norms, even if not investing would correlate to better genetic fitness.

Similar thoughts apply to fairness considerations. They are not included in the list, because they seem to be equally difficult to grasp as a concept as is altruism. Sometimes they are concerned with splitting some outcome ("fair share") and sometimes they are concerned with the rules in the process of splitting ("fair rule"). The difficulty is whether fairness is itself a social instinct, or whether it is rather instrumental in that it merely supports, e.g., in an emotional way, other basic instincts like reciprocity or giving and sharing. If the latter is indeed the case, then fairness considerations would always be linked to immediate emotional reactions like anger about unfair shares for oneself or others; but these emotions are not the same as the direct impulses to act, i.e., they are not the same as instincts. To be sure, fairness does by no means imply equal share. Hence, an inequality aversion occurs only in situations where the measures of need and desert, being the two important criteria for judging fair shares, have rendered equal shares the fair distribution. Hence, situational factors especially play a role in fairness considerations. There exists a self-serving bias by stakeholders whereas disinterested observers may reach a rather unbiased consensus on fairness judgments (Konow 2000). A further aspect of situational factors is that preferences in transactions seem to depend on the perceived relationships (market or family) and involve related concepts of fairness (Bowles 1998: 87). These facts demonstrate again the psychological-motivational foundations of preferences in interaction, and fairness considerations are one important factor of mediating the instinctive impulse to act in a social situation.

Another and very important form of preference related to social interaction is a specific "rule preference" which is cognitively anchored: preferred rules have to be simple, salient, and clear. In this way, rule preference is of an essentially esthetic nature, which is ultimately prompted by our psychological – and cognitive – make-up (Schlicht 2000: 39, FN 10). It is likely that humans have a genetic predisposition to accept certain specific forms of rules as pertinent rules, which is connected to the specific cognitive-mental conditions in humans. If the human mind is endowed with an adaptive learning capacity and a corresponding flexibility of decision-making, then it should also be adaptive to be guided by some rules that make decisions easier to achieve, i.e., to have rule preferences of a certain kind.

Social instincts in interaction are also linked to positive and negative emotive reactions, respectively, such as sympathy, envy, anger, and others.[14] These feelings represent the mechanisms that produce a hedonic state, that is, a pleasant or unpleasant sensation. This bears some relation to "visceral factors" referring "to a wide range of negative emotions (e.g., anger, fear), drive states (e.g., hunger, thirst, sexual desire), and feeling states (e.g., pain), that grab people's attention and motivate them to engage in specific behaviours. (...) Visceral factors (...) can alter desires rapidly because they themselves are affected by changing internal bodily states and external stimuli" (Loewenstein 2000: 426). Such emotive reactions bear a direct relation to attitudes as one major factor of motivation to act. Attitudes are equally based on beliefs as well as (emotive) evaluations. They are the second – and changeable – pillar on which preferences for institutions rest.

5.2.2   Attitudes

In contrast to social instincts and basic needs as unchanging substance of preferences the variable bases of preferences relate to changeable attitudes. Attitudes are "learned predispositions to respond in a consistently favorable or unfavorable manner with respect to a given object" (Fishbein and Ajzen 1975: 6, emphasis omitted, U.-M.N.). In other words, attitudes represent a person's general feeling of favorableness or unfavorableness toward some stimulus object.[15] As a person forms beliefs about an object, she automatically and simultaneously acquires an attitude toward that object. The relation is such that each belief links the object to some attribute, and the person's attitude toward the object is a function of her evaluations of these attributes (ibid.: 216). Since attitudes are learned predispositions, they are moldable. They change with experience (also mentally) of the stimulus objects, i.e., with goods and services and with social rules or institutions. Attitudes as evaluations can easily be likened to a psychological interpretation of preferences as "expressions of an affective response" rather than the reflectively reasoned orderings in economics (Kahneman 2003: 1463).[16] In the same manner, attitudes are defined by the affective value of (the mental representation of) objects and not by choices (Kahneman *et al.* 1999: 206).

Attitude formation is a function of the beliefs, i.e., subjective probabilities, about an object (cf. for this aspect Fishbein and Ajzen 1975: ch. 6). Briefly, the scheme is as follows:

> [F]rom direct observation, other sources of information, and inference, a person forms beliefs about the attributes of an object. Beliefs are thus statements about whether or not, or in what ways, the object possesses certain attributes. Attributes are evaluated independently in terms of their "favourableness" or "unfavourableness". Both beliefs and evaluations are taken to be exogeneously [sic!] and independently determined. The person's attitude toward an object then depends on his beliefs about the attributes of that object together

with his evaluations of those attributes. Attitudes, in turn, generate intentions, and intentions determine behaviour.

(Katzner 1989: 136)

In the course of a person's life, her experiences lead to the formation of many different beliefs about various objects, actions, and events. These beliefs may result from direct observation or from inference processes as forms of cognitive learning. Some beliefs may persist over time, others are less stable, and new beliefs may be formed. This is due to a growing body of experiences and knowledge accumulation. However, rapid growth of knowledge may cause problems to stability of beliefs. This may also cause instability in attitudes, which in turn may paralyse action because of uncertainty. For example, with rapidly changing or heterogeneous institutions economic actors seem to "wait and see".

Change of both positive and evaluative components of attitudes, namely beliefs and evaluations, depends upon (expected) experience of pleasure and pain from the stimulus objects. This experience is connected to primary reinforcers.[17]

Primary reinforcers imply genetically programmed neural pathways that classify some sensations as pleasant and others as unpleasant. In this sense the primary reinforcers correspond to (...) "innate, built-in values". Specific primary reinforcers arouse sensations that humans call feelings or emotions (...) Emotions and the reinforcers that evoke them are indicators of comfort and, as such, are bases for evaluating experiences.

(Pulliam and Dunford 1980: 25f.)

In essence, all goods, services, and interaction, which serve to satisfy basic needs, can be primarily reinforcing. Also former neutral or unknown stimuli can become (secondary) reinforcers, when they are experienced with primary ones.[18] In other words: Reinforcement processes are at work as a basic learning mechanism in changing attitudes.

Hence, because of reinforcement "attitudes may unwittingly be coloured by the context in which an object has been experienced" (Stroebe and Jonas 1996: 244). Furthermore, "the plasticity of people's memories may turn unexpected consequences into conscious aims, and the malleability of their preferences may make formations they once feared or opposed desirable after the fact" (Kuran 1991: 269). This mechanism helps to reduce cognitive dissonance, or regret. Mere exposure to the same – novel – stimuli effects a (positive) change in attitudes, whereas exposure to familiar stimuli does not have such an effect (Fishbein and Ajzen 1975: 281ff.).[19] Thus, the same object may evoke different valuations depending on its description or framing and on the context in which it is evaluated (Kahneman *et al.* 1999: 206).

The formation of attitudes in the sense discussed above is something inherently social. To stress the social components in attitude change the role of social interaction in learning mechanisms has to be emphasized. As Witt (2003: 12) elaborates the important fact is that in their cognitive development, individuals are not entirely autonomous. Their cognitive frames and with it, their attitudes, are influenced by communication with their social environment (as source of information) and by the socially contingent rewarding or non-rewarding experiences with certain information content (as source of valuations). This process starts early in childhood with the acquisition of language and the identification of meaning and continues during lifetime with communication and socializing with others. The more frequent and intense the interactions between agents are, the more likely it is that tacit, socially shared commonalities emerge in their subjective interpretations and valuations (Bandura 1986: ch. 2). These commonalities can also lead to socially shared models of behavior incorporating ideas of how to behave in certain social situations. These models often have normative connations. Within intensely interacting groups people tend to adopt such models for their own behavior and expect others to adopt them, too. These social-cognitive mechanisms represent the behavioral underpinnings for culturally molded preferences (via attitudes) that are relevant for the change of consumption patterns and institutions over time (see also Bandura 1986: ch. 4).

To sum up, social instincts can account for invariants in institutional arrangements, whereas mechanisms of attitude change may help to predict the variants. However, the mechanisms described above make it more ambiguous to predict social behavior from attitudes than from social instincts, since the latter are more immediate, and even behavioral, responses to stimuli, whereas attitudes are valuations of mental representations with no immediate impulse to act. But – and that makes the concept valuable – attitudes are more reliable and more tractable predictors of changing institutions than any other abstract concept of preferences. How social instincts and attitudes work together in the evolution of (formal) institutions is subject of the next section.

5.3   Evolution of preferences and institutions

This section scrutinizes, first, the invariant influences of social instincts on social behavior and institutions. To complicate matters, this perspective then has to be combined with variant influences of attitudes in order to show the mechanisms that are at work in changing real (formal) institutions. It should be noted that there need not only be a positive impact of social instincts on the evolution of institutions but that the reverse case of negative impact is also possible in the course of institutional evolution and has to be taken into account as well.

The supplementary assumption to be made in a dynamic, evolutionary setting of institutional change is technological change. Without technological change there would be no need to change systems of institutional arrangements substantially (see Service 1995). This is also what Demsetz (1967, 2002) seems to imply. There would not be much change in attitudes either. Technological as a motor of organizational change requires institutional adjustments. Thus, technological change is seen as the external, given factor. (That line of reasoning does not exclude, however, the possibility of autonomous, gradual institutional change without preceding revolutionary technological innovation.) The invariant human endowment together with technology-based variation in social organization sometimes leads to peculiar outcomes of such adjustment processes.

In this section it is shown how the set of social instincts presented before work on the development of institutional rules, or, more precisely, ownership rules. These instincts are not only of vital importance for the development of first rules in simple societies, but they are still of vital importance today. The case of property rights is chosen for illustrative purposes because of the ubiquitous presence of ownership rules in all societies or economic systems – ancient and modern, small-scale and large-scale societies. Moreover, rules of ownership also comprise some rule elements that are exceedingly important for another branch of institutional rules, namely rules of contract. Social instincts are vital to all institutions, and some especially serve specific kinds of institutions.

5.3.1 *Social instincts and institutional change*

Social instincts as innate predispositions to act are the invariant factor in institutional change. They can be superimposed by learned attitudes and behavior, but they cannot be molded like attitudes, neither can they be completely suppressed. Hence, their effect has to be reflected in formal institutional design if they should not run counter to the intention of the rules. The social instincts described in Section 5.2 are now discussed in turn as they drive the process of building institutions. These social instincts are the important initial factors driving the emergence and diffusion of first institutional rules in that they enable formulation and enhance enforcement, i.e., legitimacy, control, and sanctioning, of rules. But even today, social instincts guide rule following or hamper their dissemination. So far, the analysis will be static in the form of impact analysis. Dynamic elements will be added with attitudinal change in the next section.

When the impact of social instincts and changing attitudes is examined in the contexts of informal and formal institutions, respectively, the line of argument differs slightly for both cases. Whereas informal institutions relate to social norms and develop spontaneously via coordination or simple regularity of behavior, formal institutions need a formal apparatus of both sanctioning and changing the rules. The only difference in the context of change, though, is that with formal institutions an additional layer of political process with some external agent adds to the basic processes of informal, group internal change. The impact of social instincts on both, informal and formal, processes seems to have the same relevance, however, if not exactly the same mechanisms. Corresponding to the title of this chapter the analysis will concentrate on formal institutions.

Social instincts have an impact on different rule dimensions. They influence the definition of a rule – in terms of the two basic relations of property or contract. They also influence rule propagation and rule following, also in form of defection from existing rules. Lastly, they influence the sanctioning of rule deviators. The social instincts given in the list in Section 5.2 are now analyzed for their impact on the process of definition, legitimization, and sanction of ownership rules.

The first and most basic instinct is reciprocity in cooperation and retaliation. Reciprocity is a precondition for exchange; and exchange is beneficial in a world of unequal distribution of scarce resources (see also Service 1995 for a discussion). Without the impulse to retaliate no promises (as an informal institution) would be kept initially, which is a precondition to keep contracts (as a formal institution). As is well known, the potential to sanction deviate behavior is vital for the initial occurrence of cooperation, not merely being self-enforcing coordination. For ownership rules exactly this impulse to retaliate, but also to respect what seems the other's due, is the initial force of formation. In other words, beside reciprocity as retaliation allowing natural and reflexive modes of sanctioning, its positive form supports the definition of contract, i.e., (together with fairness considerations) it helps defining equity. How retaliatory behavior still comes through even today can be seen with some dysfunctional reflection in modern legal systems. There are forms of excessively filling the courts with lawsuits of which the subliminal or sub-threshold motives seem to be retaliatory in character. This phenomenon cannot be explained by simple incentive or cost-benefit arguments. The probability of losing one's case does not really seem to be assessed in these cases. Another point in terms of negative impact is retaliatory impulses or moral aggression in modern times of the state assuming the central coercive power to sanction deviation. Taking the law in one's own hand or even mob law may be the consequences. On the other hand, this is an expression of returning back to simple (informal) modes of individual or group sanction when the state is not considered to be the reliable force any more (as in times of revolutionary changes in politics and the law). Then, returning back to simple modes of behavior would be quite an adaptive strategy.

Possessive behavior is the next element to be discussed, which has a direct bearing on defining and maintaining property rights. Although there is no direct bearing of possessiveness on the concrete *rules* of ownership (Service 1995: 90), property rights in general help ensure continuing control over the objects of possessive behavior, i.e., the natural and social resources for satisfying basic needs and for ensuring survival and reproduction, even if there is no direct proximity of the proprietor to his or her property (Niederle 2004). Respect of property requires recognition of a lasting owner-object bond (Kummer 1991: 81, see also Ellis 1985: 115). Possessive behavior in conjunction with human insatiability and the seemingly endless creation of new wants parallel to technological advances, however, plays a trick on sustainable economic growth today and on the formation of "sustainable" institutions as well to cope with it. Although these genetic traits have been fitness enhancing in terms of risk averseness (keep it, once you have it) and adaptive in extreme environments of scarcity and low levels of subsistence, now they seem to take human society towards their ecological limits.

The third instinct to be discussed is giving and sharing. As a form of helping others it defines the limits to exclusive property rights. Therefore, giving and sharing has an indirect effect on the institutions of allocating property and of distribution.

Service (1995) notes, that the "pooling and sharing of goods [...] is suggestive of the nature of property in primitive society. Individuals obviously must *have* the goods before they can share them, and others must *want* the goods (love to possess them) in order to receive them willingly." (ibid.: 91) Obviously, possessive behavior stays in sharp contrast to this instinct and often overrules it; and many rules are formulated in order to overcome this tendency.

The fourth item is "rule preference". The concrete form that rules take is cognitively anchored in such a rule preference for – to repeat – simple, salient, and clear rules. This preference guides rule definition as well as rule propagation and following. Rule preference limits the kind of rules that are accepted informally or agreed to formally to certain types. An example is the ubiquitous rule of first possession in property law. Clearly, this cognitive bias limits the complexity of rule systems that humans can cope with, and often, the law systems of modern societies go beyond. An indicator for that may be the increasing amount of constitutional complaints and challenges.

Status as fifth element is a factor of propagating rules, which can also take the form of defecting from former, existing rules. This applies to all rules, of course, not only to rules of ownership. (For a discussion in co-evolutionary terms of prosocial commitment see Richerson and Boyd 2001.) Individuals with high status, e.g., political or religious leaders in stratified societies, have the power to bring new rules on the agenda and promote them (for an example from anthropology see Ensminger and Knight 1997). In egalitarian simple societies mediators or arbitrators do not have the same coercive power to act on rules, but their authority serves the customary resolution of disputes. Thus, by adjudication automatically new rules are articulated, just as today's judges set precedents in some form or another (see Benson 1988). Whether new rules do indeed disseminate is also determined by the other social instincts just discussed, but promotion of rules by high status authorities serves to legitimize rules and furthers acceptance. Unquestioning faith in rules and authority is the other side of the coin.

Dominance and violence have been present in the progressive development of overt status differentiation in larger social groups in sedentary societies (see Knauft 1991: 395ff. on this and the following). Since property and possession increase with sedentism, with it, various forms of (competitive) leadership and status hierarchy to control resources emerge. While simple hunter-gatherer societies are organized strongly egalitarian, some form of leadership is needed to coordinate action among larger social groups in sedentary societies. While dominance (and competitive) behavior is suppressed in the early and simple societies for reasons of risk-minimizing and equal access to resources for all members, in societies where a surplus can be gained dominance comes to the fore again in order to control (and possess) resources. Hence, dominance of elites can be traced in (formal) institutional arrangements of property since then.

Lastly, the individual aspiration to status and prestige in a group also influences commitment and loyalty to the group and to the respective rules prevailing there. (For the co-evolutionary mechanisms see again Richerson and Boyd 2001.) Commitment and loyalty obviously foster the respect for given rules in a group.

The same is true for behaving conformingly in a group. Conformity enhances diffusion of rules through imitation in order to stay uniform. The negative aspect here is that conservative conformity hampers the emergence and spread of new rules. Another negative aspect is that, sometimes, sub-group rules and norms stand against rules of the whole group so that conformity and/or commitment/ loyalty to these sub-group norms means defecting from other, institutional rules. It may be the case, for example, that for the sake of conforming to cultural sub-groups social or institutional rules are broken wilfully, e.g., damage to private or public property and vandalism.

All the instincts that have been discussed here serve to formulate and enforce the rules necessary for a society to function – be it small or big, simple or complex. They work on a very fundamental basis of unconscious behavioral reactions to existing and new rules as well as deviations from these rules. Their varying visibility in institutions is due to cultural shaping of attitudes and learned behavior that superimpose the genetically coded layer of instincts.

5.3.2   *The role of attitudes in changing formal institutions*

This section analyzes the role of attitudes as *the* basis of preferences that translate into institutional change. The questions to be answered are: How does change in attitudes come about? And how does this attitudinal change influence the variation of old and acceptance of novel institutional rules?

In economics, there exist two main influences on action (when preferences are given initially): first, perceived utility and, second, the perception of constraints. For the analysis here, utility is measured in terms of expected pleasure and pain, and sources of constraints are budget, technology, social norms and law, but also "human nature", i.e., social instincts that are not to be totally suppressed. The traditional list of constraints is extended with this last element, because it constrains behavior in a similar manner as the other elements do, albeit being itself a preference determinant. It is the only constraint that is internal to the human make-up and cannot be changed. The other – external – constraints are subject to change themselves. And so are endogenous preferences, incorporating attitudes.

Now, attitudes can help evaluating utility and constraints. In that, they serve an important function for developing preferences over objects and outcomes. They help categorizing incoming information, such as new experiences, along established evaluative dimensions (Stahlberg and Frey 1996). In that way, attitudes help to simplify and understand the complex world around us. To repeat, attitudes include beliefs about the characteristics and functioning of the object or outcome under consideration as well as some (also emotional) evaluation (positive or negative) towards the object or outcome under evaluation. Change of these two components of attitudes seems to be at the core of changing preferences and behavior.

On the meso or macro level about generalized attitudes and their components, one can aggregate beliefs about the world to "world views" and the evaluations can be summed up to "values" of a time. These two aspects of general attitudes, being expressed as world views and values, can be made use of in a generalized model of change of formal and informal institutions.[20] Then, values are a function of world views, and world views are a function of technical and scientific standards. Hence, world views seem to be more elementary than the resulting values, because, for example, knowledge of the world's functioning influences elementary religious beliefs and the rules of conduct springing from them. One of the most famous examples for general change of attitudes is the impact that Galileo's (1564–1642) fundamental discoveries had on the view of the world thereafter. In spite of his conflict with the church concerning the geocentric model of the universe the scientific revolution was not to be repressed. Main discoveries in astronomy at that time were tied to advances in optical technologies, e.g., the telescope. In turn, with the recognition of the heliocentric model the view of man's place in the universe changed and with it social values of man's due changed as well. For example, with the advent of Renaissance and its new scientific findings people, became much more worldly and self-oriented, emphasizing their own happiness in this life instead of waiting for happiness in the hereafter. Another fundamental example is the agricultural revolution with the invention of the plough effecting a whole host of social changes starting from property rights in land to social stratification and leadership. In the remainder of this section more of this macro perspective will be focused upon while incorporating the micro mechanisms of attitudinal change, which have already been shortly addressed in Section 5.2.

Showing the starting point of institutional change the highly simplified theoretical account runs as follows: humans have basic and unchangeable needs in terms of purely bodily needs and social-cognitive needs. When satisfying them they have to take into account that they have to interact with other individuals. Since the pleasure-pain calculus is applicable to *all* human behavior, also in human interaction, people must try to conform to their basic social instincts when satisfying these basic needs. That means, individual actors are constrained, first, by the available (technical) means for satisfying needs and, second, by the social determinants of need satisfaction, like identity in relation to others and respect or even envy by others. Both of these constraints form general attitudes of a time towards consumption and institutions. The constraints are in turn subject to change. The primary force of change is technological innovation (cf. also Redmond 2003: 665). The search for new technologies is driven by curiosity and a drive for still better solutions to problems of need satisfaction, if possible in the existing environment and existing mode of economy.[21] In this interpretation, ultimately (basic) needs drive the process of innovation and diffusion; they are (qualitatively) insatiable,[22] because of their aforementioned social dimension.

It is assumed here that new technologies are at the center of creative purposes.[23] Radically new behavior in the form of new institutional rules in social interaction does not seem to be a plausible starting point of new and revolutionary development, because whenever radical changes in human social groups took place, they were accompanied, or even initiated by technological innovations or at least technological imports (Nugent 1993, Gudeman 1986: ch. 1). Institutional change is

Institutional rule

	Old	New
Negative	Negative experience/ dissatisfaction	Negative expectation
Evaluation/ attitude		
Positive	Positive experience, habituation	Positive expectation, exposure

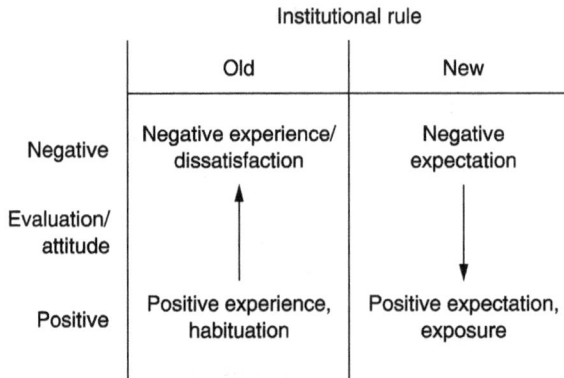

Figure 5.1 Direction of attitude change for changing institutional rules from old to new ones.

foremost induced by the spread of new technologies and the new forms of production and specialization they generate (see McKendrick 1982a, 1982b for an illustration of social change). These new forms of organization plus external effects of new technologies entail new regulation of social interaction. Foremost, new property and new liability rules have to be arranged informally or formally in order to internalize these external effects. More precisely, they have to bring to bear the costs of negative effects and to appropriate the gains of positive effects. Thus, behavioral innovation, or better, adaptation, follows rather than precedes technological innovation.

The aspect of changing attitudes towards some existing technology that triggers innovative activities is not scrutinized here, neither the aspect of changing attitudes towards some new technology in the diffusion process. The process of changing the underlying attitudes inducing institutional change, however, is of central importance. Change in this respect seems to follow quite intuitive processes of positive/negative experience with old versus positive/negative expectation from new institutional rules. (Similar processes can be identified for the area of attitudinal change towards existing and new technologies as well.)

Figure 5.1 illustrates the relation between negative versus positive attitudes towards old versus new institutional rules. Negative experience and dissatisfaction with existing institutional rules triggers negative evaluations, and, with it, negative attitudes towards these rules, whereas positive experiences and habituation rather induce positive evaluations and attitudes. Similarly, negative expectations (via negative information) about new institutional rules induce negative attitudes, whereas positive expectations and mere exposure trigger positive attitudes. In order to let a new institutional rule be propagated and disseminate two things have to occur: positive attitudes towards old rules have to change into negative ones, and potentially negative attitudes towards new rules have to be converted into positive evaluations. These two directions of change are now analyzed more closely.

When analyzing, first, the change of positive attitudes toward old rules into negative ones, two effects work in opposite directions. Dissatisfaction with the status quo caused by technological innovation works into negative direction of attitude change, while support of the existing status quo through habituation impedes this change of attitude.

To show the role of the two effects in the process of attitudinal change towards institutional rules, let us assume experience of allocative and distributive effects in the status quo versus some (potential) new situation. Attitudinal evaluations depend, on the one hand, on the perceived utility of technological progress and its institutional effects but also, on the other hand, on the affective evaluations previously held. Experiencing negative welfare effects from old rules can be expected to affect attitudes negatively, because loss of material or social position triggers dissatisfaction with this situation on a cognitive dissonance basis. It is an equally simple fact that people adapt their attitudes toward their situation. Attitudinal adaptation may also play a role in the habituation process. Counter-attitudinal and incentive- or force-induced behavior may change attitudes in a systematic way, namely to reduce cognitive dissonance springing from behavior being incoherent with original attitudes, i.e., attitudes, not behavior, will be adapted (cf. Stroebe and Jonas 1996: passim). Hence, there exists some habituation effect of the status quo on attitudes towards the status quo. This connection impedes the change to negative attitudes towards the status quo of rules at the cost of formation of positive attitudes towards new rules.

On the other hand, an effect of mere exposure to a new situation supports the formation of a positive attitude towards the situation beside the obvious positive effect that positive expectations from a new rule have. This is due to the role that reinforcement has to play in the process of attitude formation and change (Stroebe and Jonas 1996). Being exposed to ever the same argument for a new rule (in the right situation) tends to be persuasive in character and may form a positive attitude toward it. In the same manner, discontent with the status quo of existing rules opens up the mind for new rules.

Personal communication and persuasion as such work, of course, in both directions of attitude change and on both opposing counterparts of old and new rules. So-called change agents or "political entrepreneurs" play a role here. In this way, propagation or resistance cascades of rules, respectively, find their way through society. This is a complicated process of verbal reinforcement and intellectual effort; and diverse influencing factors determine its outcome. Among them are: information content, sympathy of informant or persuading person, and framing. Here, also processes of attention and distraction as well as processing abilities come into play (cf. Stroebe and Jonas 1996: passim). It is revealing, in this respect, "that variables can produce attitude change by different processes in different situations" (Petty and Wegener 1998: 369). Significantly, weak arguments by experts tend to be scrutinized more closely and be dismissed, whereas arguments by persons we like tend to be supported, and weak arguments in stressful or unpleasant situations are overlooked. All these situational factors play a role in changing attitudes. Generally, "attitudes that are changed as a result of considerable mental effort tend to be stronger than those changed with little thought and thus are more persistent, resistant to counterpersuasion, and predictive of behavior than attitudes that are changed by processes invoking little mental effort in assessing the central merits of the object" (Petty and Wegener 1998: 370). All these mechanisms seem to be a powerful source of enforcement and legitimization of social institutions. For example, public agents and the mass media are used to influence people's attitudes towards old versus new rules and institutions via communication.

In summary, several mechanisms, taken from social psychology, are involved in changing attitudes via expectation and experience: Habituation and exposure tend to trigger positive attitudes, but work in opposite directions in that the former perseveres positive attitudes towards old institutional rules, whereas the latter leads to positive attitude formation concerning new rules. Experienced loss in status quo and positive expectations influence attitudes in direction of rule change. Personal communication and persuasion have their important share in effecting these four mechanisms of attitudinal change, working in both directions.

5.4   Conclusions

This chapter contributes to the ongoing debate on the nature and endogeneity of preferences in the specific case of social interaction and institutional change. It has addressed two interrelated questions: If there is an unchanging human make-up what is its impact on the formation and change of institutional rules? When thinking about changing formal institutions – in what way do attitudes contribute to the shift from old to new rules?

To answer these questions, first, it was necessary to look for some more substantive meaning of preference. The chapter has distinguished two bases of substantive preferences that are relevant for institutional change: invariable social instincts in interaction on the one hand and a variable basis incorporating changing attitudes towards rules and institutions on the other. It has been conjectured that substantive preferences in the meaning of social instincts do not change much over time, neither individually nor historically. What does indeed change, are the bases of attitudes towards rules to guide social behavior. These bases are determined by the technological standards of a time; technological progress triggers the process of changing attitudes. In generalized terms, world views and the resulting values of a time do change. This may sound like "technological determinism", but there is still no inescapable and unilateral connection between scientific-technological progress and social-cognitive change.

As to the question why unchanging human social instincts and changing human attitudes are factors necessary to take into account, the answer is, on the one hand, that attitudes mediate the process of building "situational" preferences in a real choice situation. They are based on beliefs and (emotional) evaluations about stimulus objects, such as social interaction. In that, they mediate between utility considerations concerning the goals (pleasure and pain) and constraints (technology, etc.). This is a point of systematic, but subjective, variability that traditional decision and utility theory have not taken or cannot take into account. On the other hand, it is sometimes overlooked that there are features of deep human make-up, in the form of social instincts, that make certain paths of institutional development more or less impassable and others predestined.

This has implications for the theory of institutional design: Efficiency and welfare problems of allocating property rights are often not as simple as economic theories try to make believe. Human nature sometimes does not seem to be made for efficient solutions in monetary terms. Taking this restriction into account would save resources in terms of costs of deviation from and enforcement of formal institutions. This is a problem that informal institutions are not likely to encounter to the same extent, since regular behavior of a voluntary kind leads to norm formation and the building of institutions. Voluntary adoption of a rule is likely to conform to human social instincts and people's attitudes.

Notes

1 I would like to thank Klaus Rathe for most valuable suggestions to the present conception of this chapter. I would also like to thank Martin Binder for very fruitful analytical discussions.
2 In contrast, another, and more flexible, human endowment is the human capacity to learn.
3 There, he puts forward three conditions that foster the development of private property arrangements, namely 1. less compactness, i.e., high number and less closeness of persons involved in a resource allocation problem, 2. enhanced productivity resulting from technical change and specialization, and 3. growing complexity of economic organization that creates a need for coordination and control. These three factors are the driving forces for the rule of private law in great modern societies.
4 It seems that, in fact, Becker has translated to some extent insights from the other disciplines into simple economic modelling. It would be an interesting task to analyze his model of personal and social capital in terms of theories of learning. It could be seen to correspond to some very simplistic version of reinforcement and social learning, this being elementary to account for changing preferences in reality. Becker's utility interpretation, when stripped off its purely rational economic connotation, is rather the reward spending element in the reinforcement or learning mechanism.
5 Basic needs comprise physical as well as psychological needs.
6 This perspective stays in contrast to the formal view of utility theory. Preferences in decision theoretic terms are always relational, meaning "x is preferred over y". Then, a more or less complete ordering of preferences can be derived by two by two comparisons. The concept of preference in economic theory is closely intertwined with the concept of choosing rationally and consistently. (The problems this approach poses are discussed in Sen 1986 and March 1986.) What is meant here, however, are preferences in a more "Benthamitian utility sense", i.e., in the meaning of deriving pleasure and pain from an (inter-)action (Bentham 1948); see also Kahneman (2003: 1457). One could liken the first variant of preference to "choosing by rule" while the second variant conforms to "choosing by liking" (Kahneman 2003: 1467). The latter preferences focus on some substantive individual need basis with its different dimensions.
7 A list of basic needs may contain air, water or other drinkable liquid, sleep, means of maintaining body temperature, nutrition, sexual activity, maternal care, shelter, cognitive arousal or entertainment, and others (cf. Witt 2001).
8 The (genetic) evolution of strong reciprocity, as a component in the repertoire of human preferences, in the sense of adhering to a social norm and punishing violators is shown

in Bowles and Gintis (2000). The inclination to punish deviators is also termed "moralistic aggression". (See also Cialdini and Trost 1998: 175ff.) for a discussion of reciprocation as a universal norm.)

The coming about of these basic social preferences or instincts via natural evolution is not subject of this paper however.

9 Cialdini and Trost (1998: 167).
10 See Richerson and Boyd (2001).
11 See for this social instinct Darwin (1981: 72).
12 As Darwin (1981: 165) termed it: "love of praise and the dread of blame" in social interaction.
13 See Niederle (2004) for an analysis.
14 The four major emotions, however, are happiness/joy, anger/rage, sadness/dejection, and fear/terror (Scherer 1996: 298).
15 Such a stimulus object can also consist of a means-end-relationship.
16 The concept of attitudes seems to be very near to what I termed world views and values elsewhere (Niederle 2003: 216ff.). World views can be interpreted in terms of beliefs about the actual functioning of the world. Values closely correspond to resulting expressions of like/dislike or good/bad evaluations of the world's functioning. In a way, they follow or are a function of the world views which seem to precede them. Both have an emotional aspect. Together they resemble the concept of attitudes as a whole.
17 Reinforcement, in Becker (1996: ch. 1), is seen as complementarities of past and present consumption (or investments in personal capital).
18 See also Witt (2001: 28ff., 2000: 12ff.) for accounts of change via conditioning processes such as operant learning. In contrast to this paper, the focus there is on changing wants themselves, not attitudes.
19 This seems to have something in common with an agenda setting effect in that, e.g., new behavioral rules may be eventually accepted simply because they are extensively propagated.
20 A more formal completion of such a model is reserved to a different paper.
21 cf. again Redmond (2003), see also Cordes (2005); for a list of restrictions to innovation cf. Mokyr (1990: ch. 7).
22 A further and related question would be whether the parallel creation of seemingly new wants with technological advances bears any biological fitness basis. Is this form of human insatiability an inherently adaptive characteristic of man or is it simply a side effect of the human make up, which allows for so much useful flexibility but plays a trick in this respect?
23 In connection with creativity, new technology is indeed like "manna from heaven" in the neoclassical sense. It cannot be directly promoted, since what will once become an innovation is not known beforehand. What can be encouraged instead by institutions, is, in general, search for new solutions to known problems. Put the other way round, institutions can impede creativity based technological progress but cannot prevent it forever.

References

Anderson, L.C. and Swimmer, E. (1997) 'Some empirical evidence on property rights of first peoples', *Journal of Economic Behavior and Organization*, 33: 1–22.

Bandura, A. (1986) *Social Foundations of Thought and Action*, Englewood Cliffs: Prentice Hall.

Becker, G.S. (1976) *The Economic Approach to Human Behavior*, Chicago: The University of Chicago Press.

Becker, G.S. (1996) *Accounting for Tastes*, Cambridge, MA, London: Harvard University Press.

Benson, B.L. (1988) 'Legal Evolution in Primitive Societies', *Journal of Institutional and Theoretical Economics*, 144: 772–88.

Bentham, J. (1948) *An Introduction to the Principles of Morals and Legislation*, New York: Hafner Publishing Company.

Bowles, S. (1998) 'Endogenous Preferences: The Cultural Consequences of Markets and Other Economic Institutions', *Journal of Economic Literature*, 36: 75–111.

Bowles, S. (2001) 'Individual Interactions, Group Conflicts, and the Evolution of Preferences', in S.N. Durlauf and H. P. Young (eds) *Social dynamics*, Cambridge, MA, London: MIT Press, pp. 155–90.

Bowles, S. and Gintis, H. (2000) 'The Evolution of Strong Reciprocity', mimeo, University of Massachusetts, Amherst.

Cialdini, R.B. and Trost, M.R. (1998) 'Social Influence: Social Norms, Conformity, and Compliance', in D.T. Gilbert, S.T. Fiske and G. Lindzey (eds) *The Handbook of Social Psychology*, 4th ed., Boston: McGraw-Hill, pp. 151–92.

Cordes, C. (2005) 'Veblen's "Instinct of Workmanship", its Cognitive Foundations, and Some Implications for Economic Theory', *Journal of Economic Issues*, 39: 1–20.

Cosmides, L. and Tooby, J. (1994) 'Better than Rational: Evolutionary Psychology and the Invisible Hand', *American Economic Review, Papers and Proceedings*, 84: 327–32.

Darwin, C. (1981) *The Descent of Man, and Selection in Relation to Sex*, Princeton: Princeton University Press.

Demsetz, H. (1967) 'Toward a Theory of Property Rights', *American Economic Review*, 57: 347–59.

Demsetz, H. (2002) 'Toward a Theory of Property Rights II: The Competition between Private and Collective Ownership', *Journal of Legal Studies*, 31: 653–72.

Ellis, L. (1985) 'On the Rudiments of Possession and Property', *Social Science Information*, 24: 113–43.

Ensminger, J. and Knight, J. (1997) 'Changing Social Norms: Common Property, Bridewealth, and Clan Exogamy', *Current Anthropology*, 38: 1–24.

Epstein, R.A. (1979) 'Possession as the Root of Title', *Georgia Law Review*, 13: 1221–43.

Fishbein, M. and Ajzen, I. (1975) *Belief, Attitude, Intention and Behavior: An Introduction to Theory and Research*, Reading, Menlo Park, London: Addison-Wesley.

Frey, B.S. 'Institutions shape preferences: The approach of "Psychology & Economics"', this volume.

Gudeman, S. (1986) *Economics as Culture: Models and Metaphors of Livelihood*, London, Boston and Henley: Routledge and Kegan Paul.

Henrich, J., Boyd, R., Bowles, S., Camerer, C., Fehr, E., Gintis, H. and McElreath, R. (2001) 'In Search of Homo Economicus: Behavioral Experiments in 15 Small-Scale Societies', *American Economic Review, Papers and Proceedings*, 91: 73–8.

Jones, O.D. (2001) 'Time-shifted Rationality and the Law of Law's Leverage: Behavioral Economics meets Behavioral Biology', *Northwestern University Law Review*, 95: 1141–205.

Kahneman, D. (2003) 'Maps of Bounded Rationality: Psychology for Behavioral Economics', *American Economic Review*, 93: 1449–75.

Kahneman, D., Ritov, I. and Schkade, D. (1999) 'Economic Preferences or Attitude Expression? An Analysis of Dollar Responses to Public Issues', *Journal of Risk and Uncertainty*, 19: 203–35.

Katzner, D.W. (1989) 'Attitudes, Rationality and Consumer Demand', in J.A. Kregel (ed.) *Inflation and Income Distribution in Capitalist Crisis. Essays in Memory of Sidney Weintraub*, New York: New York University Press, pp. 133–53.

Knauft, B.M. (1991) 'Violence and Sociality in Human Evolution', *Current Anthropology*, 32: 391–428.

Konow, J. (2000) 'Fair Shares: Accountability and Cognitive Dissonance in Allocation Decisions', *American Economic Review*, 90: 1072–91.

Kummer, H. (1991) 'Evolutionary Transformations of Possessive Behavior', *Journal of Social Behavior and Personality*, 6: 75–83.

Kuran, T. (1991) 'Cognitive Limitations and Preference Evolution', *Journal of Institutional and Theoretical Economics*, 147: 241–73.

Loewenstein, G. (2000) 'Emotions in Economic Theory and Economic Behavior', *American Economic Review, Papers and Proceedings*, 90: 426–32.

McKendrick, N. (1982a) 'The Commercialization of Fashion', in N. McKendrick, J. Brewer and J.H. Plumb (eds) *The Birth of a Consumer Society: The Commercialization of Eighteenth-Century England*, Bloomington: Indiana University Press, pp. 34–99.

McKendrick, N. (1982b) 'The Consumer Revolution of Eighteenth-Century England', in N. McKendrick, J. Brewer and J.H. Plumb (eds) *The Birth of a Consumer Society: The Commercialization of Eighteenth-Century England*, Bloomington: Indiana University Press, pp. 9–33.

March, J.G. (1986) 'Bounded Rationality, Ambiguity, and the Engineering of Choice', in J. Elster (ed.) *Rational Choice*, New York: New York University Press, pp. 142–70.

Mokyr, J. (1990) *The Lever of Riches: Technological Creativity and Economic Progress*, Oxford: Oxford University Press.

Niederle, U.-M. (2003) *Institutionenwandel am Beispiel von vertraglicher Versicherung: Elemente einer allgemeinen Theorie*, Marburg: Metropolis-Verlag.

Niederle, U.-M. (2004) 'From Possession to Property: Preferences and the Role of Culture', in J. Finch and M. Orillard (eds) *Complexity and the Economy. Implications for Economic Policy*, Cheltenham: Edward Elgar.

Nugent, D. (1993) 'Property Relations, Production Relations, and Inequality: Anthropology, Political Economy, and the Blackfeet', *American Ethnologist*, 20: 336–62.

Petty, R.E. and Wegener, D.T. (1998) 'Attitude Change: Multiple Roles for Persuasion Variables', in D.T. Gilbert, S.T. Fiske and G. Lindzey (eds) *The Handbook of Social Psychology*, 4th ed., Boston: McGraw-Hill, pp. 323–90.

Pulliam, H. R. and Dunford, C. (1980) *Programmed to Learn. An Essay on the Evolution of Culture*, New York: Columbia University Press.

Redmond, W.H. (2003) 'Innovation, Diffusion, and Institutional Change', *Journal of Economic Issues*, 37: 665–79.

Richerson, P.J. and Boyd, R. (2001) 'The Evolution of Subjective Commitment to Groups: A Tribal Instincts Hypothesis', in R.M. Nesse (ed.) *Evolution and the Capacity for Commitment*, New York: Russell Sage Foundation, pp. 186–220.

Scherer, K.R. (1996) 'Emotion', in M. Hewstone, W. Stroebe and G.M. Stephenson (eds) *Introduction to Social Psychology: a European Perspective*, Oxford, Cambridge, MA: Blackwell Publishers, pp. 279–315.

Schlicht, E. (2000) 'Aestheticism in the Theory of Custom', *Journal des Economistes et des Etudes Humaines*, 10: 33–51.

Sen, A.K. (1986) 'Behavior and the Concept of Preference', in J. Elster (ed.) *Rational Choice*, New York: New York University Press, pp. 60–81.

Service, E.R. (1995) 'Technology and Economy', in T. Megarry (ed.) *From the Caves to Capital. Readings in Historical and Comparative Sociology*, Greenwich: Greenwich University Press, pp. 79–97.

Sober, E. and Wilson, D.S. (1998) *Unto Others: The Evolution and Psychology of Unselfish Behavior*, Cambridge, MA, London: Harvard University Press.

Stahlberg, D. and Frey, D. (1996) 'Attitudes: Structure, Measurement and Functions', in M. Hewstone, W. Stroebe and G.M. Stephenson (eds) *Introduction to Social Psychology: A European Perspective*, Oxford and Cambridge: Blackwell Publishers, pp. 205–39.

Stigler, G.J. and Becker, G.S. (1977) 'De Gustibus Non Est Disputandum', *American Economic Review*, 67, 76–90.

Stroebe, W. and Jonas, K. (1996) 'Principles of Attitude Formation and Strategies of Change', in M. Hewstone, W. Stroebe and G.M. Stephenson (eds) *Introduction to Social Psychology: A European Perspective*, Oxford and Cambridge: Blackwell Publishers, pp. 240–75.

Witt, U. (2000) 'Genes, Culture, and Utility', *Papers on Economics & Evolution* # 0009, Max-Planck-Institute of Economics, Jena.

Witt, U. (2001) 'Learning to Consume – A Theory of Wants and the Growth of Demand', *Journal of Evolutionary Economics*, 11, 23–36.

Witt, U. 'Animal Instincts and Moral Sentiments – Institutional Evolution and Its Behavioral Underpinnings', paper presented at the Conference on Economic Behavior and Organization, honouring Richard H. Day, USC Los Angeles, April 2003.

6 The complexity of rules and how they may evolve over time

Elinor Ostrom

An extraordinary number of field studies have found that local groups of resource users have created a wide diversity of institutional arrangements for coping with common-pool resources when they have not been prevented from doing so by central authorities (McCay and Acheson 1987, Fortmann and Bruce 1988, Berkes 1989, V. Ostrom *et al.* 1993, Netting 1993, Bromley *et al.* 1992, Tang 1992, Blomquist 1992). These empirical studies document successful self-organized resource governance systems in diverse sectors in all parts of the world. Examples also exist of commons dilemmas that have continued unabated. From the extensive empirical evidence, one can conclude that overuse and destruction of common-pool resources do not always occur, but it also is not an inescapable outcome when multiple users face a commons dilemma. While many groups succeed, others fail in their efforts to do so, and overcoming a commons dilemma is always a struggle (Dietz *et al.* 2003).[1]

Overcoming commons dilemmas is a struggle for several reasons: First, the problem in a field setting is complex. A formal game is a useful simplification of a common-pool problem, and the range of decisions faced in efforts to change the structure of a commons. The biophysical world faced in field settings is complex, however, and the array of rules that could be used to modify the incentives of participants is extraordinarily large – as I show later in this chapter.

Second, even if all those involved in making rule changes have the same interests, it will rarely be possible for them to predict the consequences of using a particular set of rules in a specific setting – especially when they are first starting to organize themselves. The consequences depend on whether (1) appropriators understand how a particular set of rules partitions the strategies available to them, (2) they tend to follow the rules or look for ways of avoiding the rules, (3) the rules are monitored and enforced so that appropriators slowly learn a common understanding of the rules, (4) sanctions are imposed for non-conformance, and (5) the biophysical system responds in the way originally predicted when rules were adopted. Surprises resulting from the operation of a new rule set are highly likely until participants have learned from their own experience how these rules operate in a particular setting.

Third, participants have the same underlying interests in getting more valuable resource units or contributing less. When it comes to preferences related to changing rules so as to improve the probability of sustaining a resource, however, preferences are apt to differ substantially among participants. Those who have used a resource for a long time will prefer rules that allocate use rights to those with a long history of use. Those who can make strong economic returns from harvesting from the resource will prefer rules that allocate use rights to those who purchase those rights.

Fourth, conditions change both in regard to the resource under consideration and in regard to the external economic and social settings. If a governance system cannot adopt new rules to adjust to these changes, a system that worked well initially may generate less and less satisfactory results over time. Of course, changes in rules do not guarantee better performance. They could make things worse!

Given the substantial progress that has already been made in understanding how individuals have struggled with these problems, I wish first to summarize what we have learned about the variety of rules adopted in the field in efforts to manage common-pool resources. In light of this extensive empirical research, I will call into question the presumption used in many policy circles that we can conduct complete analyzes to design optimal rule systems in a top-down manner. In the last section of the chapter, I share some of my own speculations about the process of experimenting with rules in ongoing processes. Here, I draw on research on complex adaptive processes to posit how rules may evolve when those involved can try out various rules to ascertain what works in a local ecological and cultural process. But, first, let me quickly review how many of us associated with the Workshop in Political Theory and Policy Analysis analyze operational action situations and the rules that affect their structure.

6.1   What is common to all operational action situations where individuals interact

6.1.1   The internal structure

Whenever two or more individuals are faced with a set of potential actions that jointly produce outcomes, these individuals can be said to be "in" an "action situation". Typical action situations include markets, work teams, committees, and bureaucratic structures. In regard to the common-pool resources, typical action situations relate to harvesting, maintenance, and investment in infrastructure.

The structure of all of these situations – and many more – can be described and analyzed by using a common set of variables or working parts: (1) the set of participants, (2) the specific positions to be filled by participants, (3) the potential range of outcomes (or static variables in the world), (4) the set of allowable actions and the function that maps actions onto outcomes, (5) the control that an individual has in regard to this function, (6) the information available to participants about the structure of the action situation, and (7) the costs and benefits – which serve as incentives and deterrents – assigned to actions and outcomes (see E. Ostrom *et al.* 1994, E. Ostrom 1999, 2005).

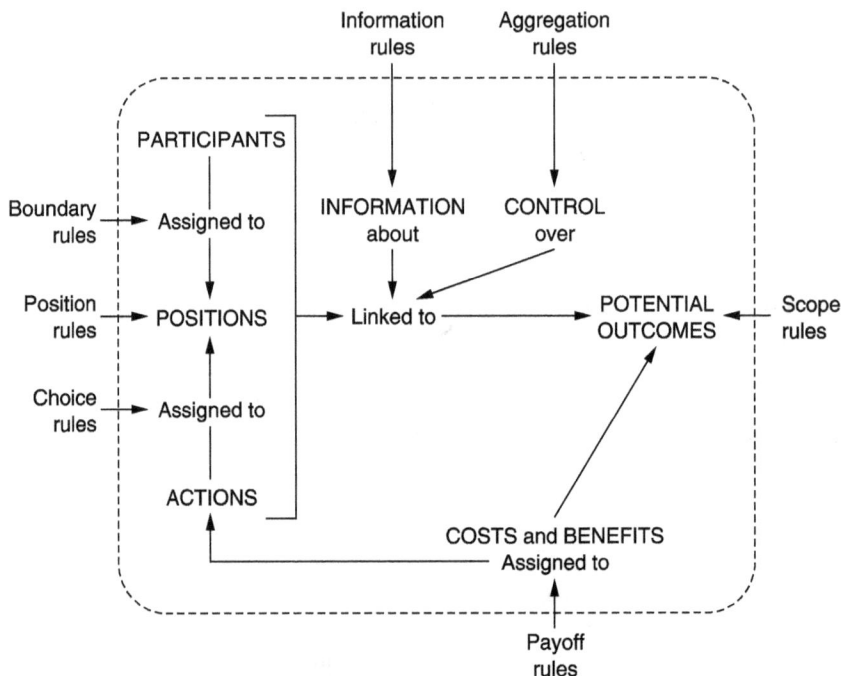

Figure 6.1 How rules affect the working parts of action situations (E. Ostrom 2005: 189).

The abstract internal structure of an action situation can be represented as shown inside the rectangle of dashed lines of Figure 6.1. In addition to the internal structure, whether a situation will occur once, a known and finite number of times, or indefinitely affects the strategies of individuals. The working parts of an action situation are similar to the elements identified by game theorists to construct formal game models (see Gardner 2003, Gintis 2000). A formal description of a game is thus one way of describing a subset of all action situations.

If one wants to change the behavior of individuals interacting in a situation, one method is to change one or more of these working parts. One way of beginning to understand this process is to ask about the rules that affect each of the working parts of an action situation. These are displayed around the outside of the rectangle of Figure 6.1.

6.1.2   *Changing the structure of operational action situations*

To answer questions about how to *change* the structure of a situation, the analyst must dig deeper into how sets of rules combine with the attributes of goods and of the community of individuals participating to generate the structure of a particular situation. By rules, I mean prescriptions about what a participant in a particular situation is obliged, forbidden, or permitted to do at a particular juncture in a larger decision process (Crawford and E. Ostrom 1995/2005). In a formal game, a rule affects the actions the game theorist posits are available to actors. If a physically possible action is represented in the choice set, the actor is permitted to choose among a set of potential actions. Usually, if an action is obligatory, it is *not* shown in a game tree and is assumed to be taken. If a physically possible action is forbidden, it is also *not* shown as a choice available to the player. In other words, formal game theory represents permitted choices but does not consider forbidden choices or mandatory actions.[2]

Rules add choices to those available in the physical world – such as creating the possibility of voting for a candidate. Rules also enable individuals to acquire rights to property for which many individuals have strong feelings (Stake 2004). Rules forbid choices from those available in the physical world – such as driving 100 miles an hour in a residential zone, or taking possession of someone else's property without their approval. While it is still physically possible to do this using many modern vehicles, a person expects that they will face a large fine if they are found doing so. If the rules are well monitored, perceived to be legitimate, and carry a sanction, most individuals do not routinely consider choices that involve breaking rules. Individuals do take actions that are forbidden and do not take actions that are mandatory from time to time, but there is the strong possibility of being monitored and sanctioned. Further, when the rules are perceived to be legitimate, the individual places a normative weight on these actions that tends to make them feel guilty when they break a rule or feel proud when they follow a rule at a substantial personal cost (Crawford and E. Ostrom 1995/2005).

In our empirical studies, we have found it useful to cluster generic types of rules according to which component of an action situation the rule directly affects. A rule may affect other working parts of an action situation as a secondary effect. This leads to the initial identification of seven broad groupings of rules: position rules, boundary rules, choice rules, aggregation rules, scope rules, information rules, and payoff rules.

Position rules define the set of relevant positions in a situation (such as boss, employee, advisor, etc.). *Boundary rules* affect how individuals are assigned to or leave positions. *Choice rules* affect the assignment of particular action sets to positions. *Aggregation rules* affect the level of control that individual participants exercise at a linkage within or across situations. *Scope rules* affect which outcomes may, must, or must not be affected within a domain. *Information rules* affect the level of information that participants may provide to each other and what is common knowledge about actions and the link between actions and outcomes. *Payoff rules* affect the benefits and costs assigned to outcomes given the actions chosen. If a prescription is a rule, rather than a norm that individuals share, some payoff rule must exist that adds a sanction to an action that breaks the rule. The direct relationship among rules and the components of an action situation is shown in Figure 6.1 as the set of arrows connecting rules to specific parts of an action situation.

6.1.3   Using rules to cope with the commons

One way to understand the rules that appropriators use in the field is to read and do a meta analysis of the extensive case study literature written about local common-pool resources by anthropologists, agricultural economists, historians, sociologists, and political scientists. Colleagues at the Workshop have collected an immense archive of original case studies written by many scholars on all resource sectors (see Hess 1999 and http://www.indiana.edu/~workshop/wsl/wsl.html). We have developed structured coding forms to help us identify the specific kind of action situations faced in the field as well as the rules that users have evolved over time to try to govern their resource effectively (see E. Ostrom 1999). In light of our coding many cases, we can examine the kinds of boundary, position, choice, and payoff rules used in field settings. These four clusters of rules are the major tools used to affect commons dilemmas in field settings while information, scope, and aggregation rules are additional tools used to complement changes induced by these four rules.

6.1.4   Affecting the attributes of users through boundary rules[3]

Boundary rules define the attributes and conditions required of those who enter an action situation. In field settings there are many action situations related to common-pool resources, but we will focus our attention on the appropriation situation: Who appropriates (harvests) how many resource units from which common-pool resource? Boundary rules, thus, define who has a right to enter and use a resource as an "authorized appropriator" – the term we will use for this most general position that exists in multiple settings. Boundary rules affect the types of participants with whom other participants will interact. If contingent cooperation is perceived to be a possibility, then an important way to enhance the likelihood of using reciprocity norms is to increase the proportion of appropriators who are well known in a community. These participants have a long-term stake in that community and would find it costly to have their reputation for trustworthiness harmed in that community. Reducing the number of users but opening the resource to strangers willing to pay a license fee, as is frequently recommended in the policy literature, introduces appropriators who lack a long-term interest in the sustainability of a particular resource. Using licenses to regulate entry may reduce the level of trust among participants and their willingness to use reciprocity and thus increase enforcement costs substantially.

From our initial reading and our own fieldwork, we expected to find boundary rules that focused on local residency so as to increase the opportunity for reciprocity. What amazed us, however, as we read the extensive case studies describing diverse inshore fisheries, irrigation systems, and forests was the variety of attributes and conditions used to define who could be an authorized appropriator. As shown in Table 6.1, we identified 23 attributes of individuals and 13 conditions described by case-study authors as having been used in at least one common-pool resource somewhere in the world (E. Ostrom *et al.* 1989). While

Table 6.1 Attributes and conditions used in boundary rules to define who is authorized to appropriate from a common-pool resource

Attributes		Conditions
Residency or membership	*Personal characteristics*	*Relationship with resource*
National	Ascribed	Continued use of resource
Regional	Age	
Local community	Caste	Long-term rights based on:
Organization (e.g., co-op)	Clan	Ownership of a proportion
	Class	of annual flow of
	Ethnicity	resource units
	Gender	Ownership of land
	Race	Ownership of non-land
		asset (e.g., berth)
	Acquired	Ownership of shares in a
	Education level	private organization
	Skill test	Ownership of a share of the
		resource system
		Temporary use-rights acquired
		through:
		Auction
		Per-use fee
		Licenses
		Lottery
		Registration
		Seasonal fees
		Use of specified technology

Source: E. Ostrom (1999).

some systems use only a single attribute or condition, many use a combination of two or three of these rules.

Boundary rules used in the field can broadly be grouped in three general classes related to how individuals gain authority to enter and harvest resource units from a common-pool resource. The first type of boundary rule focuses on acquired attributes of an individual such as an individual's citizenship, residency, or membership in a particular organization. Many forestry and fishing user groups require members to have been born in a particular location. A second broad group of attributes relates to individual ascribed personal attributes. User groups may require that appropriation depends on age, ethnicity, clan, or caste. A third group of boundary rules relates to the conditions of use relating an appropriator with the resource itself. Using a particular technology or acquiring appropriation rights through an auction or a lottery are examples of this type of condition.

In a systematic coding of those case studies for which sufficient information existed about rules used related to inshore fisheries in many parts of the world, Schlager (1990, 1994) coded 33 user groups out of the 44 groups identified as having at least some boundary rules regarding the use of the resource. All 33 groups depended on a combination of 14 attributes or conditions (Schlager 1994: 258). None of these groups relied on a single attribute or condition. Thirty out of 33 groups (91 percent) limited fishing to those individuals who lived in a nearby community, while 13 groups also required membership in a local organization. Consequently, most inshore fisheries organized by the users themselves restrict fishing to those individuals who are well known to each other, have a relatively long-term time horizon, and are connected to one another in multiple ways (see Taylor 1982, Singleton and Taylor 1992).

After residency, the next most frequent attribute or condition, used in two-thirds of the organized subgroups, involves the condition that the appropriator would use a particular type of technology. These rules are often criticized by policy analysts, since gear restrictions tend to reduce the "efficiency" of fishing. Gear restrictions have many consequences, however. Used in combination with choice rules that assign fishers using one type of gear to one area of the fishing groups and fishers using another type of gear to a second area, they solve conflicts among non-compatible technologies. Many gear restrictions also reduce the quantity of fish that can be harvested.

Other rules were also used. A scattering of groups used ascribed characteristics (age – two groups; ethnicity – three groups; race – five groups). Three types of temporary use rights included government licenses (three groups), lottery (five groups), and registration (four groups). Seven groups required participants to have purchased an asset such as a fishing berth, while three groups required ownership of nearby land as a condition of appropriation. Schlager did not find that any particular attribute or condition was correlated with higher performance levels, but she did find that the 33 groups who had at least one boundary rule tended to be able to solve common-pool problems more effectively than the 11 groups who had not crafted boundary rules.

In a closely related study of 43 small- to medium-sized irrigation systems managed by farmers or by government agencies, Tang (1992) found that the variety of attributes or conditions used in irrigation was smaller than among inshore fisheries. The single most frequently used boundary rule, used in 32 of the 43 systems (74 percent), was that an irrigator must own land in the service area of an irrigation system (ibid.: 84–5). All of the government-owned and operated irrigation systems relied on this attribute and *only* this attribute. Many of the user-organized systems relied on other attributes and conditions or land ownership combined with other rules. Among the other rules used were ownership of a proportion of the flow of the resource, membership in a local organization, and a per-use fee.

Tang (ibid.: 87) found a strong negative relationship between reliance on land as the *sole* boundary requirement and performance. Over 90 percent of the systems using other boundary rules or a combination of rules including land ownership, were rated positively in the level of maintenance achieved and in the level of rule conformance, while less than 40 percent of those systems relying solely on land ownership were rated at a high performance level ($p = .001$). This puzzling result can be understood by a deeper analysis of the incentives facing engineers who plan irrigation systems. Many government systems are designed on paper to serve an area larger than they are actually able to serve when in operation, due to a variety of factors including the need to show as many posited beneficiaries as possible to justify the cost of construction (see Palanisami 1982, Repetto 1986). The government then uses ownership in the authorized service area as the criterion for possessing a right to water. After construction, authorized irrigators find water to be very scarce because of the unrealistic plans. Frequently, they are then unwilling to abide by rules limiting the amount of water they take or to contribute to the maintenance of the system.

Thus, many of the rich diversity of boundary rules used by appropriators in the field attempt to ensure that the appropriators will be relating to others who live nearby and have a long-term interest in sustaining the productivity of the resource. One way of coping with social dilemmas is thus to change the composition of who uses a common-pool resource to increase the proportion of participants who have a long-term interest, are more likely to use reciprocity, and who can be trusted. Central governments tend to use a smaller set of rules and some of these may open up a resource to strangers without a longer-term commitment to the resource or generate conflict and an unwillingness to abide by any rules.

6.1.5 Affecting the set of allowable actions through creating position rules

The above discussion of boundary rules focused on the general position of authorized appropriator. Many times, this is not self-consciously established, but entry rules do specify who is authorized to enter this position. In some self-organized resource governance systems, they also create a second position of guard or monitor. Many different names are used.

Self-organized fisheries tend to rely on self-monitoring more than the creation of a formal position of guard. Most inshore fishers now use short-wave radios as a routine part of their day-to-day operations allowing a form of instant monitoring to occur. An official of a West Coast Indian tribe reports, for example, that "it is not uncommon to hear messages such as 'Did you see so-and-so flying all that net?' over the short-wave frequency – a clear reference to a violation of specified gear limits" (cited in Singleton 1998: 134). Given that most fishers will be listening to their short-wave radio, "such publicity is tantamount to creating a flashing neon sign over the boat of the offender. Such treatment might be preceded or followed by a direct approach to the rule violator, advising him to resolve the problem. In some tribes, a group of fishermen might delegate themselves to speak to the person" (ibid.).

Among self-organizing forest governance systems, creating and supporting a position as guard is frequently essential since resource units are highly valuable and a few hours of stealth can generate substantial illicit income. Monitoring rule conformance among forest users by officially designated and paid guards may make the difference between a resource in good condition and one that has become degraded. In a study of 279 forest *panchayats* in the Kumaon region of India, Agrawal and Yadama (1997) found that the number of months a guard was hired was the most important variable affecting forest conditions. The other variables that affected forest conditions included the number of meetings held by the forest council (a time when infractions are discussed) and the number of residents in the village. "It is evident from the analysis that the capacity of a forest council to monitor and impose sanctions on rule-breakers is paramount to maintaining the forest in good condition. Nor should the presence of a guard be taken simply as a formal mechanism that ensures greater protection. It is also an indication of the informal commitment of the *panchayat* and the village community to protect their forests. Hiring a guard costs money. The funds have to be generated within the village and earmarked for protection of the resource. If there was scant interest in protecting the forest, villagers would have little interest in setting aside the money necessary to hire a guard" (Agrawal and Yadama 1997: 455).

6.1.6   *Affecting the set of allowable actions through choice rules*

Choice rules are also a major type of rule used to regulate common-pool resources. In the CPR coding manual, we identified a diversity of choice rules used in field settings. Some rules involve a simple formula as a way of devising how many resource units appropriators may obtain. Many forest resources, for example, are closed to all forms of harvesting during one portion of the year and open for extraction by all who meet the boundary rules during an open season. Most choice rules, however, have two components.

In Table 6.2, the eight allocation formulas used in the field are shown in the left column. A fisher might be assigned to a fixed location (a fishing spot) or to a fixed rotational schedule, a member of the founding clan may be authorized to cut timber anywhere in a forest, while an irrigator might be assigned to a fixed percentage of the total water available during a season or to a fixed time slot. In addition to the formula used in a choice rule, most also attached a condition as a basis for the assignment. For example, a fisher might be assigned to a fixed location based on a number drawn in a lottery, on the purchase of that spot in an auction, or on the basis of his or her historical use. An irrigator might be assigned to a fixed rotation based on the amount of land owned, the amount of water used historically, or the specific location of the irrigator.

If all of the conditions were equally likely to be combined with all of the formulas, there would be 112 different choice rules (8 allocation formulas × 14 bases). A further complication is that the rules for one product may differ from those of another product in the same resource. In regard to forest resources, for example, children may be authorized to pick fruit from any tree located in a forest so long as it is for their own consumption, women may be authorized to collect so many head-loads of dead wood for domestic firewood and certain plants for making crafts, while *shaman* are the only ones authorized to collect medicinal plants from a particular location in a forest (Fortmann and Bruce 1988). Appropriation rights to fish are frequently related to a specific species. Thus, the exact number of rules that are actually used in the field is difficult to compute since not all base conditions are used with all formulas.

Table 6.2 Types of choice rules

Allocation formula for appropriation rights	Basis for allocation formula
Percentage of total available units per period	Amount of land held
Quantity of resource units per period	Amount of historical use
Location	Location of appropriator
Time slot	Quantity of shares of resource owned
Rotational order	Proportion of resource flow owned
Appropriate only during open seasons	Purchase of periodic rights at auction
Appropriate only resource units meeting criteria	Rights acquired through periodic lottery
Appropriate whenever and wherever	Technology used
	License issued by a governmental authority
	Equal division to all appropriators
	Needs of appropriators (e.g., type of crop)
	Ascribed characteristic of appropriator
	Membership in organization
	Assessment of resource condition

Source: E. Ostrom (1999).

Schlager (1994: 259–60) found that all 33 organized subgroups used one of the five basic formulas in their choice rules. Every user group included in her study assigned fishers to specific locations using a diversity of bases including technology, lottery, or historical use. Thus, spatial demarcations are a critical variable for inshore fisheries. Nine user groups required fishers to limit their harvest to fish that met a specific size requirement, while seven groups allocated fishers to fishing spots using a rotation system and seven other groups allowed fishing locations to be used only during a specific season. Four groups allocated fishing spots for a particular time period (a fishing day or a fishing season).

An important finding – given the puzzles addressed in this chapter – is that the choice rule most frequently recommended by policy analysts (see Anderson 1986, 1992, Copes 1986) is *not* used in any of the coastal fisheries included in Schlager's study. No attempts were made by the fishers using an inshore fishery coded by Schlager to regulate the quantity of fish harvested per year based on an estimate of the yield. "This is particularly surprising given that the most frequently recommended policy prescription made by fishery economists is the use of individual transferable quotas (ITQs) based on estimates on the economically optimal quantity of fish to be harvested over the long run" (Schlager 1994: 265).

In an independent study of 30 traditional fishery societies, James Wilson and colleagues also noted the surprising absence of quota rules: "All of the rules and practices we found in these 30 societies regulate 'how' fishing is done. That is, they limit the times fish may be caught, the locations where fishing is allowed, the technology permitted, and the stage of the life cycle during which fish may be taken. None of these societies limits the 'amount' of various species that can be caught. Quotas – the single most important concept and tools of scientific management – is conspicuous by its absence" (Acheson *et al.* 1998: 397, see Wilson *et al.* 1994).

Local inshore fishers, when allowed to manage a riparian area, thus use rules that differ substantially from those recommended by advocates of scientific management. Of course, just because the rule is not used by inshore fishers does not eliminate the possibility that an ITQ might be an optimal rule in some contexts.

Fishers have to know a great deal about the ecology of their inshore region including spawning areas, nursery areas, the migration routes of different species, and seasonal patterns just in order to succeed as fishers. Over time, they learn how "to maintain these critical life-cycle processes with rules controlling technology, fishing locations, and fishing times. Such rules in their view are based on biological reality" (Acheson *et al.* 1998: 405).

In the irrigation systems studied by Tang (1992: 90–1), three types of choice rules are used most frequently: (1) a fixed time slot is assigned to each irrigator (19 out of the 37 cases for which data is available, and in 10 out of 12 government-owned systems), (2) a fixed order for a rotation system among irrigators (13 cases), and (3) a fixed percentage (or quota) of the total water available during a period of time (5 cases). Three poorly performing systems with high levels of conflict had not crafted any choice rule at all. A variety of conditions were used in these rules such as "amount of land held, amount of water needed to cultivate existing crops, number of shares held, location of field, or official discretion" (Tang 1994: 233). Farmers also do not use rules that assign a specific quantity of water to irrigators other than in the rare circumstances where they control substantial amounts of water in storage (see Maass and Anderson 1986).

Fixed time slot rules allow farmers considerable certainty as to when they will receive water without an equivalent certainty about the quantity of water that will be available in the canal. Fixed time allocation systems are criticized as inefficient since water is not allocated to the farmers with the highest productivity. This condition does, however, economize greatly on the amount of knowledge farmers have to have about the entire system and on monitoring costs. Spooner (1974) and Netting (1974) described long-lived irrigation systems in Iran and in Switzerland where there was perfect agreement on the order and time allotted to all farmers located on a segment of the system, but no one knew the entire sequence for the system as a whole.

Tang also found that many irrigation systems use different sets of rules depending on the availability of water. During the most abundant season, for example, irrigators may be authorized to take water whenever they need it. During a season when water is moderately available, farmers may use a rotation system where every farmer is authorized to take water for a fixed amount of time during the week based on the amount of land to be irrigated. During scarcity, the irrigation system may employ a special water distributor who is authorized to allocate water to those farmers who are growing crops authorized by the irrigation system and are most in need.

In addition to devising choice rules specifying how resource units may be harvested, many systems also have to devise rules for how resources will be mobilized. These types of choice rules specify duties as contrasted to rights. As examined in E. Ostrom (1990), robust common-property regimes tend to rely on a close match between the formulae used for harvesting and the formulae used for input requirements.

The diversity of rules devised by users greatly exceeds the limited rules recommended in textbook treatments of this problem. Appropriators cope with the commons by a wide variety of rules affecting the actions available to participants and thus their basic set of strategies. Given this wide diversity of rules, it is particularly noteworthy that rules assigning appropriators a right to a specific quantity of a resource are used so infrequently in inshore fisheries and irrigation systems. (They are used more frequently when allocating forest products where the quantity available, as well as the quantity harvested, are much easier to measure (Agrawal 1994).) To assign an appropriator a specific quantity of a resource unit requires that those making the assignment know the total available units. In water resources where there is storage of water from one season to another and reliable information about the quantity of water is available, such rules are more frequently utilized (Blomquist 1992, Schlager *et al.* 1994).

6.1.7 Affecting outcomes through payoff rules

One way to reduce or redirect the appropriations made from a common-pool resource is to change payoff rules so as to add a penalty to actions that are prohibited. Many user groups also adopt norms that those who are rule breakers should be socially ostracized or shunned and individual appropriators tend to monitor each other's behavior rather intensively. Three broad types of payoff rules are used extensively in the field: (1) the imposition of a fine, (2) the loss of appropriation rights, and (3) incarceration. The severity of each of these types of sanctions can range from very low to very high and tends to start out on the low end of the scale. Inshore fisheries studied by Schlager relied heavily on shunning and other social norms and less on formal sanctions. Thirty-six of the 43 irrigation systems studied by Tang used one of these three rules and also relied on vigorous monitoring of each other's behavior and shunning of rule breakers. The seven systems that did not self-consciously punish rule infractions were all rated as having poor performance. Fines were most typically used (in 21 cases) and incarceration the least (in only 2 cases). Fines tend to be graduated depending on the seriousness of the infractions and the number of prior infractions. The fines used for a first or second offence tend to be very low.

Once a position of guard is created, payoff rules must also change so as to be able to remunerate a guard. Several formulas are used. On government-owned irrigation systems, guards are normally paid a monthly wage that is not dependent on the performance of a system or farmers' satisfaction. In South India, Wade (1994) describes self-organized systems where the water distributor-guard is paid in kind as the harvest is reaped by going to each farmer to collect his share based on the amount of land owned by the farmer. Sengupta (1991: 104) describes another system where immediately after appointment, the guards "are taken to the temple for oath taking to remain impartial. With this vow, they break a coconut. They are paid in cash at the rate of Rs 10 per acre per month by the cultivators. The *neerpaichys* themselves collect the money." This system requires the monitor (the *neerpaichy*) to interact on a face-to-face basis with those he serves. If they are unsatisfied, they can withhold a portion of their payment to him. Thus, the farmers monitor the monitor directly.

Boundary and choice rules also affect how easy or difficult it is to monitor activities and impose sanctions on rule infractions. Closing a forest or an inshore fishery for a substantial amount of time, for example, has multiple impacts. It protects particular plants or fish during critical growing periods and allows the entire system time to regenerate without a harvesting disturbance. Further, during the closed season, rule infractions are highly obvious to anyone as any appropriator in the resource is almost certainly breaking the rules. Similarly, requiring appropriators to use a particular technology may reduce the pressure on the resource, help to solve conflicts among users of incompatible technologies, and also make it very easy to ascertain if rules are being followed. Many irrigation systems set up rotation systems so that only two persons need to monitor actions at any one time and thus keep monitoring costs lower than they would otherwise be. Changing payoff rules is the most direct way of coping with commons dilemmas. In many instances, dilemma games can be transformed into assurance games – a much easier situation to solve.

6.1.8   *Affecting outcomes through changes in information, scope, and aggregation rules*

These rules tend to be used in ways that complement changes in boundary, choice, payoff, and position rules. Individual systems vary radically in regard to the mandatory information that they require. Many smaller and informal systems rely entirely on a voluntary exchange of information and on mutual monitoring. Where resource units are very valuable and the size of the group is larger, more and more requirements are added regarding the information that must be kept by appropriators or their officials. Scope rules are used to limit harvesting activities in some regions that are being treated as refugia. By not allowing any appropriation from these locations, the regenerative capacity of a system can be enhanced. Aggregation rules are used extensively in collective-choice processes and less extensively in operational settings, but one aggregation rule that is found in diverse systems is a requirement that harvesting activities be done in teams. This increases the opportunity for mutual monitoring and reduces the need to hire special guards.

6.2   Policies as experiments

6.2.1   *The daunting search for better rules*

It is important to note that we have not yet found any *particular* rules to have a statistically positive relationship to performance. Further, the search for rules that improve the outcomes obtained in commons dilemmas is an incredibly complex task involving a potentially infinite combination of specific rules that could be adopted. To ascertain whether one has found an optimal set of rules to improve the outcomes achieved in a single situation, one would need to analyze how diverse rules affect each of the seven components of such a situation and as a result, the likely effect of a reformed structure on incentives, strategies, and outcomes. Since there are multiple rules that affect each of the seven components, conducting such an analysis would be an incredibly time and resource-consuming process. No set of policy analysts (or even all of the game theorists in the world today) has sufficient time or resources to analyze the number of feasible combinations of rule changes, let alone all of the variance in these situations due to biophysical differences.

The complexity we have found in regard to common-pool resources in the field is not in any way unique to the study of resource policy. Social scientists have for too long viewed the physics of static, simple systems as the model of science we should try to emulate. Those who want to emulate the science of static, simple systems are grossly out-of-date when it comes to understanding contemporary science and particular contemporary engineering. The engineers responsible for the design of airplanes and bridges – and now computers – have long coped with complex dynamic systems. The Boeing 777, for example, has 150,000 distinct subsystems that are composed, in some instances, of highly complex components.

Design engineers of complex systems long-ago gave up hope of ever doing complete analyzes of all combinations of subsystems under all combinations of external environmental conditions. Obviously, they invest heavily in trying out diverse design elements under a variety of conditions. Various ways of testing out designs including wind tunnels and now computer simulations increase the like-lihood that they can produce a viable combination of design elements that are robust under many conditions. They also invest in complex back-up systems that enable these designed systems to achieve a high degree of robustness – meaning the capacity to maintain some desired system characteristic under changing cir-cumstances. All such robust systems are, however, fragile to a variety of small perturbations (Carlson and Doyle 2002). Small, rare perturbation can cause a disastrous cascade of failure in any highly complex, designed system.

Instead of assuming that designing rules that approach optimality, or even improve performance, is a relatively simple analytical task that can be undertaken by distant, objective analysts, we need to understand the policy design process as involving an effort to tinker with a large number of component parts (see Jacob 1977). Those who tinker with any tools – including rules – are trying to find com-binations that work together more effectively than other combinations. Policy changes are experiments based on more or less informed expectations about potential outcomes and the distribution of these outcomes for participants across time and space (Campbell 1969, 1975). Whenever individuals agree to add a rule, change a rule, or adopt someone else's proposed rule set, they are conducting a policy experiment. Further, the complexity of the ever-changing biophysical world combined with the complexity of rule systems means that any proposed rule change faces a non-trivial probability of error.

6.2.2   Self-organized resource governance systems as complex adaptive systems

In contrast to forms of organization that are the result of central direction, most self-organized groups – including the types of locally organized fisheries, forests, grazing areas, and irrigation systems discussed in this chapter – are better viewed as complex adaptive systems. Complex adaptive systems are composed of a large number of active elements whose rich patterns of interactions produce emergent properties that are not easy to predict by analyzing the separate parts of a system. Holland (1995: 10) views complex adaptive systems as "systems composed of interacting agents described in terms of rules. These agents adapt by changing their rules as experience accumulates." Complex adaptive systems "exhibit coherence under change, via conditional action and anticipation, and they do so without central direction" (ibid.: 38–9). Holland points out that complex adaptive systems differ from physical systems that are not adaptive. It is the physical sciences that have been the model for many aspects of contemporary social science. Thus, the concepts needed to understand the adaptivity of systems are not yet well developed by social scientists.

6.3   Changing rules in an adaptive process

Given the logic of combinatorics, it is impossible – as discussed above – to conduct a complete analysis of the expected performance of all of the potential rule changes that could be made by the individuals served by a self-organized resource governance system trying to improve its performance. A similar impossibility also exists for many biological systems. Let us explore these similarities.

Self-organizing resource governance systems have two structures that are somewhat parallel in their function to the concepts of a genotype and a phenotype in biological systems. Phenotypic structures characterize an expressed organism – how bones, organs, and muscles develop, relate, and function in an organism in a particular environment. The components of an action situation characterize an expressed situation – how the number of participants, the information available, and their opportunities and costs create incentives, and how incentives lead to types of outcomes in a particular environment. The genotypic structure characterizes the set of instructions encoded in DNA to produce an organism with a particular phenotypic structure. A rule configuration is a set of instructions for how to produce the structure of relationships among individuals in an action situation that is also affected by the biophysical world and the kind of community or culture in which an action situation is located. These instructions are not, of course, embedded in a biological structure and do not evolve in the same way as genes.

In a biological system, mutations in a gene are not carried forward over multiple generations unless the change is relatively harmonious with the other genes that are present. When harmful, the phenotype carrying the gene has less chance of surviving into future generations. A change of a rule, however, may reduce effectiveness of a human governance system without participants recognizing the source of lowered performance. Further, specific rule changes may be forwarded and supported by those with more decision-making power in the hopes of increasing net benefits to them.

While many scholars tend to think of rules as being designed by some central planner, most rule systems involve some combination of design and evolution. The mechanisms involved in the evolution of rules and other "cultural phenomena" follow different mechanisms from the evolution of species (Boyd and Richerson 1985, Richerson *et al.* 2002, Campbell 1975, Nelson and Winter 1982). As an evolutionary process, of course, new alternatives need to be generated, new and old combinations of structural attributes need to be selected, and those combinations of attributes that are successful in a particular environment need to be retained.

Instead of blind variation, human agents try to use reason, persuasion, and power in their efforts to devise better rules for themselves and potentially others, but the process of choice always involves experimentation. Self-organized resource governance systems use many types of decision rules to make collective choices ranging from deferring to the judgment of one person or elders, to using majority voting, to relying on unanimity (E. Ostrom 1998, Walker *et al.* 2000). In all of our efforts to study the performance of common-pool resource systems in the field, however, we have not found a particular set of collective-choice rules developed by resource users as uniformly superior than others. We and other scholars have consistently found, however, that rules developed with considerable input (if not fully their own decision) of the resource users themselves, achieve a higher performance rate than systems where the rules entirely are fully determined by external authorities (Lam 1998, Tang 1992, Bardhan 2000, E. Ostrom *et al.* 1994).

The process of trying to develop or modify rules can be thought of as being very similar to the process that faces any adaptive system. As Holland (1975) points out, to understand how complex adaptive systems improve performance over time, one needs to identify several components of such a system. For an operational situation, these include:

- The environment, E, of the system undergoing adaptation.
- The adaptive plan, A, whereby the system's structure is modified to achieve improvement.
- A measure, M, of performance – thought of as the fitness of the structure for the environment involved – like the net benefits of a game.

The problem for complex adaptive systems is that no one has complete information about the adaptive plans, A, that are the most fit when they start this process. Somehow they have to test out the performance of different structures in the particular set of relevant environments.

One needs to think of a class, epsilon, of possible environments. Different environments in epsilon elicit different performance from any given adaptive plan (or in our case, set of rules). There will be a different performance measure of each alpha in each environment. Holland (ibid.) points out that there are many obstacles for any adaptive system to overcome.

- The set of adaptive plans is large – as we have seen with the number of rules discussed above.
- The structures in alpha are complicated – particularly because of epistasis. No simple way to apportion credit to an individual part of an adapted plan (*allele* for genes, individual rule for a rule configuration). A good rule in one environment may be disastrous in another environment or with another set of rules.
- The performance measures are always complicated functions with many interdependent parameters.

6.4   Adaptive plans, rules, and genes

The central thesis that I have been pursuing is that rules are sets of instructions for creating an action situation (or, when an action situation is represented using game theory, a game). As such, rules are broadly analogous to genes, which are sets of instructions for creating a phenotype. Rules are memes rather than genes, but it is helpful to think about some of the similarities between genes and memes (Dawkins 1976, Stake 2001). One can represent a rule configuration as a string variable listing those rules that are relevant to a particular situation. The deontic operators – obligated, permitted, forbidden – are the "alphabet" of a rule configuration (see von Wright 1951). Colleagues, who are flabbergasted at the complexity of rules as I am positing them here, need to take some comfort in a recognition that a rule configuration can be thought about as a string variable similar to a gene string (for an example, see Gardner and E. Ostrom 1991, and E. Ostrom *et al.* 1994). For rule strings, we do not have the kind of biophysical structure that is present in DNA, but it is possible to list the specific rules used to create a situation. All games, for example, come with rules defining what is a legal move, how players must be involved, and how winning and losing is determined.

When Darwin first began thinking about evolution, however, he did not have a particular mode of transmission in mind. When Mendel first began exploring the relationship between various species of plants and their attributes, he gave a new name to a previously unknown element of a string variable – that of *allele*. He thought of an *allele* as being associated on a one-to-one basis with some attribute of a plant. This is broadly similar to thinking about a particular boundary rule being associated with a particular kind of membership in an action situation. As biologists have discovered, only some genes have a direct one-to-one relationship with a trait in an organism. Rules also operate in a configural manner.

It took a long time to struggle through an understanding of how the information coded in a long and complex gene string could possibly create the series of proteins that combine to constitute a particular organism. I do not want to get into the history of biological thought here, as so much useful information has been written about it elsewhere (see Mayr 1982, for example). It took a long time to understand the mechanisms of transmittal. As Boyd and Richerson (1985) have so carefully documented, the mechanisms of transmission of cultural information are not similar to the mechanisms of genetic transfer. Their theory of cultural transmission is useful for thinking about rule transmission, but it is focused primarily at the individual level.

Thus, we face some major problems in doing further analysis of the evolution of rules. The first problem is defining our "organism", its "birth and death", and thus its life's history. When does an action situation come into being? In doing theory, we posit a game and analyze it. We may then analyze several rules as they affect the incentives inside the game. But, we don't know when individuals create a new action situation in a field setting. We can count individual living beings using a variety of census techniques. None of these are fully accurate but we do have a good sense of population dynamics for many organisms. We do not have any empirical measures of population dynamics for action situations – even for those related to common-pool resources where considerable fieldwork has been undertaken.

Nor do we yet have a real tight definition of "fitness" for an action situation level. Scholars associated with the Resilience Alliance are struggling with exactly this puzzle of what attributes of a combined rule system and ecological system affect its long-term performance. Biologists long ago defined fitness as the capacity of a single individual to reproduce and pass their genes on to a new generation. One can think of the fitness of a rule system as it affects an ecological system as the capacity to cope effectively (or withstand) major disturbances and stresses from inside and outside the system. Economists would tend to use the concept of efficiency at a system level to deal with the concept of fitness. Other scholars would be concerned with legitimacy, equity and distribution, accountability, and adaptability over time (see E. Ostrom *et al.* 1993).

Thus, we have a long way to go in developing a theory of the evolution of rules. This chapter, however, hopefully provides some of the theoretical and empirical grist needed for further work. Given the focus of the last several decades on static analysis of relatively simple games, moving to this point will hopefully help us take the next steps. We now have a method for arraying rule configurations. Whether the rule configurations create situations that enable the participants to appropriate from their resource in a sustainable and efficient manner cannot be ascertained from simply learning about the rules alone. We are also beginning to develop models of the processes of rule proposal and rule change (Janssen and E. Ostrom, forthcoming). This is an important step, but more needs to be done.

Whether a set of rules enhances performance depends on the structure of the biophysical system itself. Each of these rule configurations creates a very interesting action situation; and if enough information were known about the structure of the environment, it would be possible to model each of these appropriation situations as a game (see Gardner and E. Ostrom 1991, Weissing and E. Ostrom 1991b, 1993). Representing rules as a string variable, however, we can begin to see how experimenting with rules may be similar to changes in adaptive plans affecting other types of complex adaptive systems.

Most systems are likely to start with one or two very simple rules. An obvious first candidate is to close the boundary to outsiders so that the likelihood of contingent cooperation and conformance to agreements will be enhanced. By only changing a few rules at the beginning, everyone can come to understand those rules while they are evaluating how they work. A second obvious candidate is to use the shared model of the environment built up through years of interaction in an environment to refine where appropriation should be undertaken and when. Space and time are obvious candidates for allocating access to resources in a manner that is relatively low cost to sustain. If the community is small enough and shares common norms at a high enough level, creating formal sanctions, guards, records, and other rules may not be necessary. Thus, one can imagine a process where a rule configuration with few entries slowly converts over time to a rule configuration with many entries specifying who must (or must not) do what at what juncture (with what likely sanction).

Changes in specific rules may come about through accident (forgetting or innovating on the spot) or through specific collective-choice processes where considerable time and effort is devoted to considering why performance needs to be enhanced and which rules might be changed. Since many appropriators will have experience with more than one resource, rules tried out in regard to one resource may be tried in regard to others if they were successful. Migration of individuals into a community brings individuals with repertoires of different rules used in other locations. Commerce with other groups lets appropriators see and learn about other groups who may be doing better (or worse) than they in regulating a sustainable and efficient resource system. Thus, a self-organized resource governance system with a higher level of in-migration or greater communication with other localities is more likely to adapt and change rules over time than one where few new ideas concerning how to use rules as tools are brought into the system. Trial-and-error processes may give relatively rapid feedback about rules that obviously do not work in a particular environment, but this is not always the case when the effect of human action on the environment has a long time-delay. If all self-organized resource governance systems are totally independent and there is no communication among them, then each has to learn through its own trial-and-error process. Many will find that rules that they have tried do not work. Some will fail entirely.

The rate of change will differ among self-organized resource governance systems. As with all learning theories, the rate of change is an important variable affecting performance over time. If change occurs too rapidly, little is learned from each experiment before another experiment is launched. Respect for tradition and even religious mystification has been used to increase the retention of rules considered by at least some participants as being better working. If the heavy hand of tradition is, however, too heavy and squelches innovation, a system that may have been well adapted to a past environment may find itself faltering as external changes occur without internal changes also occurring.

The institutions used for conflict resolution will also affect the rate and direction of change. If participants are able to enter further action situations before a judge, traditional leader, or a "boss", the incentives of those initiating a "case" and of the individual revolving conflicts will affect the decision made. It is likely that the individuals who initiate concern about rules are those somewhat disadvantaged by the current rules (or interpretation of them) and want to see a change to a rule more favorable to them and potentially to others. The "judge" may be motivated toward keeping with precedents (slowing down change), to avoiding future conflicts (potentially selecting better rules over time), or to making money by accepting bribes (changing rules to favor the rich) (see McGinnis 2002).

6.5   Conclusion

Once one accepts the view that one cannot create the perfect set of rules and that all efforts at reforms must be viewed as experiments, one recognizes that policy analysis can never find "the" answer. We can certainly expand knowledge about the rich diversity of rules used in practice. Appropriators in field settings across time and space have already devised an incredible richness in the rules they use. We need to learn more about this heritage so as to be better facilitators of better institutional designs – in contrast to presuming we are the experts who can devise the optimal design to solve a complex problem.

Acknowledgments

An earlier version was presented at the Workshop on "The Evolution of Designed Institutions", held at the Max-Planck-Institute of Economics, Jena, Germany, February 19–20, 2004. Support from the National Science Foundation (SES-0083511), the Ford Foundation, and the MacArthur Foundation is gratefully acknowledged. Comments by and discussions with Marco Janssen, Michael Price, Derek Reiners, and Jeffrey Stake were stimulating and very helpful. The comments of an anonymous reviewer were useful as was the comments of Christian Schubert and Georg von Wangenheim and the participants at the Jena conference. As always, I deeply appreciate the editing skills of Patty Lezotte.

Notes

1 Unfortunately, we do not have any reliable source of information regarding the relative numbers of successes versus failures. No census of user groups exists for any sector. The International Forestry Resources and Institutions (IFRI) research program has been established to track forest user groups over time to understand dynamic change in order to understand why some groups succeed and others fail over time.
2 When Franz Weissing and I modeled rule breaking, monitoring, and sanctioning a decade ago using formal game-theory tools, we had to write a special methodological note that we were allowing players to break the rules of the resource use game we were analyzing (see Weissing and E. Ostrom 1991a, 1993). We still assumed that players could not take any actions other than those we represented and thus could not break a set of logical rules we imposed.
3 This section draws on E. Ostrom (1999).

120 *Elinor Ostrom*

References

Acheson, J.M., Wilson, J.A. and Steneck, R.S. (1998) 'Managing Chaotic Fisheries,' in F. Berkes and C. Folke (eds) *Linking Social and Ecological Systems. Management Practices and Social Mechanisms for Building Resilience*, Cambridge, MA: Cambridge University Press, pp. 390–413.

Agrawal, A. (1994) 'Rules, Rule Making, and Rule Breaking: Examining the Fit between Rule Systems and Resource Use', in E. Ostrom, R. Gardner and J. Walker (eds) *Rules, Games, and Common-Pool Resources*, Ann Arbor: University of Michigan Press, pp. 267–82.

Agrawal, A. and Yadama, G.N. (1997) 'How Do Local Institutions Mediate Market and Population Pressures on Resources? Forest *Panchayats* in Kumaon, India', *Development and Change*, 28: 435–65.

Anderson, L.G. (1986) *The Economics of Fisheries Management*, rev. edn, Baltimore, MD: Johns Hopkins University Press.

Anderson, L.G. (1992) 'Consideration of the Potential Use of Individual Transferable Quotas in U.S. Fisheries', *The National ITQ Study Report*, 1: 1–71.

Bardhan, P.K. (2000) 'Irrigation and Cooperation: An Empirical Analysis of 48 Irrigation Communities in South India', *Economic Development and Cultural Change*, 48: 847–65.

Berkes, F. (ed.) (1989) *Common Property Resources: Ecology and Community-Based Sustainable Development*, London: Belhaven Press.

Blomquist, W. (1992) *Dividing the Waters: Governing Groundwater in Southern California*, Oakland, CA: ICS Press.

Boyd, R. and Richerson, P.J. (1985) *Culture and the Evolutionary Process*, Chicago: University of Chicago Press.

Bromley, D.W., Feeny, D., McKean, M., Peters, P., Gilles, J., Oakerson, R., Runge, C.F. and Thomson, J. (eds) (1992) *Making the Commons Work: Theory, Practice, and Policy*, San Francisco, CA: ICS Press.

Campbell, D.T. (1969) 'Reforms as Experiments', *American Psychologist* 24: 409–29.

Campbell, D.T. (1975) 'On the Conflicts between Biological and Social Evolution and between Psychology and Moral Tradition', *American Psychologist*, 30: 1103–26.

Carlson, J.M. and Doyle, J. (2002) 'Complexity and Robustness', *Proceedings of the National Academy of Sciences*, 9: 2499–545.

Copes, P. (1986) 'A Critical Review of the Individual Quota as a Device in Fisheries Management', *Land Economics*, 62: 278–91.

Crawford, S.E.S. and Ostrom, E. (1995) 'A Grammar of Institutions', *American Political Science Review* 89: 582–600; reprinted in E. Ostrom (ed.) (2005) *Understanding Institutional Diversity*, Princeton, NJ: Princeton University Press.

Dawkins, R. (1976) *The Selfish Gene*, Oxford: Oxford University Press.

Dietz, T., Ostrom, E. and Stern, P. (2003) 'The Struggle to Govern the Commons', *Science*, 302: 1907–12.

Fortmann, L. and Bruce, J.W. (1988) *Whose Trees? Proprietary Dimensions of Forestry*, Boulder, CO: Westview Press.

Gardner, R. (2003) *Games for Business and Economics*, 2nd edn, New York: Wiley.

Gardner, R. and Ostrom, E. (1991) 'Rules and Games', *Public Choice*, 70: 121–49.

Gintis, H. (2000) *Game Theory Evolving: A Problem-Centered Introduction to Modeling Strategic Interaction*, Princeton, NJ: Princeton University Press.

Hess, C. (1999) *A Comprehensive Bibliography of Common Pool Resources*, (CD-ROM) Bloomington: Indiana University, Workshop in Political Theory and Policy Analysis.

Holland, J.H. (1975) *Adaptation in Natural and Artificial Systems*, Ann Arbor: University of Michigan Press.

Holland, J.H. (1995) *Hidden Order: How Adaptation Builds Complexity*, Reading, MA: Addison-Wesley.

Jacob, F. (1977) 'Evolution and Tinkering', *Science* 196: 1161–6.

Janssen, M. and Ostrom, E. (forthcoming) 'Adoption of a New Regulation for the Governance of Common-Pool Resources by a Heterogeneous Population', in J.M. Baland, P. Bardhan and S. Bowles (eds) *Inequality, Collective Action and Environmental Sustainability*, Princeton, NJ: Princeton University Press.

Lam, W.F. (1998) *Governing Irrigation Systems in Nepal: Institutions, Infrastructure, and Collective Action*, Oakland, CA: ICS Press.

Maass, A. and Anderson, R.L. (1986) *. . . and the Desert Shall Rejoice: Conflict, Growth, and Justice in Arid Environments*, Malabar, FL: RE Krieger.

McCay, B.J. and Acheson, J.M. (1987) *The Question of the Commons: The Culture and Ecology of Communal Resources*, Tucson: University of Arizona Press.

McGinnis, M. (2002) 'Choice and Selection in the Evolution of Law', *Working paper*, Bloomington: Indiana University, Workshop in Political Theory and Policy Analysis.

Mayr, E. (1982) *The Growth of Biological Thought: Diversity, Evolution, and Inheritance*, Cambridge, MA: Harvard University Press.

Nelson, R.R. and Winter, S.G. (1982) *An Evolutionary Theory of Economic Change*, Cambridge, MA: Harvard University Press.

Netting, R.M. (1974) 'The System Nobody Knows: Village Irrigation in the Swiss Alps', in T.E. Downing and M. Gibson (eds) *Irrigation's Impact on Society*, Tucson: University of Arizona Press, pp. 67–75.

Netting, R.M. (1993) *Smallholders, Householders: Farm Families and the Ecology of Intensive, Sustainable Agriculture*, Stanford, CA: Stanford University Press.

Ostrom, E. (1990) *Governing the Commons: The Evolution of Institutions for Collective Action*, New York: Cambridge University Press.

Ostrom, E. (1998) 'Institutional Analysis, Design Principles, and Threats to Sustainable Community Governance and Management of Commons', in E. Berge and N.C. Stenseth (eds) *Law and the Governance of Renewable Resources: Studies from Northern Europe and Africa*, Oakland, CA: ICS Press, pp. 27–53.

Ostrom, E. (1999) 'Coping with Tragedies of the Commons', *Annual Review of Political Science*, 2: 493–535.

Ostrom, E. (2005) *Understanding Institutional Diversity*. Princeton, NJ: Princeton University Press.

Ostrom, E., Agrawal, A., Blomquist, W., Schlager, E. and Tang, S.Y. (1989) *CPR Coding Manual*, Bloomington: Indiana University, Workshop in Political Theory and Policy Analysis.

Ostrom, E., Gardner, R. and Walker, J. (eds) (1994) *Rules, Games, and Common-Pool Resources*, Ann Arbor: University of Michigan Press.

Ostrom, E., Schroeder, L. and Wynne, S. (1993) *Institutional Incentives and Sustainable Development: Infrastructure Policies in Perspective*, Boulder, CO: Westview Press.

Ostrom, V., Feeny, D. and Picht, H. (eds) (1993) *Rethinking Institutional Analysis and Development: Issues, Alternatives, and Choices*, 2nd edn, Oakland, CA: ICS Press.

Palanisami, K. 'Managing Tank Irrigation Systems: Basic Issues and Implications for Improvement', paper presented at workshop on Tank Irrigation: Problems and Prospects. Bogor, Indonesia: CIFOR, 1982.

Repetto, R. (1986) *Skimming the Water: Rent-Seeking and the Performance of Public Irrigation Systems*, Research report No. 4, Washington, D.C.: World Resources Institute.

Richerson, P., Boyd, R. and Paciotti, B. (2002) 'An Evolutionary Theory of Commons Management', in E. Ostrom, T. Dietz, N. Dolšak, P.C. Stern, S. Stonich and E. Weber (eds) *The Drama of the Commons*, Washington, D.C.: National Research Council, National Academy Press, pp. 327–59.

Schlager, E. (1990) *Model Specification and Policy Analysis: The Governance of Coastal Fisheries*, Ph.D. Diss., Indiana University.

Schlager, E. (1994) 'Fishers' Institutional Responses to Common-Pool Resource Dilemmas', in E. Ostrom, R. Gardner and J. Walker (eds) *Rules, Games, and Common-Pool Resources*, Ann Arbor: University of Michigan Press, pp. 247–66.

Schlager, E., Blomquist, W. and Tang, S.Y. (1994) 'Mobile Flows, Storage, and Self-Organized Institutions for Governing Common-Pool Resources', *Land Economics*, 70: 294–317.

Sengupta, N. (1991) *Managing Common Property: Irrigation in India and the Philippines*, New Delhi: Sage.

Singleton, S. (1998) *Constructing Cooperation: The Evolution of Institutions of Co-management in Pacific Northwest Salmon Fisheries*, Ann Arbor: University of Michigan Press.

Singleton, S. and Taylor, M. (1992) 'Common Property Economics: A General Theory and Land Use Applications', *Journal of Theoretical Politics*, 4: 309–24.

Spooner, B. (1974) 'Irrigation and Society: The Iranian Plateau', in T.E. Downing and M. Gibson (eds) *Irrigation's Impact on Society*, Tucson: University of Arizona Press, pp. 43–57.

Stake, J.E. (2001) 'Are We Buyers or Hosts? A Memetic Approach to the First Amendment', *Alabama Law Review*, 52: 1213–67.

Stake, J.E. (2004) 'The Property Instinct', *Working paper*, Bloomington: Indiana University, School of Law.

Tang, S.Y. (1992) *Institutions and Collective Action: Self-Governance in Irrigation*, Oakland, CA: ICS Press.

Tang, S.Y. (1994) 'Institutions and Performance in Irrigation Systems' in E. Ostrom, R. Gardner and J. Walker (eds) *Rules, Games, and Common-Pool Resources*, Ann Arbor: University of Michigan Press, pp. 225–45.

Taylor, M. (1982) *Community, Anarchy, and Liberty*, New York: Cambridge University Press.

von Wright, G.H. (1951) 'Deontic Logic', *Mind*, 60: 1–15.

Wade, R. (1994) *Village Republics: Economic Conditions for Collective Action in South India*, San Francisco, CA: ICS Press.

Walker, J., Gardner, R., Herr, A. and Ostrom, E. (2000) 'Collective Choice in the Commons: Experimental Results on Proposed Allocation Rules and Votes', *Economic Journal*, 110: 212–34.

Weissing, F.J. and Ostrom, E. (1991a) 'Irrigation Institutions and the Games Irrigators Play: Rule Enforcement without Guards', in R. Selten (ed.) *Game Equilibrium Models II: Methods, Morals, and Markets*, Berlin: Springer, pp. 188–262.

Weissing, F.J. and Ostrom, E. (1991b) 'Crime and Punishment', *Journal of Theoretical Politics*, 3: 343–9.

Weissing, F.J. and Ostrom, E. (1993) 'Irrigation Institutions and the Games Irrigators Play: Rule Enforcement on Government- and Farmer-Managed Systems', in F.W. Scharpf (ed.) *Games in Hierarchies and Networks: Analytical and Empirical Approaches to the Study of Governance Institutions*, Frankfurt/Main: Campus Verlag; Boulder, CO: Westview Press, pp. 387–428.

Wilson, J.A., Acheson, J.M., Kleban, M. and Metcalfe, M. (1994) 'Chaos, Complexity, and Community Management of Fisheries', *Marine Policy*, 18: 291–305.

7 Gradualism and public entrepreneurship in the evolution of formal institutions

Jan Schnellenbach

7.1 Introduction[1]

The change of formal institutions appears to be conceptually entirely different from the change of informal institutions. The latter are usually the result of processes of self-organization that can be modeled as strategic interactions in games or as frequency-dependent processes in which the payoff from adhering to a certain informal rule rises with the share of individuals who already follow this rule. A simple and familiar example is the rule of driving on the right track of the road. If one expects that the share of individuals who are right-hand drivers is close to unity, then it would obviously be individually irrational to become a left-hand driver and thereby raise the risk of an accident. A formal rule would not be necessary once an equilibrium has been reached in which the vast majority of individuals have settled to have identical expectations about the behavior of their peers (Dopfer 1991). The same frequency-dependent process works for rules clarifying how to produce a computer keyboard (David 1985). Similarly, if doing business in a certain country presupposes bribery, then strict adherence to an informal rule of non-corruption would be irrational from the perspective of an individual firm attempting to enter the market.

The reason for having an informal institution is essentially to have a reliable mode of co-operation, where it is the peculiarity of informal institutions that those who are to co-operate determine this mode of co-operation among themselves, without needing a central authority to enforce the informal rule. Which kind of rule is established may depend on a variety of influences – from simple chance in a pure frequency-dependent process to the differential power and resources available to the co-operating partners, as in the bribery example. There is no obvious reason to expect that the most efficient conceivable rule does indeed surface as the actual informal institution, although one might follow Hayek (1973) and his argument that the long-run evolution of informal institutions is accompanied by an accumulation of knowledge that is stored within these institutions.

In contrast to the rise of informal institutions, the implementation (and the change) of formal institutions involves a conscious decision. Contrary to the usually spontaneous origination of informal institutions, the establishment of a formal institution presupposes an explicit choice to phrase a rule that restricts the choices of individuals and threatens a foreseeable punishment for individuals who transgress it. The latter is sometimes seen as the constitutive difference between formal and informal institutions (Knight 1992), but the former is at least equally important: informal rules arise from decentralized individual decisions to follow them, whereas formal rules follow from a deliberate choice of an individual or a group of individuals that is endowed with the competencies to set those rules (e.g., North 1981). A formal institution is, in this sense, a technology that is deliberately chosen to solve problems of co-ordination and of control – to lower transaction costs, to provide a framework for the control of elected representatives and so on.

Moreover, under uncertainty, any implementation of a new formal institution is an experiment that produces new knowledge about the efficiency of the employed rule. Therefore, institutional change has an entirely different meaning for formal than for informal institutions: while the latter can hardly be manipulated deliberately, the change of formal institutions involves a deliberate attempt to correct rules that are perceived to perform sub-optimally. This technical property of formal institutions thus appears to be a lever for progress as a parallel process involving accumulation of knowledge and an according change of the institutional structure. The problem of how the change of formal institutions takes place is then closely related to the problem of how (or if) the efficiency of governance can be expected to increase over time.

In this chapter, it is argued that formal institutional change can be usefully understood as *syncretic* change, i.e., that institutional rules are not phrased from scratch, but that their development is usually path-dependent and involves the integration of small institutional innovations into given institutional structures that are composed of status quo formal and informal *political* institutions. If an individual feels compelled to change the institutional structure that constrains him or other individuals, then he faces constraints that do not allow him to dispense with the old institutions completely. Rather, the new institutional structure is likely to be a blend of the old institutional structure with some new rules.

The argument will proceed as follows: In Section 7.2, three ideal types of formal institutions are distinguished along functional criteria and it is argued that among the different triggers of change that are to be found in the literature, uncertainty and limited knowledge are the most interesting for the explanation of a change of consciously designed institutions. Section 7.3 argues that a distinction between short-run and long-run perspectives on formal institutional change is useful, where the short-run perspective is concerned with the evolution of formal institutions within the bounds of stable informal political institutions. Within the short-run perspective, it is argued that gradual changes of formal institutions are more likely to be adopted than more sweeping institutional reforms and that relative coherence of informal institutions facilitates formal institutional change. Section 7.4 discusses the importance of individual learning about the relative efficacy of formal institutions as well as the role so-called public entrepreneurs might play in such learning processes. Finally, Section 7.5 draws some conclusions.

7.2 Prerequisites for the change of formal institutions

7.2.1 Different types of formal institutions

As an analytical starting point, it is useful to assume a Downsian world in which the members of government or bureaucracy are perfectly controlled by the median voter (Downs 1957) on issues of institutional change. This would, for instance, be the case if a referendum on any decision by representatives to alter the institutional structure can be initiated at very low cost or is obligatory. Within the institutional structure, however, the representatives have a leeway to pursue their own interests even if they conflict with the interests of the median voter, e.g., because he is not a retrospective voter and the cost of having a referendum on any issue that is dealt with *within* the institutional structure is prohibitively high. An example is a setting in which there is a fiscal constitution, composed of rules for budgetary decision-making which cannot be modified if the median voter vetoes this change. But within the limits of these rules, which will usually be rather general (Schnellenbach 2004b), the representatives and bureaucrats have some scope to make self-interested decisions and accrue rents from government activities.

Self-interested decisions by the representatives do not necessarily conflict with the interests of the median voter. Suppose that decisions on distribution can be made entirely independent of decisions on allocation. Suppose further that government members can retain a fraction of tax revenue as rent, and that tax revenue is strictly rising with the sum of incomes generated in the economy. In this case, both the representatives and the median voter have an interest to implement those *efficiency-enhancing institutions* that are working most efficiently, because both have an interest to maximize the sum of incomes (see also Findlay and Wilson 1987).

The second type of formal institutions are *agency-related institutions* whose purpose is to set the terms for the relationship between the median voter on the one side and elected representatives and bureaucrats on the other side. Both sides are parts of a classical principal-agent-relationship, and agency-related institutions are rules that define the set of actions that can be legitimately taken by the agent. Within the setting introduced above, these rules can be thought of as constitutional rules intended to reduce the share of incomes that can be accrued as rents by the agents to a tolerable level (Brennan and Buchanan 1980 and rather critically Frey 1997). For this kind of institutions, the possibility of conflicts of interest is obvious. While the voter prefers to reduce the rent exactly to his agents' participation constraints, the agents clearly prefer rules with enough leeway to secure higher rents.

From its beginning with Buchanan and Tullock (1962), constitutional economics has been interested in the distributive consequences of formal rules. According to this approach, it is an important objective of formal institutions to narrow the scope of distributive policies in order to avoid fiscal exploitation of minorities by majorities. But *distributive institutions* as the third type of formal rules are not necessarily characterized by a negative content; they may just as well define which distributive policies are to be implemented. It is obvious that in the absence of an additional assumption such as a veil of ignorance, no consensus about distributive institutions can be expected. Whatever the institutions rationally preferred by the median voter are, he is always confronted with at least one opposing group that prefers a different set of institutions that would yield a distribution of resources that is more preferable to this group. Since both involve an element of distribution, it could be argued that agency-related institutions are a special case of distributive institutions. However, the former involve a vertical distributive conflict between principal and agent, whereas the latter involve a horizontal conflict between actual and potential principals (the winning coalition including the median voter and a more or less heterogeneous minority group).

The three types of institutions characterized here are ideal types. More often than not, a formal rule in reality serves not only one, but two or even all of the purposes described above. Nevertheless, the distinction of different types helps to highlight the origins of institutional change, which are rather different in each of the three cases.

7.2.2   *Triggers for the change of formal institutions:*
a general framework

In a world in which the ancient, although in orthodox theory still popular assumption of perfect knowledge holds, endogenous change of efficiency-enhancing institutions is virtually inconceivable. Both the principal and the agent have a clear incentive to maximize the sum of incomes by installing the most efficient set of rules, and given their overwhelming cognitive capabilities, they have no problems to find such a rule that is optimal as long as all other conditions remain stable. Under these assumptions, any change of efficiency-enhancing institutions has to be interpreted as an optimal reaction towards some exogenous change of the restrictions under which the institutions are supposed to work. The situation is not too different for the other two types of institutions. They necessarily involve conflicts of interest between individuals or groups; in the case of agency-related institutions between a majority and their agents in the public sector and in the second case between competing groups of voters. But as long as the argument stays within the boundaries of a median voter model with perfect knowledge, there is no endogenous source of instability. Once a median voter is determined and once he has installed an institutional framework that suits his interests, this constitutes an institutional equilibrium that can only be disturbed by exogenous changes.

In such an equilibrium, a thoroughly constructivist perspective on institutional economics is realized: the median voter implements a set of institutions that is optimal from his point of view. This includes a combination of distributive and efficiency-enhancing institutions that maximizes his income, accounting for the implicit trade-off between efficiency and (re-)distribution, and agency-related rules that are familiar from the theory of optimal contracts (Laffont 2001). The institutional structure that arises through this rational choice is deficient from a normative point of view if it is measured by the customary benchmarks. It is not pareto optimal, since the median voter will usually sacrifice some efficiency in favor of distributive measures that increase his income, and it is not a "fair" set of rules since it is conceived in the light of particular interests rather than behind a veil of ignorance. But more importantly, such an approach is not satisfactory because it produces positive statements that are empirically doubtful. Exogenous disturbances are certainly an important influence to explain institutional change, as for instance technological changes may affect relative prices and thereby alter the relative bargaining power of different groups (North 1990), which here would result in a median voter with a different income and therefore different institutional preferences. But endogenous change of formal institutions appears to be also a historical fact, and consequently a theory of institutional change ought to offer an explanation for it. Another empirical fact is that institutional changes do not necessarily follow exogenous disturbances, even if such changes would appear to be advantageous – there is no automatism of institutional change as a rational reaction to exogenous changes, which must seem odd from the perspective of a perfect knowledge approach.

It appears to be an obvious remedy to leave the Downsian framework behind and recognize the complexities of actual political processes. This in itself does, however, not solve the problem. As an example, suppose that the assumptions sketched above are now changed so that the median voter's complete control over the institutional structure does no longer persist. The median voter is then not able to implement the set of agency-related institutions that are optimal from his point of view. Rather, the institutional structure will depend on the relative bargaining power between those who are governing and those who are governed. Differences in relative bargaining power do, to put it drastically, determine whether the resulting agency-related institutions lead to an autocracy with high levels of rent expropriation or, on the other end of the continuum of orders, to a referendum democracy with tightly controlled political agents (see already North 1981). But as long as all individuals act rationally and with complete knowledge, the institutional structure will remain stable if the bargaining power remains stable.

Similarly, one could drop the assumption that individuals in the public sector can extract a fixed share of rents of total incomes. Then, if a particular set of efficiency-enhancing institutions allows the governing agents to extract a higher share of rents than the most efficient set of rules, a government with sufficient bargaining power is tempted to install an inefficient set of institutions (e.g., an inefficient system of property rights). In all cases, relative bargaining power of principal and agent or of different groups of voters determines the institutional structure, but changes of bargaining power can only result from exogenous changes (see also Hira and Hira 2000), for instance from technological progress or from declining costs of the "exit" option for citizens. The latter has been emphasized by Landes (1998), especially in his chapters on European economic history. For Germany, Volckart (2001: ch. 5) has elaborated on the impact of the "exit" option on institutional change in economic history.

Given these arguments, another noteworthy possibility to endogenize institutional change is to assume a circular causation (or cumulative causation, Myrdal 1957) where the magnitude and direction of technological progress depends on formal institutions, and the frequency and direction of revisions of formal institutions in turn depends on technological progress. Demsetz (1967, 2002) has pointed at the relevance of technological change and specialization on the evolution of property rights, but has not explicitly subscribed to the notion of a circular causation. Such an approach, however, is attributed to Thorstein Veblen by Brette (2003). From such a theoretical perspective, (economic) history appears as a process that unfolds without showing any tendency towards equilibrium and that is character-ized by an instability of institutional structures and changing technological para-digms. But as, for instance, the Marxist concept of historical materialism shows, it is perfectly possible to construct a theory that leads to the prediction that tech-nological dynamics eventually lead to a steady state of institutional development, in this case in communism (Hodgson 1993: ch. 5). In other words, theories of institutional change involving circular causation are generally interested in processes that take place out of equilibrium, but they nevertheless may be thought as being directed towards an equilibrium. However, from an evolutionary per-spective, the idea of a predictable long-run equilibrium is most probably unac-ceptable. Its emphasis is on change and on the generation of novelty (Witt 2003, Hodgson 1995), which necessarily introduces uncertainty about the long-run evolution of institutions and technologies. Even if there is a long-run equilibrium towards which the dynamics converge, a theorist has to admit being agnostic regarding its detailed properties, since they depend on yet unknown novelty which is to be generated on the path towards equilibrium – one is restricted to pattern predictions (Hayek 1972).

This hints towards a second, and probably more important, source of endoge-nous institutional change, namely incomplete knowledge, which is not to be con-fused with incomplete, asymmetrically distributed information. The latter is a problem that can be met with an appropriate design of optimal contracts, whereas the former is a fundamental property underlying any human decision-making that is implied by the fact that there are always two sets of actions (or of institutions) to choose from: a set of known actions (institutions) whose consequences are cer-tain or risky at worst, and a set of yet unknown actions (institutions) waiting to be discovered whose consequences are completely unknown. If this empirical fact is introduced as an additional assumption into the simple model sketched above, there is room for endogenous change from learning about new, previously untested institutional rules and new combinations of already known rules into novel insti-tutional structures. This, however, introduces indeterminacy into the model (Witt 1994) – as long as there are new institutional arrangements to be discovered, the future is open (Popper 1957).

7.3   Gradualism in the change of designed institutions

The closing arguments of the preceding section suggested that a theory explain-ing the change of formal institutions ought to focus not only on institutional change resulting from changed bargaining powers, but also on learning processes. In this section, some remarks are made regarding the restrictions on processes of institutional change that follow from the fact that individuals first of all have to change their mind regarding the relative usefulness of alternative institutional structures.

7.3.1 The syncretic change of formal institutions

The term "syncretic" is borrowed from theology, where it denotes the merging of elements from one religious belief system into a different belief system. It usually carries a negative connotation, because it threatens the coherence of belief systems and is often seen as the starting point of a dissolution of distinct faiths into fuzzy ambiguity. Such negative connotations are explicitly not intended when the term is used in an economic context. As a general definition, it can be stated that "Syncretism is the reconciliation of two or more cultural systems or elements, with the modification of both" (H.G. Burger cited from Röpke 1970: 88). The concept of syncretic institutional change has been introduced into economics by Röpke (1970) within the context of development economics. It was used to explain processes of cultural change beyond modernization that is forced, for instance, by a colonial power, i.e., cultural change that is based on the voluntary acceptance of new cultural rules by individuals living in primitive economies.

It is important to note that the amalgamation of systems of rules is an entirely subjective process in this framework. In the development context, it does not imply that a developed society learns from a primitive society in the same way as the primitive society learns from the developed society so that both actual institutional structures eventually change. Instead, the concept of syncretic change is meant to imply that a change of designed institutions presupposes the reconciliation of a status quo institutional structure with perceived alternative rules *within the minds* of individuals that initiate institutional change. And this reconciliation does, in turn, usually also require the modification of the perceived alternative if a coherent new institutional structure – including the relevant informal institutions – is to be achieved.

Syncretic institutional change thus implies that a given institutional structure is not substituted as a whole, but rather modified by substituting elements (one rule or a few particular rules) of it with new rules. Speaking of new rules does imply here that they have not so far been a part of the institutional structure. This definition is similar to the definition of policy innovations that is commonplace in the political science literature: a policy innovation takes place when a polity adopts a policy that is new *to that polity* (originally Walker 1969). Institutional novelty is therefore meant to be purely subjective; it does not necessarily denote the production of objectively new institutional rules that have not been known before to any individual, although a production of objectively new rules would obviously also generate institutional novelty. Closely related to the Schumpeterian concept of innovations, an institutional innovation can then be defined as the new combination of institutional rules which themselves *may* have already been known. But contrary to the Schumpeterian concept, there is no distinction between innovation and invention.

It is an important property of syncretic institutional change that it is to be understood as a historical process in which the past matters. Any given institutional structure in modern economies is the result of a very long running process of institutional changes. It therefore certainly reflects political traditions of a polity and it does, on the other hand, also stabilize traditions by formally expressing how the political process is expected to work, how incomes are expected to be distributed within the economy and so on. But it does not *only* reflect tradition. Rather, it is also the result of long-lasting distributive struggles of the past that are continued in the present. Therefore, it is inadequate to hold a Panglossian perspective on formal institutions. What is, is not necessarily efficient or fair, since there is no veil of ignorance involved in the actual evolution of formal institutions. At any given point in time, individuals are acting within some institutional status quo and know very well of their individual role in the economy under this status quo. If they decide to initiate processes of formal institutional change, they do so because they expect it to yield benefits for themselves. Nevertheless, as we shall see later, the individuals who are acting within a given institutional structure may consider this structure to be both efficient and fair, even if their notion of fairness can, if at all, only coincidentally match that which would be reached behind a constitutional veil of ignorance.

Given these considerations, syncretic institutional change is superficially similar to the gradualism proposed by Douglass C. North, who also claims that institutional change works slowly and incremental. He does, at one point, assert that the change of formal institutions is mainly the result of a change of informal institutions: "The move, lengthy and uneven, from unwritten traditions and customs to written law has been unidirectional as we have moved from less to more complex societies (...)" (North 1990: 46). However, there are also some instances where the causation is reversed and formal institutions are thought of as an influence on informal institutions. For example, informal rules are considered as extensions of formal rules to cases where the latter do not offer clear guidance. Similar to the circular causation that characterizes the relationship between technology and formal institutions, North reckons a circular feedback mechanism between formal and informal institutions. This institutional circular causation can be understood as a possibly perpetual sequence of gradual changes in formal institutions, which in turn lead to an adjustment of informal institutions that once again yields an accommodation formal rules, and so on.

Another property of institutional change according to North is the fact that informal institutions are assumed to change at a slower pace than formal institutions. This is intuitively plausible given the possibility to change formal institutions in a conscious act, while altering informal institutions requires a change of expectations of a multitude of individuals. In the theory of North, this may lead to a situation where formal and informal institutions are incoherent, which produces additional tensions leading either to further institutional change or to higher uncertainty, because individuals have to decide which set of rules they want to follow. It may, however, be a fruitful effort to distinguish the evolution of formal institutions within constraints from the evolution of formal institutions with parallel change of informal restrictions. In other words, the change of formal institutions within the bounds of informal institutions – a typical short-run perspective – is to be distinguished from the simultaneous change of both – a typical long-run perspective.

As long as informal institutions are stable, they constrain the scope of change for formal institutions. In our context, the most relevant informal institutions are informal *political* institutions. These include two elements: On the one hand, collectively shared hypotheses about how the economy works and about the effects that alternative sets of formal rules have on it (Schnellenbach 2005). On the other hand, they include also a normative element – political preferences, notions of fairness and so on. Clearly, this concept is another deviation from the median voter concept. Instead of having a median voter who rationally calculates his preferred quantities of public goods under a neo-classical preference ordering, the concept of informal political institutions addresses the question how such preferences form in the first place. A rationally ignorant voter can be expected to form hypotheses on efficiency-effects of alternative proposed policies through low-cost communication with his peers – technically, the spreading of opinions on policy is similar to the spreading of rumours. If it is to be approximated whether a proposed policy increases individual welfare or not, this is done by recurring to a collective belief that is widely shared within the population. Political preferences are built on collectively shared, fallible political hypotheses – and both elements together constitute informal political institutions.

In a democracy with a sufficient degree of electoral competition, the cost for an incumbent to propose a reform of formal institutions beyond the scope given by informal institutions is likely to be prohibitively high. Thus, large leaps of formal institutional change are unlikely with stable informal institutions. A breakdown of informal institutions can be understood as a prerequisite for a rapid change of formal institutions. On the other hand, informal institutions usually change at a rather slow pace: It takes substantial time to change conventions, opinions or fairness standards that are shared by a large majority of individuals. In this sense, it is useful to understand institutional change that involves a change of informal institutions as long-run phenomenon. In these cases, even if a directly observable large-scale change of formal institutions may take place quite rapidly, it has been preceded by a long-run learning process on the level of informal institutions.

From a normative perspective, this constraint on institutional change is difficult to criticize: one aspect of informal political institutions is that they are shared individual preferences over collective decision-making procedures and their outcomes, so that larger leaps cannot be justified on grounds of preference aggregation and normative individualism. When it is stated that informal institutions are a constraint, then this does not imply that formal institutions or policies that are executed within formal institutions are always necessarily in complete concurrence with informal institutions. In individual decisions, they play a similar role as all other rules: infringement may be followed by punishment (for example the denial of re-election if an institutional rule is installed that is considered unfair), but if punishment is sufficiently small or unlikely, an infringement may be favorable.

But as long as the agency-related institutions of collective-decision making provide for sufficient control, formal institutional change is limited as argued above. This argument is, of course, even reinforced if there exists an intrinsic motivation to adhere to given informal constraints – they would become even more binding in this case.

Result 1: If informal institutions are stable, a change of formal institutions is constrained to a change within the bounds of informal institutions and larger changes occur only if political competition fails so that the preferences reflected in informal institutions can be violated at low costs of electoral punishment.

Syncretic change is then a short-run phenomenon, although speaking of a short run in institutional economics certainly implies longer periods of time compared to, say, business-cycle theory. It describes a process of intentional modification of formal rules under the constraints of given informal institutions: These shared perceptions of a set of institutional rules that are considered as principally feasible and legitimate guide individual thinking about institutions. They work as a filter that determines which institutional innovations can be conducted and which are to be excluded. The concept of syncretic change therefore implies a reduction of complexity relative to North's theory of circular causation. Taking informal rules as fixed in the short run clearly leads to a more concise setting to be analyzed.

It involves, however, an increase of complexity compared to older theories of institutions such as Hayek (1960, 1973). There, the relationship between formal and informal constraints is rather rudimentary. Informal rules are assumed to evolve following an invisible-hand mechanism that preserves relatively efficient rules, where efficiency can be understood in the sense that preserved informal rules successfully help to co-ordinate individuals who themselves command only limited knowledge. In other words, the knowledge that is needed to efficiently co-ordinate individuals is embodied in rules, not in organizations or in persons. Formal rules, on the other hand, can according to Hayek be the product of discretionary collective decision-making. This leads him to an unambiguous preference for informal rules, as well as a rejection of the supposed rationalist pretensions involved in the planning of formal rules. The discussion in the following subsection however, shows that these are problematic conclusions.

7.3.2   *The scope of formal institutional change*

It has been stated above that both technology and informal institutions can be understood as constraints on the change of formal institutions. The role of technology has already been extensively discussed in the literature, often as case studies discussing how actual technological changes (the widespread use of gunpowder, the invention of the steam engine, etc.) have led to a change of the institutional structure (see the discussion and references in Section 7.2.2 of this chapter). Usually, the transmission mechanism from technological to institutional change is the assumption that the former alters the relative bargaining power of organizations or interest groups.

Given the taxonomy of formal institutions that has been introduced above, this can either be directed towards agency-related or distributional institutions. The purposeful change of efficiency-enhancing institutions, on the other hand, will under the assumption of homogeneous although incomplete knowledge not follow from a change of bargaining-power between groups competing for influence. A rise or decline in efficiency of the institutional structure may be a collateral result of changes that are intended to produce an institutional structure that reflects the actual relative bargaining powers. For example, the spread of new and more efficient production technologies following the invention of the steam engine enabled the rise of an economically powerful *bourgeoisie*. This shift of relative bargaining power away from the gentry has in turn led to a changed institutional structure that has ultimately led to a dissolution of the feudal order. One might argue that this implied a rise of efficiency by establishing more secure property rights that were no longer threatened by aristocratic political power. But the rise of efficiency is probably not much more than a welcome side effect, while the driving force to promote institutional change was to play a zero-sum game and secure benefits from rival groups, i.e., to adapt agency-related institutions to the actual relative bargaining power between *bourgoisie* and nobility.

If a deliberate change of efficiency-enhancing institutions is to be explained, then there are two options, which are not mutually exclusive: one is to maintain technological change as the trigger of a shift of relative bargaining powers, but to additionally assume that the groups or organizations that compete for institutional influence are characterized by heterogeneous stocks of institution-related knowledge; the other is to assume that a change of bargaining power is not necessary at all, but that the group or organization that sets the agenda for institutional change gets convinced that its given stock of knowledge is partially false and that its own utility can be increased by installing a different set of efficiency-enhancing rules. Both of these options constitute knowledge-based institutional change, while a change of institutions that *only* arises from a shift of bargaining power can be only interest-driven. On the other hand, knowledge-driven institutional change can also be directed at manipulating agency-related or distributive institutions if the related stock of knowledge of the institutional agenda-setter changes. To all of these various types of institutional changes, informal institutions act as a more broad constraint. As noted in the introduction, informal institutions can be understood as rules that spontaneously arise in order to solve co-ordination problems between individuals. There may, however, also be informal institutions that are distinctly political, because they define a set of political outcomes that are generally considered fair and acceptable by most (although certainly not by all) individuals in a polity (Schnellenbach 2004a: ch. 8). The emergence of such informal political institutions can generally be explained by assuming a cumulative process of communication. Individuals need to form some expectation about which institutional framework produces results that are relatively advantageous to them, and they need to determine an aspiration level by figuring out which level of utility they can realistically expect under a suitable set of institutions. In other words, individuals need a political-economic theory, however rudimentary it may be, that tells them what outcomes they can expect under a large number of different institutional structures that are all principally possible to implement. As long as experience is not available or very scarce, the diffusion of such theories within a group of individuals or a polity is similar to a frequency-dependent propagation process, be it through direct peer-to-peer communication, via mass media or through other channels of communication.

For example, a situation is easily conceivable in which the average citizen knows almost nothing about the public sector production function. Nevertheless, there will usually exist a large set of policies, each consisting of a tax burden and a quantity of public goods, that he considers to be principally acceptable. On the other hand, there will be combinations of high tax burdens and low quantities of public goods that the citizen considers to be a clear signal for an unacceptable appropriation of rents within the public sector – the aspiration level, that follows from theories about the public sector, is missed. The stock of knowledge, which through communication is shared by a large majority of individuals, is the foundation for simple informal rules that discriminate between acceptable and unacceptable policies. If in our example unacceptable policies are frequently implemented, this clearly serves as an impulse to organize formal institutional change, here of agency-related formal institutions, in order to avoid such outcomes in the future. This mechanism described here is therefore quite similar to the idea of learning about the efficiency of constitutional rules, as proposed by Vanberg and Buchanan (1991).

Similarly, there may be widespread common ideals of fairness, for example of a fair distribution of incomes. These are usually not coherent theories of fairness, as contract theories of the state attempt to produce them, but widespread rules of thumb. A certain spectrum of income redistribution may for example be defined as legitimate by these rules, while amounts above or below this legitimate range are interpreted either as insufficient or as an over-accommodation of the recipients. The result is again that there are formal distributive institutions that yield policies within these informal institutions and also formal institutions that yield policies that are out of bounds. In the short run, with given informal institutions, distributive conflicts are therefore likely to happen within the set of distributive results that is defined by informal institutions. Formal institutions are phrased in order to secure that a subset of results that are considered to be fair is enforced; *which* subset depends on relative bargaining powers.

On first sight, the case is even more straightforward for efficiency-enhancing institutions: given their stock of knowledge, individuals believe that certain institutions (e.g., a certain definition of property rights) foster efficiency, and they believe that some policies increase efficiency while others do not. If it is possible to compensate losers of institutional change, rational individuals can be expected to prefer institutions that are considered to be efficient over inefficient institutions. Similarly, they will prefer institutions that impede politicians from implementing inefficient policies over institutions that are not successful in this respect. The informal rule that principally, efficient formal rules should replace inefficient formal rules is therefore also a part of the set of informal institutions. But even if

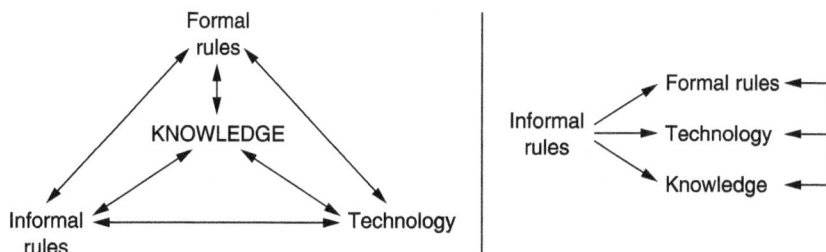

Figure 7.1 The long run and the short run in institutional change.

compensation is feasible, there is a serious problem resulting from this last informal rule. It becomes obvious at this point that the system of informal institutions itself is not necessarily coherent.

Efficiency-enhancing institutional reform may conflict with informal distributive claims, and efficiency can also collide with the wish to control a self-interested government through agency-related institutions. Even if individuals in a society share common perceptions of fairness and a common idea of how to organize the agency problems involved in representative government, the intuitively rational informal rule of *"increase efficiency if you expect such an increase to be possible"* is very likely to be (at least to some degree) inconsistent with other informal rules, particularly if perfect compensation mechanisms do not exist. The restrictions of formal institutional change thus need not be unambiguous. Rather, the tradeoffs that can be made between different informal rules are likely to be a source of conflict in itself in processes of formal institutional change. This problem will be further discussed in the following subsections.

7.3.3 The problem of institutional inertia

The discussion of the previous subsections has been summarized in Figure 7.1, with the long run perspective on institutional change on the left and the short run perspective on the right panel. In the short run, a change of formal institutions can be caused by changes of technology and of the stock of knowledge held by individuals. In turn, formal institutions are an influence on the type of technological change and, maybe a bit less obvious, on the accumulation of knowledge within the economy. All this takes place under the constraint of informal institutions that are assumed to be fixed in the short run. In a case of incoherent informal rules, i.e., when it is believed to be impossible to have an efficient institutional structure that simultaneously complies with the claims for distributive fairness and the demands for an effective control of the government through agency-related institutions, it is unavoidable that at least one informal institution is infringed. Proposals for institutional change are then likely to involve a trade-off. Additional efficiency can be achieved at the cost of reduced fairness; additional fairness can be achieved at the price of reduced efficiency and so on. This problem is aggravated by the existence of uncertainty regarding the aggregate effects of institutional change. While the effects of an institutional reform on fairness measures are often immediately clear, the magnitude of a positive expected effect on efficiency is rather uncertain. In a Downsian framework, it is doubtful whether a median voter would be willing to support such an experiment with institutional change as long as the risk of an overall failure is sufficiently large. In a framework with sufficient leeway for representatives to deviate temporarily from the median preferences, it is equally unlikely that a representative, who has been elected under the institutional status quo, is willing to conduct institutional experiments if the risk of failure and subsequent punishment (e.g., in elections) is sufficiently high. This is another very important rationale for the fact that institutional change, if it occurs, is often piecemeal change. Thus, in accordance with some of the neoclassical literature on the political economy of reform such as Dewatripont and Roland (1995) and Wei (1997), we can state the following

Result 2: Gradual changes of the formal institutional framework reduce the risk of severe failure, compared to more sweeping changes, and are therefore more likely to be implemented by self-interested agents.

Obviously, a risk of failure does also exist if there is no incoherence at all between informal institutions. Nevertheless, the case for piecemeal rather than comprehensive change is a bit different in this case. The difference is that the trade-off between raising efficiency and competing distributive or other norms does not exist here, so that institutional reform would be conducted whenever a positive effect on efficiency is expected – regardless of its magnitude. Thus, even large reforms could be implemented at no risk as long as the positive sign of their effect is certain. Put differently, uncertainty regarding the sign of the effects of institutional change is necessary to warrant piecemeal instead of large-scale reforms in economies with coherent informal institutions. In addition to these considerations, one can anticipate that there will be less politico-economic conflict to cope with in the process of changing formal institutions in the case of coherent informal institutions.

If, for example, the improvement of an efficiency-enhancing rule does not conflict with other informal institutions, then it is much more likely that such a proposal for institutional change will find broad support compared to a situation with conflicting institutions where any proposal of change has to overcome the opposition of groups or organizations with conflicting priorities.

A polity with very incoherent informal rules, on the other hand, is in danger of falling into an institutional inertia where formal institutions are changed either not at all or only as a reaction to overwhelming exogenous changes. The reason for this different propensity for institutional innovation within different constellations of informal institutions follows simply from the rising potential for political conflict with incoherent informal institutions: It is now feasible to argue against efficiency-enhancing reform on grounds of missing legitimacy. This does not imply that a polity with coherent informal rules is free of conflict altogether. There are conflicts of distribution between groups and organizations, and there are conflicts of interest between principal and agent. But the important point is that, with coherent formal institutions, it is far more difficult to question the legitimacy of formal institutional changes that are, for instance, intended and expected to increase efficiency. As soon as incoherence appears, however, informal institutional trade-offs can be exploited to de-legitimize proposed institutional change, which can possibly lead to complete institutional inertia. What follows is

Result 3: It can be expected that ceteris paribus a polity with a relatively coherent set of informal institutions produces relatively more (formal) institutional innovations than a polity with more incoherent informal rules.

7.4 Achieving formal institutional change

7.4.1 *Accumulating knowledge about institutions*

The discussion so far has shown that the triggers of institutional change are likely to depend on the type of formal institution that is to be changed. If formal institutions primarily have distributive effects or aim at managing the agency relationship between citizens and representatives, then the conflict for economic benefits between opposing groups is a permanent threat for the status quo. Following the institutional economics of, among others, Douglass C. North, a variation of bargaining powers due to exogenous changes of restrictions such as technology is the primary trigger of such institutional changes. On the other hand, the more an observed formal institution is efficiency-related, the less interesting is bargaining power as an explanation for institutional change, and the more important pure learning about the relative efficacy of institutional rules becomes.

It has been stated above that such learning involves a cognitive reconciliation of given institutional structures with perceived alternative rules by any individual who may act as a veto player to institutional reform. In an autocracy, the institution-related knowledge of a single ruler or a critical mass of individuals in a single ruling party has to change, whereas in a referendum democracy, the conjectures held by a majority of voters need to change. In a representative democracy, veto players opposed to institutional reform may be groups of decisive swing voters who fear imperfect compensation mechanisms even if overall efficiency gains are to be achieved, or who doubt that a proposed institutional reform will yield any efficiency gains at all. These examples hint at the fact that any *general* theory of a change of designed institutions has very limited scope, because much depends on the status quo structure of formal institutions from which one starts. What can be said on a very general level, however, is that individual learning processes are a necessary prerequisite for knowledge-based institutional change – whoever the relevant individuals may be in the special case.

Brenner (1999) makes a distinction between cognitive learning and associative learning. While the former refers to learning within given cognitive models, the latter denotes learning of new cognitive models or at least substantial revisions of given cognitive models. In this sense, cognitive learning can be interpreted as a routine, everyday action aiming at collecting information about the parameter values of a given model. Associative learning, on the other hand, is a less routine action that is pursued following a perceived necessity to find a new, more suitable model with higher explanatory power than the status quo model. One can easily imagine that this kind of learning is associated with relatively higher cognitive costs, since it involves potentially complex theoretical revisions compared to a simple updating of parameter values. Meier and Haury (1990) have scrutinized in greater detail how economic policy with endogenous preferences works. Their important starting point is that individual cognitive structures may change, where a cognitive structure comprehends both positive and normative statements about the world. In this chapter, we deviate from this approach in assuming that individual ends are fixed in the short-run, i.e., that individuals pursue for example a certain distributive outcome or high levels of efficiency and that these ends are, in the political sphere, represented in informal political institutions. Formal institutions are social technologies to pursue these ends, with incomplete knowledge about the relative efficacy of institutional rules.

Changing the institutional status quo does then presuppose that a sufficiently high number of individuals finds it necessary to revise their given theories on the relative usefulness of alternative institutional rules. An obvious mechanism which could lead to a revision of a given stock of knowledge is the observation of different institutional structures and their outcomes in other jurisdictions. Besley and Case (1995) have shown that such a mechanism is relevant in tax policy on the state level in the United States: if a governor raises taxes but neighboring governors do not, then he is more likely to lose the next election compared to a scenario in which neighboring governors also raise taxes. This evidence supports the assumption that individuals use experience from outside to update their stock of knowledge. The problem is, however, that the mechanism does not work for every policy issue. For example, Besley and Case show that the relative labor market performances of states have no significant impact on the probability of re-election. Another problem is that the observation and comparison of tax rates appears to be low-cost cognitive learning, whereas empirical evidence on more costly associative learning about the relative efficiency of institutional structures is not available at all thus far.

The observations by Besley and Case also hint at the problem of issue salience. Tax policy may be a popular political issue in which people are interested enough in order to invest into obtaining information about tax policy in other jurisdictions. Or changes in the tax burden are an issue that is easily accessible, compared to more complex issues where it is more difficult (where it involves higher cognitive costs) to compare the performances of differing policies and institutions. This leads to the problem of attention economies (Falkinger 2003): Attention for issues has to be supplied by individuals or groups of individuals who can draw private gains from generating such an interest. Sources of information may be found in other jurisdictions, but they may also be found in subsystems such as the scientific community, where individuals invest considerable resources and creativity into pondering about novel institutional arrangements (Witt 2003).

In any case, the important question is under which conditions knowledge that is principally available does indeed come to the attention of a sufficiently large number of individuals.

In the political sphere, the incentive structure with a tendency towards rational ignorance and the mutual re-affirming of informal institutions in social networks clearly leads to a status quo bias. From an individual perspective, a change of a collectively shared theory that may eventually lead to a reform of formal institutions is a pure public good. On the other hand, there are individual costs of such a change: There are not only cognitive costs, but also costs such as a potential alienation of other individuals who also thus far adhere to the status quo theory. There are likely to be self-stabilizing social networks, in which individuals communicate and confirm the validity of the status quo theory to each other (Schnellenbach 2004a). In such a situation, the vague prospect of improvement under an alternative set of institutions is unlikely to convince a sufficiently large number of individuals as long as they are still generally satisfied with the results produced by the status quo set. Only in a situation in which experience discredits the status quo institutions, i.e., in which the aspiration level associated with the status quo is clearly missed, can an individual willingness to critically revise the status quo theories be presupposed.

This leads, once again, to an argument explaining a disposition for gradualism in institutional change. Individuals can be relatively easily convinced of small changes that are easy to be reconciled with status quo theories. In this case, the cognitive costs of changing their minds are small and the risk of high external costs (such as alienation of a given social network) is also small. More fundamental changes, that are difficult to reconcile with the status quo, are on the other hand only likely to find support if the costs of maintaining the status quo become unbearably high – which would, as noted, be the case when experience has severely discredited the status quo theory.

Result 4: If the individual costs of learning about formal institutions increase with the difference between the status quo and the proposed alternative, then there will be a bias towards gradual changes as long as there are no strong external incentives for the individuals to abandon the theories that support the status quo set of institutions.

7.4.2 The myth of public entrepreneurship

The idea that so-called "public entrepreneurs" can manipulate the political preferences of a decisive group of voters is not new to political economy, as for example the study of Schumpeter (1942: chs 21–23) shows. As has been the case already with Schumpeter, the idea that political leadership *against* the preferences of a majority of voters is a laudable activity shows some mistrust in the capabilities of the sovereign in a democracy to make informed and rational judgments. Some contributors even go as far as Harberger (1993), who praises members of authoritarian dictatorships as "heroes" due to their role in promoting efficiency-enhancing economic reforms. One might wonder, however, what exactly the political risks were, that politicians without an election constraint are supposed to have taken to justify praise for "heroic" efforts. From a normative perspective, the concept of public entrepreneurship in the Schumpeterian sense sketched above is certainly dubious. If one is convinced of the empirical relevance of self-interested behavior in government, then a manipulation of individuals' political preferences and hypotheses on the relative efficiency of formal institutions is a cause of unease, rather than comfort. If, on the other hand, one believes in the empirical relevance of the assumption of benevolent agents in the public sector, then there is no reason to think of the tie between the governed and the governing as a principal-agent-relationship. Rational voters, knowing of the benevolence of their agents, would completely delegate all decision-making on public causes to their agents and refrain from costly mulling over these issues themselves.

In other words, public entrepreneurship would not be necessary at all because individuals would rationally grant unrestricted leeway to their benevolent agents – there would be no resistance to reform that needed to be overcome through public entrepreneurship. Hoping for public entrepreneurship, or for "heroic" economic policy-making, does then presuppose an inconsistency in the assumptions about the behavioral propensities of political agents. Thinking about economic policy-making in the spirit of Harberger and Schumpeter apparently implies to generally acknowledge widespread opportunistic behavior of public sector agents, but to hope for the occasional appearance of a benevolent agent with sufficient public entrepreneurial skills to persuade or coerce malinformed voters into accepting welfare-enhancing policies. More serious problems follow from this inconsistency of behavioral assumptions if formal institutions are proposed that facilitate what is perceived as public entrepreneurship (Heiniger *et al.* 2004 is an example). These proposals recommend a reduction of checks and balances in order to increase the set of alternatives available to the political entrepreneur and her scope to implement her preferred choices. An institutional reform along these lines is, however, obviously in contradiction with the observed fact that benevolent public entrepreneurship is an occasional phenomenon at best and that opportunistic behavior is the norm. The simple rule of constitutional economics that agency-related formal institutions ought to channel even the decisions of the worst opportunist to socially acceptable outcomes is clearly violated here.

In addition to these normative arguments, the relevance of public entrepreneurship is also doubtful from a positive perspective. In this respect, two important questions remain unanswered thus far: One is why individuals should decide to become public entrepreneurs at all, and the other is if there are further limits to institutional entrepreneurship once there are such individuals. As far as the first question is concerned, it is likely that incentives vary for different types of formal institutions. Political competition with retrospective voting (see, e.g., Hibbs 2000 for recent evidence on the importance of retrospective voting) provides *ceteris paribus* an incentive to any incumbent in office to provide efficient formal institutions. The question is, however, how strong this incentive is. Political competition is usually multidimensional and institutional change concerning specific formal institutions may be a marginalized issue. Another problem is that the incumbent may face a relatively conservative, risk-averse electorate that is generally opposed to risky institutional experiments. In such a situation, it may generally be more attractive to incumbents with a relatively high probability of winning the election to shun risky policy experiments and attempt to win the election by maintaining the institutional status quo as long as it meets the aspiration level of a majority of voters. Only with a low probability of re-election, motives such as a short-run maximization of ideological goals or sheer desperation may provide some incentives to promote institutional change. And again, if there are incoherent informal institutions, the proposal of an institutional reform that expands distributive fairness at the cost of efficiency, or vice versa, would induce additional conflicts which an incumbent prefers to avoid.

Nevertheless, there are situations in which an incumbent is likely to promote institutional change. For example, a status quo institutional framework that produces results below the aspiration level of a majority of voters clearly gives an incentive to experiment with new solutions: it is more rational to take the risk of failure in an institutional experiment compared to certainly facing a high probability of losing the next election. But it appears to be unlikely that individuals holding political offices resemble the bold personalities that Schumpeter (1942: ch. 22) describes. On the contrary, if the simple equation holds that the adoption of novelty is undertaken if the risk of non-adoption is perceived to be higher than the risk of adoption (Redmond 2003), then it is likely that a sense of crisis and urgency following from the belief that satisfying results will not be produced with the given institutional structure is necessary as an impulse for institutional change. This is also shown in some of the case studies of institutional innovation with regard to solving common pool problems by Ostrom (1990). And even individuals who appear as bold public entrepreneurs on first sight, such as Franklin D. Roosevelt or Margaret Thatcher, came forward with institutional innovation as a response to the Great Depression and the British Disease, respectively. There is indeed a large empirical evidence suggesting that crisis is a necessary prerequisite for political and institutional reform (see the contributions collected in Sturzenegger and Tommasi 1998).

At this point, it is useful to give a reminder of a fundamental distinction made by Schumpeter (1912) between the entrepreneur (the *"Unternehmer"*) and the administrator (the *"Wirt"*). The entrepreneur is the one who has an intrinsic drive to constantly search for superior solutions, a drive that is reinforced by the incentive given by (at least temporary) monopoly rents that can be accrued by those who introduce successful novelty. The administrator, on the other hand, is the one who rationally accommodates his choices to changing restrictions. According to the considerations made thus far, an incumbent in public office resembles not so much an entrepreneur, but much rather an administrator. Political or institutional innovation is then a largely defensive activity which is not undertaken by a bold public entrepreneur, but by an incumbent who is convinced that retaining the status quo under changing restrictions leads to deteriorating chances of being re-elected. Of course, a public entrepreneur does not necessarily need to be an individual holding a public office. On the contrary, Schumpeter (1942: chs 22–23) argues in favor of public entrepreneurship as an activity taken up by individuals who are interested in putting one well-defined issue onto the political agenda and in changing the preferences of individuals in their favor, but who have no further career concerns in the public sector.

It is, however, open to debate under which conditions such a deliberate creation or manipulation of informal political institutions is feasible. It has become popular in political economics to adopt the concept of social networks from sociology (see, e.g., Granovetter 1973 or Putnam 1993) and enrich these approaches with some more traditional rational choice considerations. The assumptions that learning is costly, that deviation from the point of view prevailing within a network is costly and that communication within a network leads to a mutual affirmation of the views held by the individuals in a network easily leads to the conclusion that the views shared within such a network are very stable (Schnellenbach 2004a), at least if they are views on core issues for that group (Murphy and Shleifer 2004). In such models, decentralized mechanisms of reinforcing the status quo make it highly unlikely that a public entrepreneur can deliberately change the views held by individuals within a social network once the members of the network have converged to an equilibrium view, which, in our framework, would constitute a political informal institution.

There are two levers for public entrepreneurship in such models: If there are new issues which have thus far not concerned the members of a social network and which they are indifferent about, then public entrepreneurs can "hijack" such a network to diffuse their position on such a new issue. And if there is a widespread disenchantment with the status quo view, because it produces results below the aspiration level, then this may lead to a situation where a demand for a new approach arises which can be supplied by public entrepreneurs. In both cases, there is no manipulation of citizens' preferences, as Schumpeter suggests, but a supply of points of view by interest groups, politicians or other public figures on issues for which no stable equilibrium position exists. This distinction may appear as pure pettifoggery, but it does have an important implication: public entrepreneurship is confined to the introduction of novel issues to the political process, but once an equilibrium set of informal political institutions concerning an issue exists, the internal support of the status quo within social networks makes it very unlikely that an effort to induce change succeeds. Once again, a situation of crisis which discredits the status quo and creates a demand for new solutions is a prerequisite for change and bold entrepreneurship is transformed into defensive accommodation to changed circumstances.

Result 5: Informal political institutions, understood as shared theories about and preferences for alternative sets of policies and formal institutions, are highly resistant to change once they are adopted by a large social network. Thus, entrepreneurship in the public sector is confined to the introduction of new issues, but attempts to manipulate an existing status quo are likely to fail.

This reasoning provides another rationale for the gradual nature of the change of formal institutions. We have seen that informal political institutions are stable over long periods of time and very difficult to be deliberately changed, which makes them a constraint for the change of formal institutions that even so-called public entrepreneurs can hardly circumvent as long as democratic checks and balances are in effect.

7.5 Conclusions and outlook

It has been argued that the change of formal institutions can be understood as *syncretic* change, i.e., as being based on the voluntary integration of novel institutional rules into given institutional structures. This implies that the change of formal institutions usually happens incrementally, at a slow pace and in a piecemeal fashion. Moreover, it has been argued that the ability of a polity to generate formal institutional change depends on the coherence of its informal institutions. The more coherent the informal institutional structure is, the more likely is the appearance of formal institutional innovations.

There are some further implications. The argument in this chapter can be extended to show that social constructivism, as feared by Hayek, is unlikely to occur on a large scale in the design of formal institutions. On the contrary, the change of formal institutions is constrained by informal institutions. These are the result of traditions and distinct political cultures. Constructivism is certainly not impossible, but given the arguments in this chapter, it is unlikely to occur if incumbents act rationally and are sufficiently constrained by the electorate (see also Hayek 1979) – public entrepreneurship initiated by despots and tyrants would be a subject for a different paper.

Finally, it should be remarked that gradual institutional change is likely to allow a sustained diversity of polities. If formal institutional changes are constrained by informal institutions, and if informal institutions reflect political and societal traditions that may be very peculiar and different from polity to polity, then it is unlikely that learning from the institutional policies of other jurisdictions will lead to a harmonization ex post, as it is envisioned by some approaches to institutional competition (see Siebert and Koop 1993 for an example). Instead, if informal institutions differ, then the institutional knowledge that is the basis of formal institutional change is also likely to evolve differently in different polities. It is therefore unlikely that variety in the public sphere will disappear via syncretic institutional change.

Note

1 This is an overhauled version (including a change of the title) of a paper presented at the Workshop on the Evolution of Designed Institutions at the Max-Planck-Institute of Economics (Jena), 19–21 February 2004. I would like to thank Bruno S. Frey, Wolfgang Kerber, Richard Langlois, Elinor Ostrom, Christian Schubert and Ulrich Witt for comments, but obviously the usual disclaimer applies.

References

Besley, T. and Case, A. (1995) 'Incumbent Behaviour: Vote-Seeking, Tax-Setting and Yardstick Competition', *American Economic Review*, 85: 25–45.

Brennan, G. and Buchanan, J.M. (1980) *The Power to Tax. Analytical Foundations of a Fiscal Constitution*, Cambridge: Cambridge University Press.

Brenner, T. (1999) *Modelling Learning in Economics*, Cheltenham: Elgar.

Brette, O. (2003) 'Thorstein Veblen's Theory of Institutional Change: Beyond Technological Determinism', *European Journal for the History of Economic Thought*, 10: 455–77.

Buchanan, J.M. and Tullock, G. (1962) *The Calculus of Consent. Logical Foundations of Constitutional Democracy*, Ann Arbor: University of Michigan Press.

David, P.A. (1985) 'Clio and the Economics of QWERTY', *American Economic Review*, 75: 332–7.

Demsetz, H. (1967) 'Toward a Theory of Property Rights', *American Economic Review, Papers and Proceedings*, 57: 347–59.

Demsetz, H. (2002) 'Toward a Theory of Property Rights II: The Competition Between Private and Collective Ownership', *Journal of Legal Studies*, 31: 653–72.

Dewatripont, M. and Roland, G. (1995) 'The Design of Reform Packages Under Uncertainty', *American Economic Review*, 85: 1207–23.

Dopfer, K. (1991) 'Toward a Theory of Economic Institutions: Synergy and Path Dependency', *Journal of Economic Issues*, 25: 535–50.

Downs, A. (1957) *An Economic Theory of Democracy*, New York: Harper.

Falkinger, J. (2003) 'Attention Economies', mimeo, University of Zürich.

Findlay, R. and Wilson, J.D. (1987) 'The Political Economy of Leviathan', in A. Razin and E. Sadka (eds), *Economic Policy in Theory and Practice*, New York: St. Martin's Press.

Frey, B.S. (1997) 'A Constitution for Knaves Crowds Out Civic Virtues', *Economic Journal*, 107: 1043–53.

Granovetter, M. (1973) 'The Strength of Weak Ties', *American Journal of Sociology*, 78: 1360–80.

Harberger, A. (1993) 'Secrets of Success: A Handful of Heroes', *American Economic Review, Papers and Proceedings*, 83: 343–50.

Hayek, F.A. von (1960) *The Constitution of Liberty*, London: Routledge & Kegan Paul.

Hayek, F.A. von (1972) *Zur Theorie komplexer Phänomene*, Tübingen: Mohr Siebeck.

Hayek, F.A. von (1973) *Law, Legislation and Liberty, vol. 1: Rules and Order*, London: Routledge.

Hayek, F.A. von (1979) *Law, Legislation and Liberty, vol. 3: The Political Order of a Free People*, London: Routledge.

Heiniger, Y., Straubhaar, T., Rentsch, H., Flückiger, S. and Held, T. (2004) *Ökonomik der Reform. Wege zu mehr Wachstum in Deutschland*, Zürich: Orell Füssli.

Hibbs, D.A. (2000) 'Bread and Peace Voting in US Presidential Elections', *Public Choice*, 104: 149–80.

Hira, A. and Hira, R. (2000) 'The New Institutionalism: Contradictory Notions of Change', *American Journal of Economics and Sociology*, 59: 267–82.

Hodgson, G.M. (1993) *Economics and Evolution. Bringing Life Back into Economics*, Cambridge: Polity Press.

Hodgson, G.M. (1995) 'The Evolution of Evolutionary Economics', *Scottish Journal of Political Economy*, 42: 469–88.

Knight, J. (1992) *Institutions and Social Conflict*, Cambridge: Cambridge University Press.

Laffont, J.-J. (2001) *Incentives and Political Economy*, Oxford: Oxford University Press.

Landes, D.S. (1998) *The Wealth and Poverty of Nations. Why Some Are So Rich and Some Are So Poor*, New York: W.W. Norton.

Meier, A. and Haury, S. (1990) 'A Cognitive-Evolutionary Theory of Economic Policy', in: K. Dopfer and K.-F. Raible (eds) *The Evolution of Economic Systems*, London: Macmillan.

Murphy, K.M. and Shleifer, A. (2004) 'Persuasion in Politics', *American Economic Review, Papers and Proceedings*, 94: 435–39.

Myrdal, G. (1957) *Economic Theory and Underdeveloped Regions*, London: Duckworth.

North, D.C. (1981) *Structure and Change in Economic History*, New York: W.W. Norton.

North, D.C. (1990) *Institutions, Institutional Change and Economic Performance*, Cambridge: Cambridge University Press.

Ostrom, E. (1990) *Governing the Commons. The Evolution of Institutions for Collective Action*, Cambridge: Cambridge University Press.

Popper, K.R. (1957) *The Poverty of Historicism*, reprint, London: Routledge, 1999.

Putnam, R. (1993) *Making Democracy Work: Civil Traditions in Modern Italy*, Princeton: Princeton University Press.

Redmond, W.H. (2003) 'Innovation, Diffusion and Institutional Change', *Journal of Economic Issues*, 37: 665–80.

Röpke, J. (1970) *Primitive Wirtschaft, Kulturwandel und die Diffusion von Neuerungen*, Tübingen: Mohr Siebeck.

Schnellenbach, J. (2004a) *Dezentrale Finanzpolitik und Modellunsicherheit. Eine theoretische Untersuchung zur Rolle des fiskalischen Wettbewerbs als Wissen generierender Prozess*, Tübingen: Mohr Siebeck.

Schnellenbach, J. (2004b) 'The Evolution of a Fiscal Constitution when Individuals are Theoretically Uncertain', *European Journal of Law and Economics*, 17: 97–115.

Schnellenbach, J. (2005) 'Model Uncertainty and the Rationality of Economic Policy', *Journal of Evolutionary Economics*, 15: 101–16.

Schumpeter, J.A. (1912) *Theorie der wirtschaftlichen Entwicklung*, Leipzig: Duncker & Humblot.

Schumpeter, J.A. (1942) *Capitalism, Socialism and Democracy*, New York: Harper.

Siebert, H. and Koop, M.J. (1993) 'Institutional Competition versus Centralization: Quo Vadis Europe?', *Oxford Review of Economic Policy*, 9: 15–30.

Sturzenegger, F. and Tommasi, M. (eds.) (1998) *The Political Economy of Reform*, Cambridge, MA: MIT Press.

Vanberg, V.J. and Buchanan, J.M. (1991) 'Constitutional Choice, Rational Ignorance and the Limits of Reason', *Jahrbuch für Neue Politische Ökonomie*, 10: 65–78.

Volckart, O. (2001) *Wettbewerb und Wettbewerbsbeschränkung im vormodernen Deutschland 1000–1800*, Tübingen: Mohr Siebeck.

Walker, J. (1969) 'The Diffusion of Innovation among the American States', *American Political Science Review*, 63: 880–99.

Wei, S.-J. (1997) 'Gradualism versus Big Bang: Speed and Sustainability of Reforms', *Canadian Journal of Economics*, 30: 1234–47.

Witt, U. (1994) 'Endogenous Change – Causes and Contingencies', *Advances in Austrian Economics*, 1: 105–17.

Witt, U. (2003) 'Evolutionary Economics and the Extension of Evolution to the Economy', in U. Witt (ed.) *The Evolving Economy. Essays on the Evolutionary Approach to Economics*, Cheltenham: Elgar.

Part III
Normative perspectives

8 A contractarian view on institutional evolution

Christian Schubert

8.1 Introduction[1]

While the positive evolution of consciously and purposefully designed institutions (i.e., the products of society's political and legal rule-making processes) has so far been widely neglected within Evolutionary Economics, their *normative* evaluation has received even less attention. To evaluate an empirically given or theoretically conceived designed institution presupposes a normative judgment concerning the "goodness" of a socio-economic state or process that the designed institution under review is assumed to be able to influence. Developing the basis for such judgments is the task of *normative economics*. Until now, this venerable field of research has hardly aroused the interest of evolutionary economists. This chapter proposes a way how they might venture into this uncharted territory. Put differently, the chapter attempts to elaborate on some possible foundations of a – yet to be fully developed – normative branch within Evolutionary Economics.

Normative Economics is currently dominated by welfare theoretic approaches that in turn are based on a quasi-utilitarian methodology (Hausman and McPherson 1996, Sen 1996a). Starting from the (often implicit) ontological assumption of a static economic system with a given and closed set of individual preferences and resources, the normative statement is put forward that policy-makers should design the economy's institutional framework (and thereby the economy's incentive structure) in such a way that resources will be allocated in a welfare-maximizing way.

Besides welfare theory, there are three other more or less mature normative approaches which play a (limited) role within contemporary normative economics. First, the *Constitutional Economics* school, being strongly influenced by the contractarian tradition of social philosophy, is based on the idea that a society's "rules of the game" should be designed in such a way that they can be plausibly reconstructed as being voluntarily agreed upon by all individuals concerned (Buchanan 1975, Vanberg 1999). Second, the use of *neo-pragmatist* ideas has been proposed by, e.g., Knight (2001) and Posner (1998), in particular in the context of research on Law and Economics topics. Third and finally, *Austrian* economists have developed their own views concerning the appropriate (non-)design of political and legal institutions (Langlois and Sabooglu 2001, Denis 2002).

Within evolutionary economics, the need to autonomously engage in normative theorizing (on the explicit background of an evolutionary view on economic processes) in order to be able to develop and justify policy implications has been most prominently put forward by Witt (1996, 2003). Similar ideas have recently been voiced by a leading exponent of the New Institutional Economics, flirting with evolutionary ideas (North 1999).

North summarizes both the unease of heterodox approaches with the normative orientation of mainstream economics and the motivation to think about an alternative perspective by stating that "[e]conomic theory is static; and in the world in which we live a static body of theory consistently and persistently yields the wrong policy prescriptions".[2] Hence, the static orientation of positive economics is identified as being the main obstacle on the way toward a theory that is able to yield well-founded statements about political or constitutional implications (see Pelikan 2002 for a similar assessment); such a theory has of course to presuppose or, better yet, to explicitly develop and justify normative statements which are plausible and convincing from an evolutionary perspective. To specify this argument (and North's intuition), a meta-theoretical concept is necessary that clarifies the relationship between positive and normative statements as well as the latter's scientific status. For if we (1) criticize orthodox welfare theory's normative concept and its resulting statements, and (2) work out an alternative concept that yields alternative statements, we are inspired by or rely on Evolutionary Economics' *positive* insights into the nature of economic behavior and economic processes. There is thus a link between the positive and the normative sphere whose nature has to be clarified. This endeavor may eventually result in a normative approach that is compatible with an overall evolutionary world-view – put differently, it may lead us to a "normative branch" within Evolutionary Economics.

The chapter is organized as follows. In Section 8.2, the two basic concepts of the following argument are briefly introduced: the "evolutionary" perspective on socio-economic systems and the peculiarities of normative theorizing. Concerning the latter, a meta-theoretical framework, i.e., a basic model of normative reasoning, is introduced which is borrowed from the social philosophy of Critical Rationalism, based on the work of Karl Popper, among others. This meta-theory provides us with the basic tools that we need in order to examine the plausibility of alternative normative approaches from an evolutionary perspective. On a less abstract level, i.e., on the level of concrete normative (or justificatory) theories, Section 8.3 proposes to use the contractarian approach as the foundation of a normative branch within Evolutionary Economics, for it is arguably the most *general* one among all possible candidates, i.e., it can be plausibly interpreted as encompassing most other approaches.[3] There are, however, two main deficiencies that should be remedied in order for this approach to be "evolution-proof". The two conditions that are thereby identified render it possible to delineate the range of contractarian theories which are compatible with an evolutionary perspective on economic processes. Hence, this section delineates the contours of a normative branch within Evolutionary Economics by way of critically assessing the theoretical potential of contractarianism from an evolutionary point of view. In Section 8.4, the approach of the political philosopher *John Rawls* is argued to fall into the range of theories that are acceptable in this sense – provided that it is interpreted in a conventionalist ("Humean") way, i.e., provided that Rawls' contractarianism puts the historically contingent informal *social norms* (such as, e.g., norms of distributive justice or property conventions) of a given society at center stage. Section 8.5 concludes.

8.2   Preparing the ground: The evolutionary and the normative viewpoint

8.2.1   The evolutionary perspective

Before the potential of normative thinking can be discussed from an evolutionary perspective, some preliminary remarks are in order as to what characterizes an "evolutionary" perspective on the economy. The next section (8.2.2) will deal with the peculiarities of *normative* theorizing.

In what follows, an evolutionary perspective on economic behavior and its systemic (macro) implications will comprise essentially three points. First, the socio-economic system is seen as an open one that evolves endogenously in historical, i.e., irreversible time. Social order is understood as being generated and continuously adapted by spontaneous processes of self-organization. In the course of these order-generating processes, genuine novelty emerges whose implications can only imperfectly be anticipated.

Second, individual economic behavior is not to be understood as an exercise in permanent optimization, but rather as the attempt to adapt to ever changing circumstances by learning and imitation. Humans acquire knowledge in a cumulative way, in particular by imitating other individuals' behavior which is perceived as relatively successful. In order to cope with uncertainty, individuals consciously and unconsciously follow institutions that are either self-enforcing ("conventions") or decentrally enforced by moral sanctions ("social norms"). In Ferguson's famous words, these institutions are themselves the non-anticipated product of "human action, but not human design".

Third and closely related to the second point, individual preferences change over time. Concerning both preferences in consumption and preferences in social interaction, there is a basic universal component which is directly related to the results of human genetic evolution. This component can be thought of as consisting of a set of "basic wants", such as, e.g., the want for sweeteners or the want for social status. Building on this, the relatively much more rapid processes of cultural evolution have led to a complex differentiation of human preferences (Witt 2000). These processes have been driven by cultural transmission mechanisms (in particular imitative or observational learning) whose basic structure is the product of genetic evolution, too. Concerning the class of preferences in social interaction, cultural learning processes have, e.g., generated culturally contingent attitudes on the "justice" (or "fairness") of socio-economic states or processes or, for that matter, collective decision-making procedures (Sartorius 2002, Binmore 1997, Frey *et al.* 1996).

By itself, the characteristics of an evolutionary "world-view" do not logically imply any normative conclusions at all. They do however render some normative theories (such as utilitarianism or contractarianism) or normative statements (such as propositions on policy goals) more or less *plausible*. To illustrate, from an evolutionary perspective it becomes highly implausible to develop normative statements on the basis of a justificatory approach that presupposes the concept of an aprioristic "Archimedean" viewpoint outside time and space, i.e., outside processes of cultural evolution. Since the attempt to venture into normative territory from an explicitly evolutionary perspective has hardly been made in the relevant literature (Witt 2003), some basics on what it means to argue normatively are in order.

8.2.2   *The normative perspective*

Normative or "ought"-statements are categorically different form positive or "is"-statements. This insight is at the basis of David Hume's famous dictum that no normative statement can be logically deduced from exclusively positive premises. Technically, this insight, often called "Hume's Law", derives from the logical impossibility of inductive conclusions: positive statements concern single events of the past, while normative statements claim to be universally valid in the future. He who tries to cross the divide between is and ought with logical means commits what has been later called (by Moore, in a slightly different context) the "naturalistic fallacy".[4]

Which implications does this fundamental logical insight bear for the task of normative reasoning? There are widely conflicting views on this. On the one hand, it has been argued that genuinely scientific statements can only be developed at all within the sphere of purely positive theories. From this skepticist perspective, it is nothing but arbitrariness that reigns on the normative side of the is-ought-divide. On the other hand, according to ethical cognitivism, normative statements can possess the same certitude and truth-value as positive ones, for in this view, there exist "moral facts" which can be identified analogously to positive facts.

Both polar views are rejected as implausible by the social philosophy of *Critical Rationalism* (Albert 1988, Popper 1992). According to it, neither is it reasonable to assume that normative statements can be deduced from a cognitively accessible sphere of moral facts (and hence, can be true or false), nor does it make sense to conclude from this rejection of cognitivism that normative statements are purely arbitrary expressions of "tastes".

What Critical Rationalism proposes in order to overcome the dichotomy between moral skepticism and cognitivism is inspired by two essential empirical observations. First, most real-world individuals who formulate normative statements do not actually interpret them as being analogous to expressions of pure subjective tastes, but rather as implying a claim to inter-subjective validity. Most often, they want other individuals to be *persuaded* by them. Second, when arguing about alternative normative statements, most real-world individuals consciously or unconsciously follow a basic discursive rule, according to which this claim is the more plausible, the more the underlying normative statement is perceived as having been developed from an ideal perspective of *impartiality*. Hence, from the viewpoint of the individuals concerned, normative statements are viewed as possessing a variable degree of plausibility or quality, i.e., they can be more or less well-founded. These observations point to the idea that there must be *more* to them than being mere expressions of arbitrarily formed tastes – even if there is admittedly *less* to them than ethical cognitivism suggests. Note that by identifying a general methodology to rationally discuss alternative normative statements, the meta-theoretical viewpoint taken here rejects at least a strong version of *moral relativism*, according to which there does not exist any universally valid method whatsoever to develop meaningful and justified judgments about competing normative claims (i.e., claims that may for instance have been developed in different cultural contexts).

According to the social philosophy of Critical Rationalism, this idea can be rationally reconstructed by analyzing the internal structure of normative statements. In principle, normative statements contain at least one positive component, i.e., they are based on at least one underlying (often implicit) factual hypothesis. This component can be rationally examined and criticized in a "value-free" way, thereby opening the way toward a rational discussion of the normative statement itself. Apart from this positive component, normative statements are also generally based on one or several more abstract normative principles. This insight points to a second option to examine them, namely, by testing the consistency between the normative statement itself and the (allegedly) underlying abstract principle. Moreover, this principle itself can of course again be examined in the same way as a simple normative statement – i.e., by investigating its positive component (or components) and its underlying, even more abstract, principle (or principles).

Third and finally, a given normative statement can be examined as to its compatibility with those moral intuitions and social norms that govern the real-world individuals' behavior, particularly their voting behavior when they are to decide on constitutional issues. Analyzing the origin and content of these intuitions and norms is of course a task of, inter alia, positive economics. In light of critical rationalism, a society's prevailing social norms should not only count as a valid touchstone of normative statements – the development of any moral (or, for that matter, social) philosophy should also explicitly take into account insights into the moral intuitions and motivations of man. This is a meta-theoretical advice that aims at preventing moral and social philosophy from losing contact to what determines the moral attitudes and constitutional preferences of real individuals. Note that this advice has to be handled with care: Insights from economics, evolutionary biology or moral psychology into the determinants of moral behavior cannot *per se* establish any claim to normative validity. Philosophy and empirical science ask fundamentally different questions about morality (Dworkin 1998).

Summing up, there are essentially three tools available to examine the plausibility of alternative normative statements. By using these tools, Evolutionary Economics may arrive at well-founded judgments on the quality of those normative statements (about, for example, appropriate policy goals) that have been proposed by mainstream welfare theory. From the viewpoint of the present chapter, the investigation into the quality of their positive components ought, of course, to be informed by insights of Evolutionary Economics into the nature and determinants of economic behavior and economic processes. The discussion of the plausibility of underlying, more abstract normative principles may also be informed by those insights.

To be sure, what can be achieved by the critical discussion of alternative normative statements are hypotheses of the form "Given what we (hypothetically) know so far about the positive nature of economic behavior, policy goal X is more plausible than policy goal Y". Since no (positive or normative) statement can ever be perfectly justified in the sense of the "principle of sufficient reason" (Popper 1992), the scientific status of the results of normative reasoning are of conjectural character only. Put differently, since no rock-solid *logical* bridge can bring us from the sphere of factual statements to normative territory, we have to use weaker *methodological* bridges. This softens the status of the results of our theoretical efforts. Hence, this methodology of normative reasoning avoids Hume's naturalistic fallacy. No logical conclusions are derived from the sphere of factuality alone for the sphere of normativity. Hence, positive theoretical insights are not sufficient to resolve normative disputes – but they can at least help to clarify the discussion, to influence the preferences of participants of the constitutional discourse, and to establish convincing claims about the quality of alternative normative statements. Logic can only play a role when the participants at the normative discourse have not only agreed upon facts, but also upon at least one ("basic") *normative* statement, for "[g]ranted that an *ought* cannot be derived from an *is*, it is still possible to derive an *ought* from an *is* in conjunction with another *ought*" (Schlicht 1998: 290, emphasis in the original).

The critical rationalist toolbox sketched above allows us (1) to systematically examine the normative statements that have been put forward by alternative economic schools of thought, such as utilitarian Welfare Theory (and its applied sub-disciplines, such as Public Choice or Law and Economics), contractarian Constitutional Economics, Austrian Economics and Evolutionary Economics. It helps us (2) to avoid committing the naturalistic fallacy which looms large when, e.g., a Panglossian stance is taken, or the categorical difference between the *empirical prevalence* of social norms and their *moral validity* is confounded, as is often the case in the literature on "Evolutionary Ethics" (Dworkin 1998). Both tendencies hinder the development of a plausible normative theory within economics in general and Evolutionary Economics in particular.

In order to develop substantive normative statements concerning the "goodness" of economic states and processes (a precondition to evaluate given or theoretically conceived designed institutions), a normative theory is needed that structures the justification of evaluative statements and that guarantees the plausibility of the latter – given what we know about the evolutionary nature of economic behavior. Once normative statements have been developed that are plausible in this sense, they form, in combination with positive insights into, for example, means-ends-relationships within the economy or the working properties of political

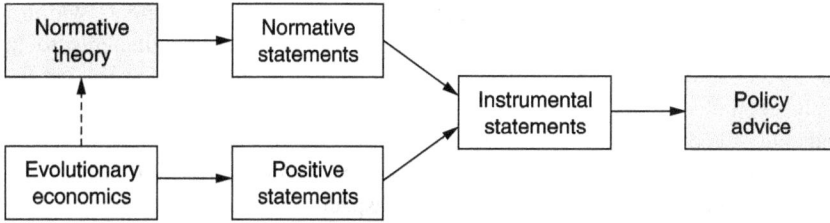

Figure 8.1 The derivation of policy advice. (The dashed line indicates no logical, but only a "weak" indicative relationship.)

or legal rules, the basis of *instrumental* statements which in turn serve as a direct input into the process of policy consulting (see Figure 8.1).

An approach that may serve as a basis for such a normative theory will be sketched in the following section (8.3). Before that can be done, though, we need to introduce a basic concept that indicates in a very general way what it shall mean to say that an economic state or process is "good" or "bad".

Almost the totality of normative economics takes the principle of *Normative Individualism* as its most fundamental normative premise. From the perspective of Critical Rationalism, sketched above, this principle is to be understood as a hypothetical imperative. It is formulated on the background of our hypothetical knowledge on the plausibility of its positive component and the consistency of its underlying, even more abstract normative principles (which lie outside the realm of economics). On a very general level, according to the principle of Normative Individualism, (1) the single autonomous individual is the only bearer of value judgments, i.e., her preferences are the only acceptable legitimizing force of any social order. There are no normatively valid social goals that are independent of the individually held preferences. It is in this sense that no "external ethical criteria" are accepted (Vanberg 2004). Moreover, (2), all individual preferences have exactly the same weight in the process of deriving social welfare judgments (Buchanan 1991; Vanberg 1994).[5] Hence, what is to be judged a "good" economic state or process depends exclusively on the identically weighted preferences of the individuals concerned.

To be sure, this principle can be made operational in a variety of different ways. First, we sketch the way it is applied within mainstream normative economics; then, we propose an alternative approach.

From the perspective of mainstream normative economics, the practical application of the normative individualistic principle makes use of the criterion of *Pareto efficiency*, which is linked to the concept of market failure by the first fundamental theorem of Welfare Economics. The market failure concept plays a fundamental heuristic role: Conscious institutional design is necessary if the market does not perform perfectly, as indicated by the divergence between private and social marginal costs and benefits of economic action. Zero divergence ("efficiency") is set up as a social goal in an aprioristic way. This efficiency notion has been rightly rejected by evolutionary scholars as being a static concept that can only be used to measure the arrangement of a given set of elements within a closed social system. From an evolutionary perspective, the elements to be arranged cannot be taken as given; rather, their genesis and diffusion is what has to be examined. Thus, what counts is to look at how open social systems that are capable of endogenously generating novelty *develop* in a continuous way.

If we conceptualize the economy as a complex system that exhibits continuous self-transformation, there appear to be two aspects that are normatively relevant: First, it seems plausible to conjecture that the individual users of the economic system want it to be adaptive, i.e., its principal capacity to develop endogenously and to generate novelty to be maintained. This aspect plays a key role in the few endeavors into normative territory that evolutionary economists have undertaken so far. Put simply, the corresponding goal can be labeled "adaptive efficiency" (North 1999).

There is however a second aspect that has so far been largely neglected in Evolutionary Economics: There is no reason to assume a priori that the novelty which is generated in the course of the dynamic interplay between individual agents is inherently a "good" thing. Historically, besides their doubtless beneficial long-term effects,[6] new technologies, products, and production processes have often caused hardship among a subset of the individuals concerned (see Witt 1996) – either as pecuniary externalities, or as hitherto unknown risks, or as long-term negative impacts on the diffusion of certain social norms, etc. The undesired consequences ("undesired" at least by a subset of the individuals affected) associated with innovation in a wide sense can be resumed as negative *distributional* effects. Arguably, any normative branch within Evolutionary Economics should be able to evaluate these effects as well as the adaptive efficiency aspect described above. Note, though, that there is a tension between these two goals – the first one referring to the characteristics of social processes, the second one to the characteristics of (temporary) social states.

In light of the second – distributional – aspect, the orthodox normative concept of market failure can be substituted by a concept first proposed by Buchanan (1977) and Schelling (1978: ch.1): If the spontaneously evolved macro result of the individuals' micro behavior is negatively judged by one or several individuals, then there is a prima facie case for *spontaneous disorder*. Trivial examples delivered by Buchanan and Schelling include littered beaches and un-coordinated seating arrangements in theaters and university lecture rooms: By their interdependent actions, the individual agents unconsciously produce a certain macro result, which at least some of them subjectively regard as "undesirable" ex post. If we start from the hypothetical imperative of normative individualism, these assessments certainly have to be taken seriously, i.e., they have to be considered as normatively relevant. While it is of course true that any evolving economic system will regularly generate a huge amount of spontaneous disorder, which makes this concept quite impracticable at first sight,[7] it is nonetheless useful as a heuristic device: Evolutionary economists engaged in normative reasoning should not overlook the undesirable side-effects of novelty. To be operational, the concept of spontaneous disorder needs to be complemented by a criterion as to which subset of "negative distributional patterns" should be classified as problematic. This will be the main task of the remainder of this chapter.

8.3   The contractarian approach, as seen from an evolutionary perspective

8.3.1   The general outline

It was presumably the political philosopher Thomas Hobbes who first introduced the contractarian perspective in his *Leviathan* in 1651. He argued that from within an anarchical state of nature, where he imagined life to be "solitary, poor, nasty, brutish and short" every individual would reasonably agree to set up an omnipotent sovereign power that would establish social order by fiat. A central Leviathan would, under these conditions, benefit everyone, hence be generally acceptable and, thus, *legitimate*. In the twentieth century, contractarian thought has been revitalized by Buchanan and Tullock (1965) and John Rawls (1971/1995). At the outset it should be emphasized that within its modern versions, the theoretically constructed "social contracts" that define the social order agreed to by the individuals are not meant to serve as empirical hypotheses. Rather, they have to be understood as hypothetical normative models, i.e., as "thought-experiments". For their function is not to gain empirical, but normative insights into the legitimacy of alternative policy measures.[8] Unfortunately, this basic misunderstanding is still widespread in the literature.[9]

As opposed to utilitarianism, which dominates mainstream welfare theory, contractarianism offers the "general voluntary consent" of the individuals affected as the main criterion to comparatively judge the constitutional rules of the game. This is directly derived from the principle of Normative Individualism: in the contractarian perspective, the latter implies that "the desirability, and legitimacy, of constitutional arrangements is to be judged in terms of the preferences of, and the voluntary agreement among, the individuals who live under (or are affected by) the arrangements" (Vanberg 2004: 154).

Moreover, contractarianism differs from utilitarianism in its conception of individual rights (hence, with regard to a procedural aspect): While utilitarianism aims at maximizing the *aggregate* of individual utilities, without regard to a policy's impact on individual utility levels (and, a fortiori, on individual rights positions), contractarianism aims at securing individual rights and maintaining their compatibility in the light of changing circumstances. In a very general sense, this gives it a *Kantian* orientation. Put somewhat emphatically, while utilitarianism gives priority to the Good, contractarianism puts the Right at center stage, in the sense that individual rights are legitimatorily prior to individual well-being (or utility or wealth); they demarcate the sphere within which well-being can be maximized.[10] The difference between utilitarian and Kantian approaches is a fundamental one. In his focus on procedural criteria in general, and the value of individual rights in particular, Hayek can for instance also be regarded a Kantian (Gray 1998).

Today, contractarian thinking plays a key role within Constitutional Economics.[11] It is operationalized as follows. Constitutional Economics starts from the analytical distinction between rules of the (market) game and single moves within the game. While the former are defined and continuously re-defined on the constitutional stage, the latter take place on the sub-constitutional stage. The totality of the rules of the game constitutes the market order – thus, the latter is conceptualized as a bundle of institutions. It is essential to note that the scope of gains from exchange that is realizable at any point in time is defined relative to the set of constitutional market rules. For it is the latter that define the individuals' economic opportunities to act. Hence, there is no economic (market) evolution *per se*; it is rather conceptualized as taking place under a specific set of market rules. The market's beneficial effects are of a fundamentally conditional nature. Therefore, the "efficiency" concept has to be modified – efficiency can only be defined relative to a given set of constitutional rules, i.e., relative to the specific set of opportunities that is constituted by these rules.

Thus, if economic evolution generates "undesirable" results (i.e., spontaneous disorder), this establishes a prima facie case for modifying the rules of the game. There is thus no such thing as a market failure but rather contingent cases of institutional or indeed state failure: "[T]hose market actors who are especially faced with a wealth-decreasing fall-out from the 'creative destructors'... will have an interest in changing the rules of the game against innovation or creative destruction, or in protecting 'old' (non-innovative) resource combinations" (Röpke 1990: 118). It is the rules that are the object of constitutional discourse and constitutional agreement. For by voluntarily agreeing to a set of mutual behavioral constraints, individuals can generate a cooperative surplus; this institutional exchange constitutes the social order: "[I]ndividuals choose to impose constraints on their own behavior (...) as a part of an exchange in which the restrictions on their own actions are sacrificed in return for the benefits that are anticipated from the reciprocally extended restrictions on the action of others" (Buchanan 1990: 4).

After having sketched the principal analytical outline of constitutional economics, we now have to take a closer look at the social contract notion that constitutes the core element of normative constitutional economics. In the contractarian view, collective decisions are legitimate insofar as they can plausibly be reconstructed as being the product of a (fictitious) agreement among the (real) members of society who gather in an (artificially modeled) state of nature or "original position" in order to choose among alternative rule arrangements.[12] The original position and the specific way it is modeled play a central role in the contractarian thought-experiment. It serves as a correcting device that forces the individuals to adopt an "impartial" position when deliberating and voting about alternative rules of the game. The way this impartial position is modeled constitutes the core theoretical problem of any contractarian approach. Generally, conditions of impartiality are achieved by artificially restricting the informational endowment of the individuals – they are put behind the famous *veil of ignorance*, i.e., they do not know their personal social position in the sub-constitutional market game. This model forces even rational self-interested *homines oeconomici* to adopt a moral viewpoint and to consider the interests of all individuals affected when casting their vote. Hence, rationality (in the neoclassical sense) is forced into a moral straightjacket (Kersting 1996). As a methodology for developing normative statements, modern contractarianism draws upon the decision-theoretic rationality concept of neoclassical economics. After having completed the social contract thought-experiment, constitutional economists usually proceed by formulating some hypothetical positive statement of the form "Rule R is able to command general assent among the individuals concerned". Put simply, we could call such a rule putatively *agreeable*. Note that this statement is value-free – it is only the more or less complex method by which it has been developed that is built on normative assumptions.

As this chapter aims at exploring the ground for a normative branch within Evolutionary Economics, it has to be asked if the contractarian methodology sketched above can be unconditionally employed by evolutionary economists. Unfortunately, this is not the case. For there are two powerful criticisms, voiced by Hume on the one hand and Hayek on the other hand that have to be accounted for. These criticisms delimit the scope of contractarian approaches that are principally compatible with an evolutionary world-view. To anticipate briefly, only those approaches that are naturalistic (without however violating Hume's Law) and conventionalist as well as anti-constructivist in an epistemic sense will be allowed to join the club. Hence, the kind of legitimizing theory that can be integrated into Evolutionary Economics should be discernible after both the Humean and the Hayekian hurdle are successfully overcome. These hurdles will be described in the following sections.

8.3.2 Hume's objection

David Hume has developed a general critique of contractarianism that receives more and more attention today (Engländer 2002, Müller 2002).[13] According to him, Hobbes' assumption that a centralized, omnipotent Leviathan is necessary to establish social order is fundamentally flawed. For anarchy can be (and has been historically) overcome by decentralized means, namely informal *conventions*. First of all, after Hume, these spontaneously evolving and self-enforcing institutions are historically prior to any formally designed rules. This obviously comes close to a genuinely evolutionary perspective on the economy, *avant la lettre*. By itself it is, however, no strong objection, for modern contractarians do not use Hobbes' story as an empirical hypothesis. According to Hume, though, informal conventions are also prior in a normative sense: For there is no reason to assume that a *fictitious* contract – or a real one, agreed upon centuries ago, for that matter – has any binding force per se on contemporarily living *real* individuals (see Hume 1748/1992). Even my own agreement to a contract, given yesterday, does not in itself bind me today. Assuming otherwise means to commit a logical fallacy, viz. a logically invalid inductive conclusion: If it is rational to make a certain decision in situation A (say, the original position), it does not follow that it is also rational to make the same decision in situation B (say, a real-world setting).[14] Put differently, if it is rational for agent *i* to agree upon the terms of a social contract, it does not logically follow that it would also have been rational for agent *j* to do so. Rather, in order to get the necessary binding force, some prior social norm (or "convention")[15] has to be introduced, as for instance the social norm to abide by contractual agreements ("*pacta sunt servanda*"). In his essay "Of the Original Contract", Hume rhetorically asks the reader: "[W]hy are we bound to keep our word? Nor can you give an answer, but what would, immediately, without any circuit, have accounted for our obligation to allegiance" (Hume 1748/1992: 456). This normatively expected social norm is logically prior to any formal, "artificially" set up social contract.

Thus, for Hume, the contract metaphor itself becomes obsolete: Either you abide by the contractual terms because of some internalized social norm; or it is in your pure rational self-interest to do it anyway. Hume's social philosophy disposes of the social contract altogether – it gets eliminated by Occam's razor. Concluding from this exercise in applied logic, we can say that in the long-run, constitutional rules are only viable if they are enforced by either (1) some underlying effectively binding social norm or (2) by the pure rational self-interest of the individuals concerned.

The second option, however, does not lead us very far. If we understand the "pure rational self-interest" in purely subjectivist terms, the resulting hypothetical statements about the content of the social contract will either be indeterminate and, hence, useless for our purposes (for everything depends on ad hoc assumptions about what the inhabitants of the anarchical state of nature want, or their individual bargaining power, or both),[16] or it will possibly conflict with our own moral intuitions. This is, for instance, the case with Buchanan's (1975) attempt to construct a radically subjectivist version of the contractarian model. From this perspective, even a slave-holder society may be judged legitimate if relative bargaining powers are such that in anarchy, the slave's position may be even worse than under the terms of the social contract.

Our basic model of normative reasoning (introduced in Section 8.2.2, above) allows us to see the major pitfall in this argument. The strong conflict with widely held moral intuitions indicates already that something may be wrong with Buchanan's argument. His approach can be criticized by testing its compatibility with the normative-individualistic premise that Buchanan himself of course subscribes to.[17] If the slave, given that his expected utility in anarchy would be even lower, opts for the contract that establishes a slave-holder relationship, this hardly represents a case of *voluntary* agreement. Arguably it is implausible to consider such effectively involuntary choices as normatively relevant – for they probably do not properly reveal the agent's actual preferences. Hence, the project of building the contractarian method on a radically subjectivist foundation does not deliver plausible results. Vanberg (1994) has suggested a "cost-avoidance" criterion that permits to discriminate between voluntary and forced acts: A choice counts as voluntary (and, hence, normatively relevant) if the choosing agent disposes of alternative options at "low" costs. Apart from technical problems (what does "low" mean?), it has to be stressed that this marks a first step toward a qualitative ranking of individual preferences – in this case, according to their genesis.[18] What is more, the ranking is made plausible by reference to the reader's "moral intuition" on what it means (within the reader's cultural context) to make a genuine "voluntary" choice. Thus, Buchanan's (1975) approach shows that without further qualifications, the concept of rational self-interest does not provide a sufficient basis for the contractarian argument. What is rather needed is information on (1) the genesis and (2) the content of individual preferences.[19]

Hence, the contractarian argument should be based on insights into the determinants of individual preferences. Broadly speaking, investigating these determinants requires insights into (1) the "nature of man", i.e., man's biological heritage, such as, for example, the basic learning mechanisms that have evolved during the "environment of evolutionary adaptation" (Binmore 1998). What is arguably more important, however, are (2) insights into the transmission mechanisms that are at work during the relatively rapid processes of *cultural* evolution. According to the fundamental "continuity hypothesis" (Witt 2000), the latter is to be seen as a continuation of biological evolution, albeit with different means.[20] Cultural learning mechanisms are based on, but not determined by, the results of biological processes.

In light of this account of the relationship between biological and cultural evolution, what can be achieved by introducing insights into the origin and content of individual preferences in the methodological toolbox of contractarianism may be dubbed a "naturalistic" or "conventionalist" strategy. In what follows, the second notion will be employed. Hume's critique can then be used in a constructive way by systematically linking key notions of the contractarian model to the set of informal social norms of a given society. These social norms constitute what may be dubbed society's "normative framework" (Engländer 2000). It specifies the agents' motivation to abide by the terms of the social contract. Note that this is of course not meant to deny that individuals, when reasoning about their compliance with the constitutional rules of the game, generally rely on their rational self-interest. This, however, does not tell us anything about the concrete substance of their preferences and about the way individuals perceive the components of their self-interest. Arguably, specifying those social norms that effectively constrain the agents' behavior can provide a means to discern this substance. What individuals take to be their self-interest is, among other factors, also shaped by the social norms they adopt.

Summing up, Hume's objection can be fruitfully used to derive two conditions that *any* contractarian theory should comply with. As the Humean criticism is a very general one, the conditions apply irrespectively of being viewed from an evolutionary or a neoclassical angle. As will be seen, however, the Humean conditions do have a distinctly evolutionary flavor in the sense of calling for theoretical efforts that are best delivered by Evolutionary Economics.

In order to overcome Hume's hurdle, contractarianism has to drop some ballast in the sense of qualifying two traditionally held pretensions. First, most of its conclusions will hold only for a social order that is already existing. Hence, the contractarian argument can be used to structure and guide constitutional *reforms* from within a given institutional structure.[21] Note that this does not necessarily mean that no universal statements are possible. In order to get meaningful results, on the one hand positive enquiries into the "normative framework" of the relevant population are a desideratum. This requires taking a conventionalist perspective which avoids to set a priori assumptions about the content of social norms. On the other hand, according to the continuity hypothesis it makes sense to assume that there does exist a set of fundamental human needs whose examination may help to identify some common features of human institutions, such as, for example, universally shared basic fairness norms. Conjectures on these norms may then be used to develop original position models; note, however, the difference to the traditional, non-empirically founded aprioristic way to define these models.

Second, it has to be emphasized that the methodology sketched above obviously does not circumvent Hume's logical induction problem. The contractarian thought-experiment does not allow us to make any strong deductive inferences about the relative "goodness" of alternative constitutional arrangements – rather it should be seen as a *heuristic* device that can inform and guide collective decision-making. By means of social contract theory, hypothetical statements can be formulated as to the capacity of constitutional rules to command general assent – these hypotheses serve as informed proposals that can be presented to those very individuals who, according to the premise of normative individualism, have the exclusive sovereign right to decide.

Hence, the status of contractarian statements has been qualified in two regards: First, while the basic structure of the original position model may reflect universally accepted fairness norms, practical statements may not reach any more beyond the very population or society that is the object of enquiry at any point in time. These statements are, then, culturally and historically contingent. Second, their methodological status has been somewhat downgraded: They are not to be understood as products of a deductive syllogism, i.e., as rock-solid logical insights. Rather, they should be seen as hypothetical statements. This derives from the hypothetical consensus concept that is unavoidably employed due to the prohibitive transaction costs of organizing *factual* agreements. If agreement is not understood as a practical "in-period decision rule," but as a "legitimizing principle" or, to use the Kantian term, "regulative idea",[22] the contractarian results can necessarily only claim a modest status. As Kersting puts it,

> the usefulness of the hypothetical contract metaphor as a model for the legitimization of social and political principles does not hinge on the possibility to justify the principles [derived by contractarianism, C.S.] by pointing to any factual agreement on the part of the agents concerned; rather it hinges on there being *good reasons* for the allegation that the participants ought to have *reasonably* agreed upon such a covenant, and that they therefore should comply with the principles derived from it as if they would have agreed to them personally.
>
> Kersting (1996: 265, italics in the original)[23]

8.3.3 Hayek's objection

The second major criticism raised against contractarianism is explicitly motivated by an evolutionary model of the economic system. According to Hayek, any attempt to consciously design formal institutions in order to influence the results of the market game runs the risk of damaging the market's knowledge-processing capacities. With its explicit aim to design the constitutional framework of the market order, contractarianism unavoidably became an easy target of Hayek's.[24]

Due to spatial restrictions, the complex (and sometimes contradictory) argument of his will be only sketched in what follows. For the purposes of this chapter, it is important to discuss three points. First, Hayek introduces an explicitly evolutionary (viz., epistemic) interpretation of the "welfare contribution" of complex economic systems; second, he stresses the epistemic constraints of any attempt to consciously influence market processes in order to avoid "undesired" and to bring about "desired" allocative or distributive patterns; third, he occasionally acknowledges that any spontaneous order necessarily relies also on basic formal institutional provisions (the products of "reason"), like, for example, legally enforced property rights.

Concerning the first point, Hayek stresses the difference between a closed "economic" and an open "catallactic" system. While the former (in the literal sense of the Greek "oikos") represents a constant set of fixed elements – as, for instance, economic resources – that can be re-arranged so as to yield a maximum gain, the latter represents a highly complex, continuously evolving open set of economic opportunities, where decentralized decisions by individual agents (based on their mostly tacit subjective knowledge) bring about macro phenomena in an unpredictable way. Epistemologically spoken, these macro phenomena store more knowledge than any single agent or organization could ever gather, let alone process. Thus, for Hayek, the essential feature that distinguishes the spontaneous market order is its capacity to process huge amounts of ever novel economic knowledge – rather than its capacity to allocate given resources in a welfare-maximizing way, as suggested by orthodox welfare theory. In the light of the Hayekian welfare criterion (i.e., the system's capacity to process decentralized knowledge), the degree of individual freedom, i.e., the scope of individual opportunities to act, comes to the fore. Starting thus from some fundamental epistemological insights, Hayek arrives at a Kantian-like position on individual rights – the only peculiarity being Hayek's *instrumental* justification for the (procedural) goal of maximizing the individuals' chances to attain their subjective goals.

As regards the second point, since no single agent or group of agents can ever attain the degree of economic knowledge that is involved in spontaneously emerging market patterns and results, it follows that economic policy is confronted with a fundamental epistemic dilemma. Designers of institutions, such as lawmakers, can never be perfectly certain about the direct and indirect effects of their interventions. In an open catallactic system, individual agents affected by policy measures can always find creative ways to react to them – as these reactions cannot be perfectly anticipated, there is an irreducible element of surprise involved in any attempt to intervene in the market order (Wegner 1997).

In this context, Hayek suggests that the spontaneous market order relies on a specific kind of institutional foundation – which he calls "Nomos". According to Hayek, it is only on the basis of informal "rules of just conduct" which themselves are the product of processes of cultural evolution that the market order can display its epistemic advantages. In this view, consciously designed rules ("theseis") – embodying, as they do, only theoretical knowledge, which is inferior to the *cultural* knowledge implicit in the "nomoi" – are only adequate within closed, hierarchically organized systems, such as business firms. Hence, Hayek develops normative statements about the adequate institutional framework of alternative kinds of social order.

Concerning the third point, Hayek however has at times to admit that "nomoi" rules are actually not perfectly sufficient to constitute and maintain a stable market order. There are several sections in his works where he reluctantly concedes that there may be situations where it will be necessary to consciously design rules.[25] However, in his eyes any effort to this end runs the risk of inducing the temptation to manipulate large areas of the economic system. According to Hayek, this hubristic attempt involves a "pretence of knowledge" that in turn is based on a specific rationality concept which he calls "constructivist rationalism" (CR).[26] Unfortunately, it is unclear what is exactly meant by this awe-inspiring term: While at times, Hayek interprets as CR only those grand efforts that aim at *completely* reconstructing a given social order de novo,[27] at other times he appears to classify as CR any attempt to "better" single social institutions on the basis of the best theoretical knowledge available[28] – something which Constitutional Economics undoubtedly aims at. Hayekian scholars sometimes do not seem to remark this inconsistency: For instance, Langlois and Sabooglu (2001: 239, emphasis added) define CR as the doctrine according to which "human reason is capable of constructing a set of *ideal* institutions". On the other hand, they also argue that what Hayek means by CR is any attempt "to arrive at a government *based on reason*" (ibid., emphasis added). However, the latter approach does not necessarily imply the former one. Again, that can be seen by means of our critical rationalist model of normative reasoning: It is possible to rationally discuss alternative ways to better the social order without ascribing some implausible utopian status ("*ideal* institutions") to the products of such a discourse.

To sum up, although Hayek time and again stresses the dangers of conscious policy – or constitutional rulemaking, he also repeatedly (albeit unsystematically) emphasizes the need to inject "constructivist" inputs into the process of institutional evolution. While from his scattered remarks on this issue hardly any theory can be distilled,[29] it is important to note that Hayek also introduces an "evolutionary" welfare criterion, viz. the maximization of the individuals' chances to attain their subjective goals. On the basis of this goal-setting, he then engages in an instrumental inquiry into alternative institutional arrangements. It is in this sense that Hayek may even be classified as a (crypto-)contractarian (Sugden 1993a; Gray 1998) – even if he actually does not offer a well-developed normative account.

Hence, the contractarian approach seems to be compatible in principle with a Hayekian view on economic systems. That means that we can use Hayek's objections in a constructive way by deriving two conditions that any contractarian approach should satisfy in order to be compatible with an evolutionary model of the economy. In particular, the contractarian method can be applied in order to help institutional evolution to overcome evolutionary "impasses", if

- the scope of *individual freedom* is taken to be a fundamental criterion when rules of the game are comparatively evaluated. Freedom is considered in its instrumental value to maintain the market's knowledge-generating capacity. The latter goal is best achieved when the individuals have the possibility to form *reliable expectations* as to the behavior of their partners in social interaction.[30] This in turn presupposes that institutional design proceeds in such a way that rules are only modified in a generally foreseeable way, i.e., that surprises are avoided (Lachmann 1971). In order to achieve this, the modest "immanent criticism" of given institutions is one strategy that has been proposed by Hayek himself (1976: 24). It tries to solve new policy problems by also relying on the practical knowledge inherent in the given institutional structure of society (see also Sugden 1993a);
- the precarious and fallible quality of the *governance knowledge* available, i.e., the knowledge on individual constitutional preferences as well as on the working properties of alternative rules of the game is explicitly taken into account. This is indeed a weak point of traditional Constitutional Economics: there it is often assumed that while individuals in the original position are ignorant about their own social positions in the post-constitutional stage, they do possess perfect instrumental knowledge on the effects of alternative rules, on economic means-ends-relationships, etc. Hence, in order to be "evolution-proof," contractarian theories should account for the need to generate positive and normative knowledge by, for example, experimental trial-and-error-approaches or appropriate social deliberation procedures. Put differently, they should evaluate given collective decision-making procedures as to their qualities in this respect.

8.3.4 The scope of "evolution-proof" contractarian theories

Summing up, we have identified three main conditions that any contractarian theory should fulfill in order to be employable by evolutionary economists. What we look for is a theory that

1 provides a systematic place for social norms. Thereby it may be possible to develop positive and testable hypotheses on the origin and content of the individuals' constitutional preferences. These hypotheses are taken into account when constitutional proposals on institutional design are developed. To be sure, it is up to the individuals themselves to accept or reject these proposals. Since under conditions of real-world scarcity, the general consensus can only be conceptualized as a "legitimizing principle" (rather than an

"in-period decision rule", see Vanberg 2003), collective decision-making procedures should be organized in such a way that unsatisfied individuals have adequate channels at their disposal to voice their viewpoints. Note that basing the contractarian argument on substantive hypotheses on the origin and content of individual constitutional preferences makes it harder to abuse the model in an ideological way.

2   Second, the theory should explicitly take into account the problem of how to continuously generate both positive and normative *governance knowledge*. The real-world place to do this is the system of collective decision-making procedures of a given polity. Note that the constitutional economist is only one of many policy counselling experts and "norm entrepreneurs" that attempt virtually daily to influence the individuals' attitudes and preferences on questions of institutional design. It is all the more important to make sure that her contributions be free from ideological (i.e., unfounded or disguised) value judgments.

What can be concluded from the combination of points (1) and (2) is a general preference for a gradual approach to institutional design and constitutional reform, i.e., one that proceeds along the given "normative framework" of a society ("immanent criticism") and one that allows for the experimental generation of new governance knowledge by proceeding in a piecemeal way.

3   Third and finally, the contractarian theory that is to be developed should offer us both a procedural criterion of how to value (possibly conflicting) individual rights in a non-instrumental (i.e., Kantian) way, and a criterion of how to judge alternative distributional patterns which emerge as a consequence of economic novelty. To be sure, what is to be judged are not the single temporary results of market processes *per se*, but rather those rules of the market game which influence the general pattern of market results (Vanberg 1999).

What is most important to note, though, is that in order to be compatible with an evolutionary world-view, contractarianism has to operate from within an ongoing social order, i.e., from within a given system of values, norms and preferences; this implies that it cannot attain any Archimedean point beyond specific cultural and historical contexts. In the following section, we briefly discuss one possible candidate for such a reconceptualization of the contractarian approach.

8.4   Rawls, with a twist

8.4.1   The basic idea

In what follows, a contractarian approach is discussed that arguably complies with the three conditions outlined above. It may serve as a cornerstone of a normative branch within Evolutionary Economics, because (1) it explicitly tries to embed the contractarian argument in the informal institutional framework of given social orders, (2) it aims at developing normative criteria that are to guide constitutional rule-design (rather than the manipulation of single sub-constitutional allocative and distributional patterns), and (3) it offers both a non-instrumental account of the value of individual *rights* and substantive criteria to evaluate alternative rules according to their *distributional* implications. What is more, the distributional criteria – which are a desideratum in the light of the "spontaneous disorder" problem – are both economically rational and "internally" derived from the pre-existing institutional background of the society under review.

The political philosopher John Rawls is widely referred to as the main initiator of the renaissance of contractarian thought in the late twentieth century (Kersting 1996: ch. 9). He has developed a highly original contractarian methodology which will be proposed as the cornerstone of a normative branch within Evolutionary Economics. First, the general outlook of his theory is presented. Then, a specific aspect is discussed that is neglected by most contemporary critics of Rawls' – such as, for instance, Binmore (1998). Before that can be done, though, the basic outline of his approach is described.

By means of his concept of "justice as fairness", developed in his *Theory of Justice* (Rawls 1971/1995; Rawls 1958/1999), Rawls aims at deriving a set of fundamental principles of justice that shall govern the design of society's "basic structure". The latter term encompasses all rules and procedures that regulate the distribution of basic resources, i.e., the principles of justice serve "to assign basic rights and duties and to determine the division of social benefits" (Rawls 1971/1995: 11). Thus it is not the detailed distribution of dollars or euros that is to be regulated, but rather the distribution of multi-purpose goods like rights and entitlements.[31] This distribution directly hinges on the constitutional provisions as specified in a society's "social contract".

From a general economic perspective, Rawls' approach is interesting for two main reasons. First, as seen above, his social philosophy is explicitly focused on the normative analysis of the basic institutional structure of society rather than on the normative examination of single economic interactions on the marketplace. Second, he conceptualizes society as a cooperative arrangement, i.e., as a positive-sum game: He explicitly takes account of the economic insight that there is a trade-off between allocative efficiency and distributional equity.[32] For that reason, outside completely static systems it does not make economic sense to simply equate justice with equality. In dynamic systems, growth necessarily implies deviations from the state of perfect equity.

Finally, in the light of the critical rationalist model of normative reasoning, it is worth noting that Rawls' approach explicitly starts from the assumption of a *plurality* of values. This makes it necessary to qualify the status of the contractarian results – they are meant to be derived from a *political* agreement, rather than from some metaphysical insights. As Sugden (1993b: 1957) puts it, in a pluralistic setting "[t]he political problem is to find a basis on which individuals who disagree on metaphysics and morals can nevertheless cooperate with mutual respect". Rawls looks for a genuinely political (instead of philosophical) conception of justice, since according to him, it is inadequate to aim at some higher "truth" in the realm of collective decision-making (Rawls 1999: 132f., 169f.).[33] On a fundamental level, this orientation makes his approach compatible with the critical rationalist account of normativity.

Rawls follows the basic contractarian logic in arguing that the way the benefits and costs of the processes of social cooperation are distributed is "just", if it corresponds to principles that rational agents would plausibly have agreed upon under "fair" conditions. This fairness proviso refers to the specific way the original position is modeled.

The original position model includes assumptions about the kind of information available to the individuals (the "thickness" of the veil of ignorance), the individuals' preferences (e.g., for risk), and a normative rule concerning the weight of the individual preferences in the process of deriving social welfare judgments. The whole contractarian methodology is centered around the precise specification of the original position.

Assuming that on the constitutional stage, the individuals do not dispose of any information as to the position they will take in the future sub-constitutional market game, Rawls develops two positive substantive hypotheses about the agents' choice behavior under these conditions. First, he conjectures them to behave in a very risk-averse way, i.e., to choose according to the *maximin* criterion: That is, when selecting among the available sets of constitutional rules, they will focus exclusively on their respective worst consequence – they then choose the set that displays the, for them, "best" worst consequence.

On the basis of this decision-theoretic assumption, Rawls concludes that behind the veil of ignorance, rational agents will agree upon the *Difference Principle*. It includes two sub-principles and one priority rule:

1   Each person is to have an equal right to the most extensive total system of equal basic liberties compatible with a similar system of liberty for all.
2   Social and economic inequalities are to satisfy two conditions. First, they must be attached to offices and positions open to all under conditions of fair equality and opportunity; and second, *they must be to the greatest benefit of the least advantaged members of society.*

(Rawls 1971/1995: 302, emphasis added)

He explains the second principle as follows: "[T]he higher expectations of those better situated are just if and only *if they work as part of a scheme* which improves the expectations of the least advantaged."[34]

The principles are complemented by the following priority rule: "The principles of justice are to be ranked in lexical order and therefore liberty can be restricted only for the sake of liberty." [35]

Note that the Difference Principle offers preliminary answers to the two main desiderata of any normative theory within Evolutionary Economics (as identified in Section 8.3, above): First, it determines a non-instrumental weight – or "value" – for individual rights; in this sense, it is compatible with the Hayekian concern for the extent of individual liberty. Secondly, it formulates a criterion for evaluating alternative distributional patterns; in this sense, it gives an answer to the question raised by our proposal to substitute the Buchanan-Schelling concept of spontaneous disorder for the orthodox concept of market failure.

Hence, according to Rawls, every member of society should be granted a minimum endowment of basic multi-purpose resources; at the same time, no individual should be systematically excluded from sharing in the cooperative surplus generated by the very mutual behavioral constraints that will be agreed upon on the constitutional stage.

The way the Difference Principle is derived by Rawls has been extensively criticized in the literature (Harsanyi 1975, Binmore 1998); the critics have, however, mostly missed the main point about this principle. This shall be briefly shown in the following.

Harsanyi (1975) has rightly raised the objection that behind the Rawlsian veil of ignorance (as, for that matter, in real-life situations), no rational agent, even if endowed with a reasonable degree of risk-aversion, would ever choose the maximin principle.[36] Rather, a rational individual would vote for the set of constitutional rules that maximizes her own expected utility in the sub-constitutional market game. Since by assumption, the agents do not hold any objective information about the probability of taking any sub-constitutional position, they rationally assume taking any conceivable position with *equal* probability.[37] Thus, they choose the rule (or set of rules) that maximizes *average* utility, without any regard for the distributional implications – thereby, they end up with a utilitarian welfare criterion.

While within the methodological framework of decision theory, Harsanyi is certainly right, his argument demonstrates nonetheless that there is something wrong with applying this logic for contractarian purposes. The whole problem originates in the standard contractarian approach (also taken by Rawls) to equate the agents' choice situation behind the veil of ignorance with the choice situation of an autonomous single agent in real-life settings. For if the veil is sufficiently thick, all agents dispose of identical information (or rather, non-information) concerning the characteristics of the sub-constitutional market game. In that case, their choice behavior can be reconstructed by modeling the choice behavior of a single representative agent. Thus, under these highly artificial conditions, social and individual choice become identical.[38]

It is however a *non-sequitur* to reduce social choice to individual choice, for the following reason. There is a categorical difference between individual and collective choice behavior under uncertainty.[39] In the former case, it is perfectly rational for a single agent to choose a strategy (say, driving by car) that involves a small risk of resulting in a negative payoff (a deadly accident), if the overall expected utility is still positive or sufficiently high (depending on the agent's risk preference). In the latter case, though, following this logic cannot be assumed to be collectively rational a priori. For if a utilitarian (hence, distributively blind) rule is chosen, there is a positive probability that some members of society will effectively end up in a situation where they do *not* dispose of the Rawlsian minimum resource endowment. Then, the resulting distributional pattern will not be acceptable for these agents, in the sense of not being defendable as resulting from the application of a justifiable rule. A rule that is agnostic on distributional outcomes cannot plausibly be defended on the basis of the principle of normative individualism. Seen from a non-normative angle, such a rule cannot be expected to be *viable* in the long run, because there will systematically emerge a subset of losing agents who will reject the rule.

Hence, we are stuck in a methodological dilemma. If the contractarian methodology shall rely on economic rationality concepts and decision-theoretic arguments, the original position's "fairness" conditions (i.e., the "moral straightjacket" for rational self-interest) have to be modified. Otherwise it cannot be taken for granted that applying the contractarian method systematically yields generally agreeable results (viz. normative statements implying generally acceptable constitutional principles). This is a desideratum for future research.

What is more important for the purpose of this paper, though, is the normative intuition that underlies Rawls' Difference Principle. According to Rawls, a contractual agreement is legitimate only if it can be made sure that no individual member of society will be systematically discriminated ex post (in the sense of being completely excluded from society's cooperative surplus or the benefits of novelty). In the end, the maximin principle appears to be just a technically flawed expression for a plausible normative idea – which itself will have to be further specified, to be sure. In the following subsection it is however not the material content of the Rawlsian "principles of justice", but the *procedure* by which they can be developed that plays a key role. For first and foremost, what Rawls offers is a procedural theory of justice.

8.4.2   *Toward a conventionalist development of the "original position"*

For the purpose of the present paper, the most important feature of Rawls' approach is the fact that he actually combines two different legitimization procedures in order to derive agreeable principles of justice. Besides the traditional contractual method described above, he employs a "coherentist" method (O'Neill 1998, Kersting 1996: ch. 9). This is discussed in what follows.

As shown above, the specification of the original position and its informational structure plays a key role in any contractarian theory. The informational constraints serve as a model of the "moral viewpoint" a fictitious impartial observer would adopt. Underlying this model is a set of normative statements about what kind of arguments are considered acceptable or even convincing in a normative discourse.

In order to specify such a model, one has to choose one out of two possible procedures. The model can either be defined in a non-empirical (e.g., a cognitivist) way (Harsanyi 1982). This is the approach Kant himself arguably took when he proposed the original position *cum* social contract metaphor as a model for the categorical imperative – which, in turn, was based on purely theoretical, rationalistic (i.e., non-empiristic) reasoning. According to Kant, reason alone (if engaged in by a well-minded person) can recognize the content of the "golden rule" whose reasonability he took as self-evident (Kant 1793/1977).

As an alternative, an empirically informed perspective can be taken. This in turn opens the way toward either (a) a *naturalistic* or (b) a *conventionalist* justificatory strategy. In both cases, normative reasoning has its starting point not in the social philosopher's armchair, but rather in an empirical enquiry into the moral intuitions and social norms that actually do prevail in the historical-cultural setting under consideration. Hence, the individuals' moral *common sense* is set at center stage in the contractarian argument. Its origin and content is explored in order to derive normative statements (about both the appropriate structure of the contractarian model and the contractarian conclusions) that are more in line with what in fact shapes the constitutional preferences of real-world individuals. The chances of voluntary compliance with the constitutional rules are thereby increased. While a naturalistic strategy focuses on the purely biological origins of basic moral instincts, such as the human capacity to adopt an empathic position with regard to other individuals (see, e.g., Binmore 1998),[40] a conventionalist strategy is directed toward examining how these moral instincts emerge in the course of cultural evolution.[41] Arguably, Rawls follows this second approach, when he suggests that the empirically prevailing social norms should guide the specification of the contractarian original position. Hence, instead of using an a priori definition, he proposes to explicitly develop the contents of the original position; in other words, the key component of the contractarian model is endogenized (O'Neill 1998). This *"Humean"* strategy avoids the pitfalls implied by falling back on some fictitious Archimedean position when trying to model a universally acceptable perspective of impartiality. Rather, what precisely counts as "impartial" depends on what the individuals concerned take it to be. This endogenous approach does not by itself imply anything about the relative weight of biological versus cultural factors in the development of moral intuitions and attitudes. In particular, it does not exclude the possibility that some very basic components of the moral common sense are indeed *universal* in character, while their concrete specifications differ across cultural contexts.

In the light of our basic model of normative reasoning, it becomes evident that any non-aprioristic strategy runs the risk of violating Hume's Law. The temptation to directly derive normative statements (about the adequate mode of the original position, say) from purely descriptive ones (about the empirically prevailing social norms or moral instincts) does bedevil, for instance, the emerging school of "evolutionary ethics" (Wilson 1998: ch. 11). In order to avoid this fallacy, Rawls needs to construct a methodological bridge to overcome the gap between the is- and the ought-world.[42] To this end, he suggests a *public deliberation procedure* which takes the individual moral intuitions and the collectively shared social norms of a given society as a ("crude") input and transforms them into a set of abstract principles of justice. Thereby, reflective agreement gains a systematic place within the contractarian architecture: Before normative conclusions can be drawn, empirically given social norms and moral views have to be made the object of conscious reasoning and have to be generally agreed upon.

The abstract principles of justice shall be gained in the course of a rule-guided multi-step procedure. Assume that there are three classes of individual preferences, namely ordinary preferences (with respect to consumer goods or social interaction), *constitutional* preferences, concerning matters of institutional design (they are used as input into the contractarian original position model), and *moral* preferences that concern the adequate design of the original position model itself, i.e., that reflect the fundamental moral views of the individuals.[43] Rawls proposes the following approach: The individuals, participating at a given constitutional discourse, move first by expressing their more or less well-specified moral preferences, as shaped by their underlying moral intuitions and commonly shared social norms. As this will result in a vast amount of "normative knowledge" which will be both non-operational and highly contradictory (and partly non-sensical, too), social philosophy enters the stage and gets the task of summarizing these statements, in the sense of distilling their common denominators. The few abstract principles that will have been formulated will then be suggested to the individuals, who probably will partly reject them, but who may also critically reflect on their own original statements and adjust them, etc. In the end, this interactive learning process will (ideally) result in a coherent set of abstract normative principles that properly reflect the generalizable core of the agents' moral views. These principles constitute what Rawls calls the "Reflective Equilibrium" of a polity.[44] Their main function is to guide the specification of the contractarian original position. The Reflective Equilibrium represents Rawls' idea of a genuinely political (compromise-based) agreement on normative issues, i.e., it dismisses with any metaphysical pretensions.[45] It rather reflects the essential components of society's "public political culture" (Rawls 1999) and is meant to serve as a minimum common basis for collective decision-making even within a pluralistic setting. Moreover, in spite of the misleading "equilibrium" notion, it is not meant to be developed once and to be statically valid thereafter. Rather, it serves as a device to solve normative problems, as long as it yields generally acceptable results. If this is no longer the case, it will be adjusted and modified accordingly.

Figure 8.2 illustrates the Rawlsian public deliberation process. A rule-guided (properly institutionalized) interactive learning process generates a coherent set of principles that constitute the "Reflective Equilibrium" (a). These results guide the specification of the original position device, which is still necessary in order to derive operational principles out of the day-to-day constitutional preferences of the members of society (b). Reflective Equilibrium and Original Position are to be understood as the key components of this conventionalist contractarian procedure: They are to be developed before the individuals' constitutional preferences can be processed; moreover, they are probably less variable than the constitutional preferences.

Note that in the end the Rawlsian approach is not *completely* procedural: The Reflective Equilibrium principles are also used to materially "double-check" the (relatively concrete) results of the application of the contractual device (c). Thus, in order to make sure that the results of the whole exercise are truly capable of commanding general assent, Rawls combines a procedural with a material quality control (Homann 1984). Specifying the substance of a given society's constitutional consensus turns out to be not only a complex, but also a continuously ongoing task. Finally, note that the moral intuitions and social norms of the individuals do also influence their day-to-day constitutional preferences (that are more directly involved in issues of day-to-day institutional design).

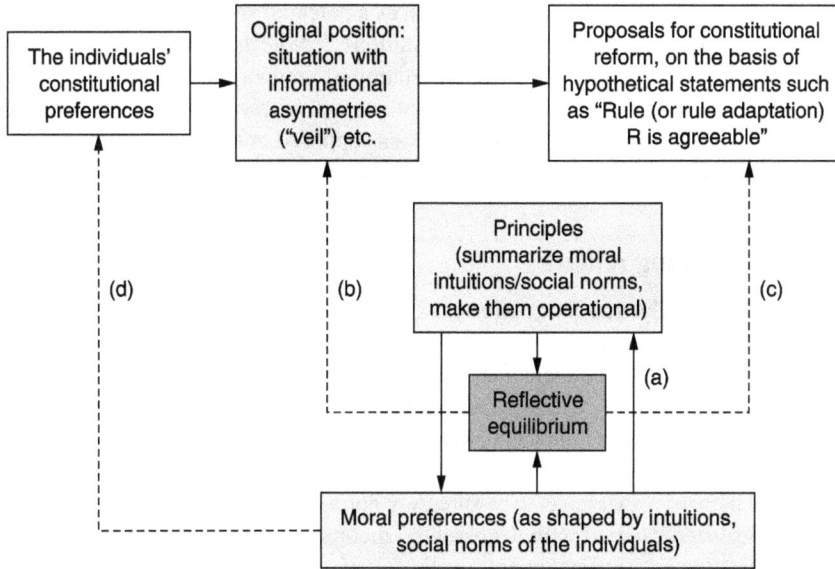

Figure 8.2 The double function of the "reflective equilibrium". Shaded boxes denote those components of the model that are to be understood as relatively less variable.

What do we actually gain by employing this conventionalist strategy? First, the contractarian methodology gets firmly rooted within the cultural context of the society under review. While this does not exclude the option to claim universal normative validity for a subset of the contractarian conclusions arrived at, it certainly implies a more relativistic stance than traditional social contract theory. Second, by anchoring the model in a given cultural context, it is now possible to "tap" the given institutional structure of society in order to derive testable hypotheses about the material content of the constitutional consensus at any point in time. Due to its radically subjectivist orientation, traditional constitutional economics is hardly able to give non-arbitrary answers to questions like, for example, what exactly is perceived as a "discriminatory" rule, what is it that makes collective decision-making procedures "fair", what constitutes a harmful "externality", or what kind of property rights contents are perceived as legitimate. Third, both a normative agnosticism as well as a constructivist introduction of external (Archimedean) normative criteria are avoided. While the individual preferences are taken to be the ultimate standard of judgment, and any social goal is only to be developed out of them, these preferences do of course change over time. In light of the complexities of matters of constitutional reform, it would make no sense to assume otherwise: "In the evolutionary perspective, the basis for normative judgments may change: ends and results of policy making are assessed in a way which itself evolves" (Witt 2003). While from the viewpoint of orthodox welfare theory, this creates tricky problems of consistency (v. Weizsäcker 2002), from the Rawlsian perspective sketched above preference change due to "constitutional learning"

(Buchanan and Vanberg 1991) is to be seen as a potential source of new productive knowledge on constitutional problem solutions.[46] Note finally that this view is also compatible with a Hayekian interpretation of democratic decision-making – which he understood as an institutionalized interactive learning process.[47] In more abstract terms, this denotes a *deliberation* – as opposed to the traditional Arrovian pure aggregation – view on individual preferences (Wohlgemuth 2002).

8.5   Concluding remarks

While it is trivially true that cultural evolution in and by itself does not pursue any "goal", i.e., cannot be conceptualized in a teleological manner, the individuals affected do ascribe their own subjective goals to it. From the viewpoint of Normative Individualism, this is normatively relevant. The individual users of socio-economic systems hold their own views about what socio-economic processes and temporary states should be avoided and which should be aimed at. These views are themselves variable, to be sure. Any normative branch within Evolutionary Economics is confronted with the essential theoretical challenge to develop well-substantiated normative statements on this slippery foundation.

The contractarian methodology, widely applied by constitutional economists, can cope with this problem if it is (1) firmly rooted in the given cultural context of society and if it (2) provides a systematic place for public deliberation processes. It is in this sense that culture as well as reason, both influenced by instinct, can be combined in the task of assessing institutional design. This allows not only to give more substance to the constitutional preferences of the individuals affected (based on testable hypotheses about the preferences' origins and material content); moreover, the *epistemic* dimension of policy-making and constitutional reform comes to the analytical fore. Collective (i.e., legislative, judiciary and administrative) decision-making procedures have to be assessed as to their capability to process and generate new constitutional knowledge. This encompasses both positive or theoretical knowledge on, for example, the working properties of alternative rules of the market game as well as normative knowledge on the preferences of the individuals. Both components cannot be assumed to be given, observable and constant a priori. This is what distinguishes the evolutionary approach to the positive and normative analysis of institutional design.

Notes

1   I am indebted to an anoymous referee and participants at the workshop on "The Evolution of Designed Institutions" for helpful comments. The usual disclaimer applies, of course.
2   North (1999: 79) who continues: "The recent interest in evolutionary economics is, however, a heartening development" (ibid.)
3   As can be demonstrated by, e.g., Harsanyi's (1982) attempt to justify utilitarianism (more precisely: the maximization of average utility levels) by contractarian means.
4   cf. Hume (1740/1978: Book III, part 1, ch. 1); for a skeptical position on this cf. Rorty (1991: ch. 11) and Wilson (1998: 238–56).

5 The term "social welfare judgment" does not by itself presuppose any "social welfare function", to be sure. The latter concept is rejected by the constitutional economics school (see, e.g., Buchanan 1959).

6 A point famously stressed by Schumpeter, see Witt (1996). Remember, however, Schumpeter's words about economic evolution implying manifold processes of "creative *destruction*".

7 Note, however, that this criticism also applies to the mainstream "market failure" approach.

8 cf. Kant (1793/1977): "Allein dieser Vertrag ist (…) keineswegs als ein Factum vorauszusetzen nöthig (ja als ein solches gar nicht möglich); (…) Sondern es ist eine *bloße Idee* der Vernunft, die aber ihre unbezweifelte (praktische) Realität hat: nämlich jeden Gesetzgeber zu verbinden, dass er seine Gesetze so gebe, als sie aus dem vereinigten Willen eines ganzen Volkes haben entspringen können, und jeden Untertan, so fern er Bürger sein will, so anzusehen, als ob er zu einem solchen Willen mit zusammen gestimmt habe. Denn das ist der Probirstein [sic] der Rechtmäßigkeit eines jeden öffentlichen Gesetzes." See also Buchanan (1977: 82, 124), Buchanan (1975: 54).

9 ... the first culprit probably being David Hume: "Almost all the governments, which exist at present, or of which there remains any record in story, have been founded originally, either on usurpation or conquest, or both, without any pretence of a fair consent, or voluntary subjection of the people." (as quoted by Kersting 1996: 250).

10 See Coleman and Murphy (1990: 71): "Kantianism, (...) very generally, is the view that the rational choice in ethics is always the choice that respects the rights of autonomous persons freely to determine their own destinies, even if this respect is bought at the cost of a loss of happiness or well-being."

11 See Vanberg (1999) for an excellent introduction.

12 cf. Buchanan (1959: 126, "presumptive efficiency"), Buchanan (1977: 129–30). If you nevertheless feel somehow uneasy about the parentheses, you are in good company – see David Hume's critique of contractarianism which will be discussed in due course.

13 Schlicht (1998) is a good introductory book on key aspects of Hume's work. See also Hayek (1991). Binmore (1998) explicitly relies on Hume's anti-contractarianism when developing his own social philosophy. See also Binmore (2001). Voigt's (1999) critique of the social contract notion is implicitly Humean.

14 cf. Müller (2002); see Sugden (1998) for an enquiry into Hume's theory of inductive inferences.

15 Strictly speaking, these notions should be properly distinguished, to be sure. In the present context, however, this would add nothing of substance to the argument.

16 Obviously, this makes the approach vulnerable to ideological abuse, cf. van Aaken/ Hegmann (2002).

17 cf. Buchanan (1990), Buchanan (1991).

18 cf. also Elster (1982) on the qualitative difference of preferences with respect to their genesis.

19 Note in passing that within welfare economics, too, the same problem has received more and more attention over the last years (Sen 1996b).

20 See also Tomasello (1999) for an elaboration of this hypothesis.

21 This is compatible with Buchanan's maxim that constitutional economists necessarily "start from here", where "here" denotes the given institutional structure of a society or the individuals' cultural context, see Buchanan (1997: 144).

22 cf. Vanberg (2003), Homann (1984).

23 My translation from: "Nicht weil die Verbindlichkeit [der kontraktualistisch abgeleiteten, C.S.] Grundsätze durch eine vertragliche Übereinkunft aller Betroffenen begründet werden könnte, kann die Vorstellung eines hypothetischen Vertrages als Modell der Rechtfertigung von sozialen und politischen Verfassungsprinzipien dienen, sondern allein deswegen, weil es *gute Gründe* für die Behauptung gibt, dass die beteiligten Parteien eine

derartige Vereinbarung *vernünftigerweise* hätten treffen sollen und dass sie darum die aus dieser Übereinkunft hervorgehenden Grundsätze betrachten sollten, als hätten sie ihnen zugestimmt."

24 cf., for instance, Hayek (1967: 86) and Hayek (1973: 10).

25 cf., e.g., Hayek (1973: 88, emphasis added): "The fact that all law arising out of the endeavour to articulate rules of conduct will of necessity possess some desirable properties not necessarily possessed by the commands of a legislator does *not* mean that in other respects such law may not develop in very undesirable directions, and that when this happens correction by deliberate legislation may not be the only practicable way out. For a variety of reasons the spontaneous process of growth may lead into an *impasse* from which it cannot extricate itself by its own forces or which it will at least not correct quickly enough." See also Hayek (1973: 45–46): "The spontaneous character of the [social] order must (...) be distinguished from the spontaneous origin of the rules on which it rests".

26 See, inter alia, Hayek (1949), Hayek (1973: 10, 24–6) and Hayek (1991).

27 In this context, Hayek (1949: 9) quotes Descartes: "[T]here is seldom so much perfection in works composed of many separate parts, upon which different hands had been employed, as in those completed by a single master."

28 See, e.g., Hayek (1967: 85).

29 cf. the assessment by Langlois and Sabooglu (2001: 241): "Hayek's position concerning social reforms is, at the very least, fuzzy."

30 Put differently, in that case "the several plans of action of different individuals become so adjusted to each other that they can be carried out in most cases" (Hayek 1973: 111).

31 From the Rawlsian point of view, it is irrelevant if the individual members of society effectively succeed in using these goods in a welfare- or autonomy-enhancing way; what counts is solely their initial assignment with basic resources.

32 See Rawls (1971/1995: 84), where he speaks of society as a "cooperative venture for mutual advantage".

33 Note the similarity to Buchanan's position, e.g., Buchanan (1959).

34 cf. Rawls (1971/1995: 75, emphasis added).

35 cf. Rawls (1971/1995: 302).

36 "If anybody really acted this way, he would soon end up in a mental institution" (ibid.: 595).

37 Here, Harsanyi relies on the Laplace rule.

38 Note the similarity to the utilitarian calculus, made by the (ideally omniscient) social planner. There, too, it is one single agent who effectively chooses what is best for the others.

39 See Hinsch (2002) for the following argument.

40 To illustrate, Binmore models empathic preferences as "Nature's answer" to the equilibrium selection problem in coordination games, see (ibid.: 209, 212).

41 Hume himself can be seen as a precursor of seeing the "rules of morality" not as pure "conclusions of our reason", but rather as the product of cultural evolution, cf. Hayek (1991).

42 On the relative applicability of methodological and logical bridges, see section 2.2, supra.

43 cf. Harsanyi's (1982) account of the "moral point of view" that individuals adopt when arguing about fundamental moral issues.

44 cf., e.g., Rawls (1971/1995: 20), Rawls (1999), O'Neill (1998), Homann (1984).

45 Its various *sources* can and often will be of metaphysical or religious character, to be sure. In the course of public deliberation, they are "translated" into the *lingua franca* of genuinely political parlance.

46 cf. also Schnellenbach (2002) for an attempt to model the diffusion of constitutional knowledge.

47 cf., for instance, Hayek (1960: 108f.).

References

Albert, H. (1988) 'Critical Rationalism: The Problem of Method in Social Sciences and Law', *Ratio Juris*, 1: 1–19.

Binmore, K. (1997) 'The Evolution of Fairness Norms', *Papers on Economics & Evolution* # 9704, Jena: Max-Planck-Institute of Economics.

Binmore, K. (1998) *Game Theory and the Social Contract, vol. II: Just Playing*, Cambridge, MA: MIT Press.

Binmore, K. (2001) 'Natural Justice and Political Stability', *Journal of Institutional and Theoretical Economics*, 157: 133–51.

Buchanan, J.M. (1959) 'Positive Economics, Welfare Economics, and Political Economy', *Journal of Law and Economics*, 2: 124–38.

Buchanan, J.M. (1975) *The Limits of Liberty*, Chicago: University of Chicago Press.

Buchanan, J.M. (1977) *Freedom in Constitutional Contract*, College Station: Texas A&M University Press.

Buchanan, J.M. (1990) 'The Domain of Constitutional Economics', *Constitutional Political Economy*, 1: 1–18.

Buchanan, J.M. (1991) 'The Foundations of Normative Individualism', in J.M. Buchanan (ed.) *The Economics and Ethics of Constitutional Order*. Ann Arbor: University of Michigan Press, pp. 221–31.

Buchanan, J.M. and Tullock, G. (1965) *Calculus of Consent*, Ann Arbor: University of Michigan Press.

Buchanan, J.M. and Vanberg, V.J. (1991) 'Constitutional Choice, Rational Ignorance and the Limits of Reason', *Jahrbuch für Neue Politische Ökonomie*, 10: 61–78.

Coleman, J.L. and Murphy, J.G. (1990) *Philosophy of Law*, Boulder: Westview Press.

Denis, A. (2002) 'Was Hayek a Panglossian Evolutionary Theorist? A Reply to Whitman', *Constitutional Political Economy*, 13: 275–85.

Dworkin, R.M. (1998) 'Darwin's New Bulldog', *Harvard Law Review*, 111: 1718–38.

Elster, J. (1982) 'Sour grapes – utilitarianism and the genesis of wants', in A.K. Sen and B. Williams (eds) *Utilitarianism and Beyond*, Cambridge: Cambridge University Press, pp. 219–38.

Engländer, A. (2000) 'Die neuen Vertragstheorien im Licht der Kontraktualismuskritik von David Hume', *Archiv für Rechts- und Sozialphilosophie*, 86: 2–28.

Frey, B.S., Oberholzer-Gee, F. and Eichenberger, R. (1996) 'The Old Lady Visits your Backyard: A Tale of Morals and Markets', *Journal of Political Economy*, 104: 1297–313.

Gray, J.N. (1998) *Hayek on Liberty*, 3rd ed. London: Routledge.

Harsanyi, J.C. (1975) 'Can the Maximin Principle Serve as a Basis for Morality? A Critique of John Rawls' Theory', *American Political Science Review*, 69: 594–606.

Harsanyi, J.C. (1982) 'Morality and the Theory of Rational Behavior', in A.K. Sen and N. Williams (eds) *Utilitarianism and Beyond*, Cambridge: Cambridge University Press, pp. 39–62.

Hausman, D.M. and McPherson, M.S. (1996) *Economic Analysis and Moral Philosophy*, Cambridge: Cambridge University Press.

Hayek, F.A. v. (1949) 'Individualism: True and False', in: *Individualism and Economic Order*, London: Routledge, pp. 1–32.

Hayek, F.A. v. (1960) *The Constitution of Liberty*, London: Routledge.

Hayek, F.A. v. (1967) *Studies in Philosophy, Politics and Economics*, Chicago: University of Chicago Press.

Hayek, F.A. v. (1973) *Law, Legislation and Liberty, vol. I: Rules and Order*, London: Routledge & Kegan Paul.

Hayek, F.A. v. (1976) *Law, Legislation and Liberty, vol. II: The Mirage of Social Justice*, Chicago: University of Chicago Press.

Hayek, F.A. v. (1991) 'The Legal and Political Philosophy of David Hume (1711–76)', in W.W. Bartley and S. Kresge (eds) *The Collected Works of F.A. Hayek*, vol. III., Chicago: University of Chicago Press, pp. 101–18.

Hegmann, H. (2000) 'Conventionalist foundations for collective action in a culturally frag-mented setting', *Hamburg University, Faculty of Economics Discussion Paper # 61*.

Hinsch, W. (2002) *Gerechtfertigte Ungleichheiten*, Berlin: De Gruyter.

Homann, K. (1984) 'Demokratie und Gerechtigkeitstheorie. J.M. Buchanans Kritik an J. Rawls', in H. Albert (ed.) *Ökonomisches Denken und soziale Ordnung*, Festschrift Boettcher, Tübingen: Mohr, pp. 133–54.

Hume, D. (1740/1978) *A Treatise of Human Nature*, 2nd ed., Oxford: Clarendon Press.

Hume, D. (1748/1992) 'Of the Original Contract', in: T. Hill Green and T.H. Grose (eds) *David Hume. The Philosophical Works*, vol. 3, Aalen: Scientia, pp. 443–60.

Kant, I. (1793/1977) 'Über den Gemeinspruch: Das mag in der Theorie richtig sein, taugt aber nicht für die Praxis' ['On the Old Saw: That May be Right in Theory, but it won't work in Practice'], in W. Weischedel (ed.) *Immanuel Kant Werkausgabe*, vol. XI., Frankfurt/Main: Suhrkamp, pp. 127–72.

Kersting, W. (1996) *Die politische Philosophie des Gesellschaftsvertrags*, Darmstadt: Primus.

Knight, J. (2001) 'A Pragmatist Approach to the Proper Scope of Government', *Journal of Institutional and Theoretical Economics*, 157, 28–48.

Lachmann, L.M. (1971) *The Legacy of Max Weber: Three Essays*, Berkeley: Glendessary.

Langlois, R.N. and Sabooglu, M.M. (2001) 'Knowledge and Meliorism in the evolution-ary theory of F.A. Hayek', in K. Dopfer (ed.) *Evolutionary Economics: Program and Scope*, Boston: Kluwer, pp. 231–51.

Müller, C. (2002) 'The methodology of contractarianism in economics', *Public Choice*, 113: 465–83.

North, D.C. (1999) 'Hayek's Contribution to Understanding the Process of Economic Change', in V.J. Vanberg (ed.) *Freiheit, Wettbewerb und Wirtschaftsordnung*, Freiburg: Haufe, pp. 79–96.

O'Neill, O. (1998) 'The Method of A Theory of Justice', in O. Höffe (ed.) *John Rawls Eine Theorie der Gerechtigkeit*, Berlin: Akademie-Verlag, pp. 27–43.

Pelikan, P. (2002) 'Why Economic Policies need comprehensive evolutionary analysis', in P. Pelikan and G. Wegner (eds) *Evolutionary Analysis of Economic Policy*, Cheltenham: E. Elgar.

Popper, K.R. (1992) *Conjectures and Refutations*, 5th ed., London: Routledge.

Posner, R.A. (1998) 'The Problematics of Moral and Legal Theory', *Harvard Law Review*, 111, 1637–93.

Rawls, J. (1958/1999) 'Justice as Fairness', in S. Freeman (ed.) *Collected Papers of John Rawls*, Cambridge, MA: Harvard University Press, pp. 47–72.

Rawls, J. (1971/1995) *A Theory of Justice*, Cambridge, MA: Belknap Press.

Rawls, J. (1999) 'The Idea of Public Reason Revisited', in J. Rawls (ed.) *The Law of Peoples*, Cambridge, MA: Harvard University Press, pp. 129–80.

Röpke, J. (1990) 'Evolution and Innovation', in K. Dopfer (ed.) *The Evolution of Systems*, London: Macmillan, pp. 111–20.

Rorty, R. (1991) *The Consequences of Pragmatism*, Minneapolis: University of Minnesota Press.

Sartorius, C. (2002) 'The Relevance of the Group for the Evolution of Social Norms and Values', *Constitutional Political Economy*, 13: 149–72.

Schelling, T. (1978) *Micromotives and Macrobehavior*, New York: W.W. Norton.

Schlicht, E. (1998) *On Custom in the Economy*, Oxford: Clarendon Press.

Schnellenbach, J. (2002) 'The Evolution of a Fiscal Constitution when individuals are theoretically uncertain', *Freiburg Discussion Papers on Constitutional Economics* # 02/6.

Sen, A.K. (1996a) 'On the Foundations of Welfare Economics: Utility, Capability, and Practical Reason', in F. Farina, F. Hahn and S. Vannucci (eds) *Ethics, Rationality, and Economic Behaviour*, Oxford: Clarendon Press, pp. 50–65.

Sen, A.K. (1996b) 'Rationality, Joy, and Freedom', *Critical Review*, 10: 481–93.

Sugden, R. (1993a) 'Normative Judgments and Spontaneous Order: The Contractarian Element in Hayek's Thought', *Constitutional Political Economy*, 4: 393–424.

Sugden, R. (1993b) 'Welfare, Resources, and Capabilities', *Journal of Economic Literature*, 31: 1947–62.

Sugden, R. (1998) 'The role of inductive reasoning in the evolution of conventions', *Law and Philosophy*, 17: 377–410.

Tomasello, M. (1999) 'The human adaptation for culture', *Annual Review of Anthropology*, 28: 509–29.

Van Aaken, A. and Hegmann, H. (2002) 'Konsens als Grundnorm?', *Archiv für Rechts- und Sozialphilosophie*, 88: 28–50.

Vanberg, V.J. (1994) 'Individual choice and institutional constraints', in V.J. Vanberg (ed.) *Rules and Choice in Economics*, London: Routledge, pp. 208–34.

Vanberg, V.J. (1999) 'Markets and Regulation: On the contrast between free-market liberalism and constitutional liberalism', *Constitutional Political Economy*, 10: 219–43.

Vanberg, V.J. (2003) 'Citizens' Sovereignty and Constitutional Commitments: Original vs. Continuing Agreement', A. Breton, G. Galeotti, P. Salmon and R. Weintrobe (eds) *Rational Foundations of Democratic Politics*, Cambridge: Cambridge University Press, pp. 198–221.

Vanberg, V.J. (2004) 'The Status Quo in Contractarian Constitutionalist Perspective', *Constitutional Political Economy*,15: 153–70.

Voigt, S. (1999) 'Breaking with the Notion of Social Contract: Constitutions as based on spontaneously arisen institutions', *Constitutional Political Economy*, 10: 283–300.

Wegner, G. (1997) 'Economic policy from an evolutionary perspective – a new approach', *Journal of Institutional and Theoretical Economics*, 153: 485–509.

Weizsäcker, C.C. v. (2002) 'Welfare Economics bei endogenen Präferenzen', *Perspektiven der Wirtschaftspolitik*, 3: 425–46.

Wilson, E.O. (1998) *Consilience. The Unity of Knowledge*, New York: Knopf.

Witt, U. (1996) 'Innovations, Externalities and the Problem of Economic Progress', *Public Choice*, 89: 113–30.

Witt, U. (2000) 'Genes, Culture and Utility', *Papers on Economics & Evolution* # 0009, Jena: Max-Planck-Institute of Economics.

Witt, U. (2003) 'Economic Policy Making in Evolutionary Perspective', *Journal of Evolutionary Economics*, 13: 77–94.

Wohlgemuth, M. (2002) 'Evolutionary approaches to politics', *Kyklos*, 55: 223–46.

9 Probing the welfare prospects of legal competition

Gerhard Wegner

9.1 Introduction

The following reflections are concerned with a form of institution subject to institutional change. I consider legal norms which are designed by governments in order to regulate market activities. Due to their legal character such norms are mandatory and cannot voluntarily be altered unless governments change the law. Rule-setting is comparable to monopoly insofar as regulatees can avoid rule-following only by abandoning the regulated economic activity, that is, if they realize an exit option. Since market exit will not change the legal norm, political decisions remain the only way to change a designed institution. It is obvious that the dependence of institutional change on the political process raises questions pertaining to welfare losses. Even if the regulation of market activities can in principle be supported by market failure arguments, it remains an open question whether the scope and extent of regulation harmonizes with individual welfare. Not only may regulators be "captured" by vested interests, as has often been indicated; they may also be overburdened by the requirement of adapting regulations to changing preferences, even if regulations are initially aligned with individual preferences. The mere fact that regulation is made by legal norms and thus depends on the political process suggests that welfare losses are possible.[1]

If one admits that legal norms may be at variance with individual preferences, that is, that regulatory failure may exist, the search for institutional safeguards suggests itself.[2] Here I consider legal competition as a potential remedy. At first glance, and in particular from a judicial point of view, the mere notion of legal competition sounds as a contradiction in itself. By definition legal norms are general as well as enforceable and cannot be subject to individual choice like coffee or cigars, let alone an option not to consume. Obviously the state itself would undergo substantial change, if not erosion, if its monopoly were replaced by competition amongst legal norms. However, legal competition is not a fictitious idea of some innocent armchair economist, but has, even though unintentionally, emerged as a practical result of the EU-Treaty, in particular of its far-reaching interpretations by the European Court (EC). Notably, the EU has not deliberately chosen the track of legal competition and has not to this day pursued this type of institutional change in its official declarations; instead, the vision of a single legal order in the EU (the so-called positive integration) is the first preference on the agenda of European Integration; nevertheless, legal competition does occur and holds out an important example of the evolution of designed institutions. For this reason, it has attracted much attention which, however, has not led to an un-ambiguous assessment. While a few scholars such as Streit and Kiwit (1999) propagate an overoptimistic view and deem legal competition to work in a Hayekian-like manner as a "discovery procedure", many others have formulated objections against the idea that governmental rule-setting should be subject to competition; critics refer to economic arguments against the workability of such competition as well as to political misgivings pertaining to the erosion of demo-cratically legitimized rule-setting, if an anonymous mechanism is supposed to replace collective decisions (Bratton et al. 1996: 2).[3] This turns out to be much more of a problem if such collective decisions are corroborated by cultural norms and find acceptance by the constituents. It is precisely this outcome which cannot be denied a priori when we concentrate on legal competition.

In this chapter, Section 9.1 focuses on legal competition in the EU which pro-vides several reasons for well-suited "meta-institutions" to launch legal competi-tion. With this done, we can depict the ideal-working of legal competition and its underlying requirements. Probing the welfare prospects of legal competition also requires making a distinction between frictions of competition on the one hand and factors which question the very possibility that legal competition can raise wel-fare; Section 9.3 is devoted to that problem. In Section 9.4, I deal with common objections to legal competition which point to the re-emergence of market failure; notably these objections have been made even in the absence of cross-border exter-nalities. In Section 9.5, I turn to a problem linked to "domestic discrimination" which is logically inherent to legal competition when the latter is designed to work as a "discovery procedure" and defies instant solution. Section 9.6 concludes.

9.2   The constitution of legal competition in the EU

In this section, I concentrate on legal norms regulating products (including services), i.e., the attributes or quality of products, or the way in which products are manufactured. Of particular interest is the nation-wide regulation of products pertaining to safety, health, environment and consumer protection (SHEC), that is product standards which quantatively make up "far the most sizeable segment of regulation in modern economies" (Galli and Pelkmans 2000: 16). Labor market regulations or competition regulations (including retail regulations) are also part of important nation-wide regulations. In a broader sense many other industry reg-ulations such as competition rules shape the economic environment affecting pro-duction costs. The importance of product regulations with which we are concerned here derives from the fact that even within a regime of free trade, governments have a real option to apply their own regulatory regime (in a non-discriminative way) or, alternatively, to accept the rules of the exporting country. In the former case governments would make their own rules mandatory for foreign imports; in the latter, in which the government recognizes the rules of the country of origin, these rules would coexist with the (possibly different) rules of the domestic country.[4] In this case, products (services) would be offered to consumers which are made under different rules, which is one (meta-) institutional precondition of legal competition. Domestic markets, however, would be open in a much deeper sense than under a regime of free trade, for free trade only demands that governments apply domestic rules equally to domestic producers; but they are not bound to accept the rules of the country of origin.

For several reasons the EU offers an important laboratory for experimenting with legal competition, namely in case of product regulation.[5] The Common Market of the EU differs from free trade in the way just explained: governments of the member states are bound to accept the regulatory standards of other member states and are not permitted to apply their own rules to imported goods, even if rules are applied equally within the territory of one member state. This meta-rule was not part of the original concept of the Treaty of Rome which only forbade discrimination with respect to nationality. Subsequently, the European Court transformed this anti-discrimination rule (Art 28 EC; formerly Art 30) into an anti-restriction rule obliging member states to accept the rules of others. Only in highly restricted cases are exceptions possible, e.g., if the protection of health or safety demands the application of domestic rules (Art 30, EC, formerly Art 36 EC). However, even in such cases member states must have good reasons for a restriction (that is the application of the domestic rules) and are not allowed to apply national rules in all areas of safety, the protection of the environment, or morals.

A further reason for the thesis that the EU offers a laboratory for legal competition is that the meta-institutional rule of mutual recognition (concerning regulations) is directly applicable, as are all rules of the European Treaty which define basic rules for economic freedom (which also include the freedom of relocating capital, the transnational right of abode as well as the freedom of movement). In contrast to free-trade agreements between nation states, economic subjects of the EU can sue for their rights laid down by the EC and are not dependent on the assistance of their own governments in doing so. In reality, obstacles exist which make a direct application of the particular EU rules difficult; for instance, firms have desisted from making use of their rights because they worry about reputation losses when they sue governments of other member states;[6] but other than that, and particularly with regard to the rest of the economic world, the European Treaty offers a powerful instrument for realising legal competition (Wilmowsky 1992, Winkler 1999, Streit and Mussler 1994, Galli and Pelkmans 2000).

To illustrate, product regulations have sometimes been regarded as a part of national culture in the respective member states and were widely accepted by producers as well as consumers in the respective states. Consider regulations concerning foodstuffs, e.g., regulations for Italian pasta or the brewing of German beer and rules concerning the ingredients of Belgian pralines. However, many regulations which prohibit certain ingredients are highly idiosyncratic; for instance, the centuries-old "purity-rule" allows not more than four substances to brew German beer.[7] Even though national industries have had an interest in impeding market entry from without, these rules from which they took profit were also rooted in cultural norms and defended accordingly by their governments, sometimes with considerable support from the public. Nevertheless, in the past, all these national product regulations restricting foreign suppliers are judged by the European Court as violations of the Common Market rules; even though member states were free to keep these rules to regulate their own industry, suppliers of other countries have to be exempted from them. A further important branch of product regulation pertains to product liability rules, although these rules were debated in much more sober sense than the above mentioned regulatory cases. Also product safety norms or environmental norms are candidates for mutual recognition.

The co-existence of legal rules as well as the country-of-origin principle constitutes the precondition of competition among legal norms. With respect to the European Union, however, we must note that legal competition provides only one possible meta-institutional alternative which has been discovered, as Streit and Mussler (1994) point out, only accidentally.[8] The alternative track of uniform European legal norm setting still exists, which would override national legal norms and consequently bring legal competition to a halt; monopolized norm setting replaces the coexistence of national norms. The European Commission pursued "positive integration" up to 1985, but in light of the mass of legal norms to be harmonized, it has been unable to continue this policy. Hence, the alternative of harmonizing (or "cartelizing") institutional rules exists alongside the alternative of legal competition. According to its official announcements the European Commission continues to display a preference for harmonization, but practical reasons leave this political choice pending.[9]

9.3   The ideal working of legal competition

One crucial characteristic of legal competition is the asymmetry of freedom of choice between the demand and supply. If government is bound to accept mutual recognition, the choice set for consumers is broadened: Consumers encounter products and services which are produced under alternative rules; this affects both the price and the quality of products as a consequence of different national norms concerning safety, health, environmental requirements etc. Consumers thus choose not only the products of firms, but also (indirectly) the institutions supplied by national governments which narrow suppliers' alternatives in accordance with rule-setters' preferences.

As a result, consumers implicitly choose among institutional alternatives. Unlike competitive federalism, the demand side can stay within the *same* jurisdiction whilst being able to substitute among *different* governmental offers.[10] On the other hand, however, the supply side is bound to comply with regulations of the nation state in which it is situated. When a national regulatory norm has been banned by the European Court, national suppliers will not enjoy this liberalization as well but are subject to "domestic discrimination". This fact constitutes the asymmetry of freedom of choice concerning demand and supply side of the market. As a result, if suppliers want to choose alternative rules, they *have* to relocate their production. Hence, capital mobility is not only an assumption (as it is portrayed in many models) but a *requirement*, while, on the other hand, consumers – who are mostly presumed to be immobile – have no need to relocate because they benefit from mutual recognition. Contrary to widely-held beliefs about globalization, consumers are privileged in this regard.

If we probe the welfare prospects of legal (here: regulatory) competition, we have to keep in mind the first step which launches competition, that is,

- the broadened choice set for consumers, and
- the "unleveled playing field" for competitors.

From the perspective of consumers, institutions are no longer monopolized but become part of the choice set. If the demand side is informed about the quality of regulation, substitution reveals preferences concerning regulations and thus generates information which one does not otherwise have: while within a regime of free trade in which the country of destination exclusively defines the regulatory setting, one can only speculate whether regulators have been captured by the regulated industry wanting to erect barriers to entry, consumer behavior offers an answer to that question. For instance, even after German regulators were obliged to permit the import of sorts of beer produced under different regulatory regimes (and not in conformity to the "purity rule" imposed on domestic producers), the German regulation prevailed. Supposedly "uninformed" consumers did not shift their demand to products of "lower quality" but retained, now voluntarily, the former regulatory regime, something which must also have surprised lobbyists of that industry who were intent on holding on to the old regime until the last minute. Although consumers cannot single out institutions for selection but have to decide on "joint offers" – comprising products as well as regulations – one additional competitive element has been introduced; this generates more information about the congruence of regulator's with consumers' preferences than is available under a regime of free trade. Besides, whether lax regulatory regimes have a competitive advantage over stricter rules, depends on both preferences for quality on the demand side and the effectiveness of rules to provide for such quality. Hitherto laxity – as is widely-feared – is far from being inevitable (I turn to this point below).

If, however, domestic suppliers suffer from a competitive disadvantage, an incentive exists to get rid of it. Relocating to a more advantageous regulatory regime as well as influencing their own government in order to withdraw disadvantageous norms are alternatives. Relocation can be interpreted as "regulatory arbitrage" processed by the suppliers. Through a transfer of capital into a more preferred regulatory regime this option is realized. This further erodes the domestic regulatory regime because suppliers relocate to other jurisdictions. If the government wants to avoid this outcome of capital transfer, it has to adapt the regulatory regime which furthers the competitiveness (more general: performance) of the domestic industry. Depending on the role which domestic competitiveness plays in the political competition, policy-makers have an incentive to redesign norms

Rule-setting in regime₁   Rule-setting in regime₂

Penetration of norms

Relocation of resources

Exporting country   Importing country

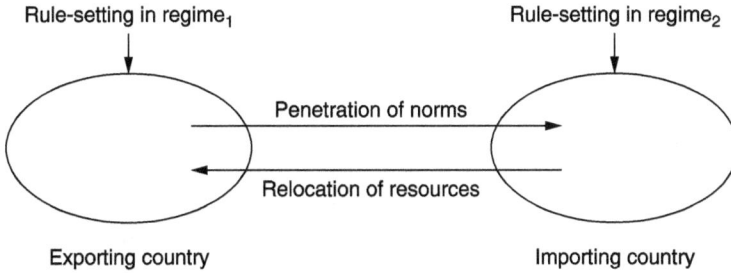

Figure 9.1 The ideal working of legal competition.

aligned with the performance of industries. This ideal conception relies on effective political competition which controls policy makers insofar as they check the adaptiveness of domestic rules; in this case it would be unattractive for them to maintain rules which impair the competitiveness of the domestic industry.

If political competition is ineffectual in this regard, however, the reality of regulatory competition will depend on the lobbying of national industries which suffer from the unleveled playing field. In this respect, Stigler's (1971) capture theory of regulation undergoes an interesting reversal with regard to regulatory competition: While under monopolized rule-setting as well as the regime of free trade capturing gives rise to rent-seeking, the abandoning of less-preferred ("inefficient") norms now *depends* on the capturing of norm setters by lobbyists. If the latter cannot any longer erect barriers to entry through norms, they have an interest in influencing norm setters to abandon those norms which impair competition, given that relocation is costly.

If these scenarios concerning adaptation of rules work, governmental rule-setting would respond to revealed consumer preferences and thus restrain government power to use norms exclusively on behalf of vested interests. Consequently, legal competition comprises a specific link between economic and political competition under particular meta-institutional rules which make legal competition possible. As "evolutionary" theories of institutional competition have argued against static conceptions of competition, the final result of mutual re-adaptation of regulatory competition is hardly predictable.[11] Rather, it becomes attractive for policy-makers to check norm-setting permanently with regard to preferences as well as to discover so far unsatisfied preferences for regulation. This political process is by no means designed to produce uniform or at least "equivalent" norms (in the sense of the European Commission), that is, a regulatory equilibrium.[12] Rather, regulatory competition invites policy-makers to behave as political entrepreneurs in a more literal sense: the discovery of preferences for regulations becomes constitutive for entrepreneurship in the realm of politics. Additionally, regulatory dynamics is also furthered by changing preferences for regulation, which includes the emergence of new cases for regulation which regulators may address. For these reasons the outcome of regulatory competition is necessarily transitory.

To summarize, the benefits of this ideal-typical regulatory competition can be seen in

- the diversity of regulatory norms amongst which consumers can choose;
- the sanctioning mechanism for policy-makers so that it becomes detrimental for them to erect market barriers through regulations;
- the installation of a permanent check of regulations according to its link to economic competition so that the feedback loop between political decision-making and economic outcomes becomes tighter;
- the re-alignment of private ends towards public welfare when industrial lobbyists strive for "better" regulations.[13]

These general statements need to be qualified. In reality, the intensity (as well as the emergence) of legal competition depends on various factors, including

- the impact of national regulation on production costs;[14]
- the existence and shape of regulatory preferences;
- the costs of relocation;
- the competitiveness of the industry in question relative to its competitors from outside, including its capability to offset costs resulting from regulations (Sun and Pelkmans 1995: 72);
- the relevance of industrial competitiveness for the current course of economic policy.
- the responsiveness of the political sphere to impairing industrial competitiveness ("political transaction cost", Dixit 1996).

Legal competition implies a fundamental link between economic performance (governed by industrial competitiveness) and political responsiveness in the sense that policy makers cannot afford to institute an economic policy detrimental to competitiveness without any sanction by voters. In the same vein, industrial competitiveness must be conceived to be a part of voter's preferences. If this precondition is fulfilled, an incentive exists to identify determinants of competitiveness, so that regulation is within the scope of review by policy-makers. The other elements mentioned above point to frictions of legal competition but do not principally militate against legal competition. Just as little as transportation costs are an argument against free trade, so are occasional shortcomings of entrepreneurial alertness or small comparative advantages in some industries which make foreign trade unattractive.[15] Pointing to frictions within competition, in particular those which will decrease in the course of competition, is not an argument against the opening of competition.

A more convincing argument against the ideal working of legal competition, at least at first sight, might point to the fact that legal norms are unsuitable for competition. While action parameters of competition such as contracts, costs, attributes of products etc. are permanently changed in order to sharpen the competitive edge of firms, legal norms unfold their character as rules as a result of certain stability.

Constantly changing rules are more likely to disorientate behavior than orientate it, but the latter is the essence of rules.[16] To some degree, as, for instance, Buchanan (1975: ch. 7) has shown, the attribute of rules relies upon the stability of rules (transaction costs caused by learning the rules play an important role to be taken into account here).

Again, this point hardly constitutes a fundamental objection against the opening of legal competition. Even though it is true that legal norms cannot undergo changes such as common action parameters in competition, this gives only hints as to the potential performance of legal competition. That the specific nature of legal norms limits entrepreneurship in this realm is something which can be learnt within the political sphere. If policy-makers continue to experiment with norms in order to identify the best ones so that firms lose their patience with hyper-active rule setters, relocation will sanction this type of untrammeled rule changing. Under these circumstances other rule setters could attract firms by advertising the relative stability of their own rules and offering a legal environment which makes longer-term economic planning on the part of firms possible again. Since the consequences of rule-setting decisions reflect on the decision-makers themselves (and are thus "internalized"), no case for market failure can be identified. Achieving a balance between adaptation of norms with regard to regulatory preferences on the one hand and stability on the other is something which can be left to the self-organising process of competition.

9.4 Will market failure (re-) emerge as a result of legal competition?

I scarcely need emphasize that the welfare prospects of legal competition rely on the absence of cross-border externalities. Product regulations on which we concentrate here fulfill this condition to a large extent. If national regulators are going to lower the standards for product quality or safety in order to attract investors to their location, they cannot externalize damage to consumers of exporting countries who prefer higher standards of regulation. Because the latter can choose among regulatory alternatives, they are not exposed to negative externalities.[17] If, however, the country with higher standards loses investors and foreign producers take advantage of lower standards so that the former country is urged to lower its standards as well, such a race to lower standards would reflect a *rise* in welfare.

Recently, Sinn (2003) has renewed his well known misgivings about regulatory competition by pointing to positive externalities when governments prescribe quality standards.

> "Consumer protection benefits the foreigners because the quality of the goods consumed by foreigners increases without their having to pay more to cover the additional costs. And for the same reason, it harms the domestic firms. Because the utility of the foreign consumers is not considered in the calculations of the national government, there is a policy bias implying

overly lax consumer protection (…) On balance, national consumer protection measures will indeed generate a positive international policy externality and will therefore remain underdeveloped."

[ibid.: 147]

I agree that national regulators can be said to produce some sort of policy externality but it is hard to see why it will make for underdeveloped regulation in the meaning of regulatory competition failure. Higher regulation increases the price of product, but consumers in countries with a lower level of regulation are not able to benefit from high quality products unless they pay for it.[18] For that reason, product regulation per se does not make for a collective good from which other consumers, in particular those from other countries, can benefit. Consequently, no objections against legal competitions can be raised. Of course, other cases for legal norms exist which do provide for supra-national collective goods so that legal competition fails to increase welfare. Cross-national environmental damage as well as the protection of international competition against cartels or the abuse of dominant market power are cases in point. Arguably, in these cases, national norm setting can benefit from lax rules and impose its negative consequences on other countries, be it in terms of environmental damage or in terms of impaired competition. Since these aspects have been extensively debated in the literature I will desist from a discussion here.[19]

However, the rationale for product regulation to be considered here is not the existence of negative external effects but asymmetric information; as a result, as textbooks tell us, consumers are unable to distinguish between alternative qualities so that regulation arguably makes consumers confident about product quality. Referring to this rationale for regulation, authors such as Tjiong (2002) and, again, Sinn (2003, 1997) have raised severe doubts about the workability of legal competition. The argument runs like this: If product regulations are introduced because consumers are unable to distinguish between low and high qualities, "it cannot be assumed that the consumers will be able to distinguish between state-regulated national quality standards" (Sinn 2003: 146).

Trachtman (1993) and Tjiong (2002) make this argument as well:

"If one assumes that the protected parties are sophisticated enough to police regulatory arbitrage, it would seem a small next step to expect them to protect themselves without any regulation" (Trachtman 1993: 67).

"… it can be argued that actual tolerance of consumers of regulatory differences in a product market, once allowed, would suggest the relative obsolescence of regulatory protection in the first place."

(Tjiong 2002: 81)

Both Sinn and Tjiong corroborate their doubts with reference to BSE infected meat, in which case regulatory competition could be harmful since consumers cannot be presupposed to make judgments as to the consequences of consuming;

hence it would be an illusion to rely on regulatory choice and consumers being well-informed about the content of alternative regulations (ibid.).

These arguments deserve scrutiny because consumer safety, the protection of health in particular, are amongst the strongest arguments for governmental regulation. At first, however, let us recall that BSE does not (only) represent an example of market failure, but even more one of the most salient cases for governmental failure. By no account were British consumers exposed to unregulated meat supplied by profit maximizing farmers exempted from any supervision, but, even worse, they were dependent on national regulators who were unwilling to discern any signs of potential damage caused by their lax regulations (on the contrary, in this case governmental regulators even encouraged consumers to rely on national regulations and to ignore warnings of their fellow regulators in the EU). For this reason alone, one may argue that regulatory choice would have improved the situation of all consumers in the UK; if they had called the capabilities of their own national regulators into question, regulatory alternatives would have been present and urged the national regulators to give reasons for their risk-loving behavior.[20] Thanks to the absence of a single EU-regulatory authority, the health of meat consumers of other EU-member states did not depend on the risk taking of one decision maker who could act as a monopolist. What can be learnt from the case of BSE-treated meat is that there are occasionally good reasons to call governmental regulations into question and to think about institutional competition as an alternative.

Furthermore, the "re-emergence-hypothesis" invokes deeper investigation. Sinn (2003, 1997), Trachtman (1993) and Tjiong (2002) make an analogy between asymmetric information with regard to unregulated products on the one hand, and products regulated under different regimes on the other. However, an important categorical difference remains which calls such an analogy into question. First of all, regulating is a *public* activity done by authorities (even though in reality private associations are involved). Even if consumers are actually less-informed about the detailed content of regulations, they are at least entitled to access to such information. Other than knowledge concerning manufacturing which is private by definition, knowledge pertaining to regulations can be attained by anyone because public authorities are obliged to reveal their regulations. As a consequence, we must make a categorical distinction between changing the quality of products as a private activity (e.g., to offer cheaper but worse or even harmful products), and changing the content of regulations. While the former represents hidden action, the latter does not; unlike suppliers who may choose to sneak products of lower quality onto the market, rule-setting is an identifiable action by nature.[21] Public authorities can hardly hope for introducing poor regulatory standards into the Common Market without public awareness. In the same vein it is implausible that governments could escape public sanction if they undercut prevailing regulatory preferences.

A second argument against the "re-emergence-hypothesis" relates to the quantitative dimension of regulatory regimes being comparable to information about product quality. Sinn (2003) worries about variety:

There are 15 countries in the current European Union, and soon there will be 25 countries or more. How can one reasonably assume that, for each lemon good, the consumers will be able to distinguish between 25 national quality standards? The hope that the consumer's confusion in the national context will not carry over to the international choice problem appears to be overly optimistic under realistic conditions.

One is tempted to agree, but against the background that product markets carry hundreds of product qualities for each market, the regulatory market seems to be rather well-ordered. This is supported by the potential behavior of some governments (of smaller countries in particular) which may copy regulations of other countries instead of affording regulations of their own; accordingly the number of regulatory regimes falls short of the number of EU member states; in that case regulatory complexity is not likely.

Third, the well-known institutional fallacy concerning information acquiring also applies to regulatory variety. Insofar as consumers are educated not to choose among alternative regulations but to rely on one regulatory regime only, ignorance as to regulation is a rational adaptation to this institutional arrangement. (As it is, for example, rational for citizens to remain uninformed about local affairs including local politicians so long as local jurisdictions lack political competence.) Once consumers have learnt that they can choose among regulatory alternatives, information acquiring becomes an attractive economic activity. The latter can also be undertaken by specialized brokers in the service sector (including informational service of non-profit-organizations such as consumer associations), so that a deepening of the division of labor could apply in order to cope with informational complexity. One also has to take into account that governments themselves have an interest to advertize their own regulations and by this reduce information cost of consumers.

For these reasons the arguments pointing to the re-emergence of market failure are not very convincing. I concur with Sinn (1997) that "no European wants to lose his hair after washing" (ibid.: 48, my translation) but such an objection against regulatory competition does not really stand up. What is concerned in the European context is not the unconditioned recognition of non-European (say Liberian) regulations but the "reserved" recognition of regulations of other member states; as a matter of evidence, regulatory preferences are not very divergent in delicate cases such as health. Even non-informed consumers can know that health will hardly be endangered if, e.g., German consumers ponder whether they could rely on Dutch regulators and vice versa. At least to some extent, reliance of democracy in other countries substitutes for knowledge about foreign regulation. However, if strong reasons indicate governmental failure as occurred in the BSE-case, member states can still protect their consumers by exempting particular regulations from mutual recognition. If such a meta-rule safeguards mutual recognition and thus hedges legal competition, misgivings about consumer protection should be dispelled.[22] In addition, as Porter and v.d. Linde (1995) account with regard to environmental regulation, firms have learnt in the past 20 years that high regulatory standards indicate a "premium location" and are well suited to signal product quality. Admittedly, industries in advanced economies have an interest in making regulatory standards more efficient as to compliance cost or to abandon non-preferred standards, but they will hardly support a strategy of lowering regulatory standards in general. Consequently governments can not afford to undercut regulatory preferences, in particular health and safety requirements, if domestic industry will lose its competitive edge as a result of maladaptation to private preferences. Rather, it is much more plausible that governments will check both regulatory cost and regulatory preferences, which includes raising standards in case new preferences emerge (both in the domestic market and in large export markets).

In short, the existence of good reasons for regulating market activities does not imply that legal competition leads back to the status quo ante and thus has to be prevented from the beginning through "harmonization" (which means one supranational legal monopoly). A realistic concept must start from "less-than-perfect" governmental behavior which prompts the search for meta-institutions for controlling norm-setting with regard to regulatory preferences. Once national norm setting has been replaced by harmonized rules, the problem of adapting norms to regulatory preferences would re-emerge on the supra-national level. Hence, welfare losses caused by heterogeneous regulatory preferences are more likely if the preferences of the citizens of several countries are to be met. Furthermore and with regard to the laborious negotiation process in the EU, the risk of "fossilized" norms cannot be overlooked, once a supra-national decision on regulations has been accomplished.[23] Most importantly, EU-policy makers will not (economically) be sanctioned if norms need to be changed and turn to barriers to market entry. The cost in terms of trade restrictions or losses of consumer welfare emerge gradually and are thus likely to escape political attention. On the other hand, industries which bear the cost of maladapted norms cannot but influence political decision making, because an exit option is unavailable. Against the background of this alternative, regulatory competition appears to be a preferable alternative to monopolized rule setting.

9.5 The distortion of economic competition as a by-product of legal competition

The arguments in support of legal competition notwithstanding, one final problem needs to be scrutinized. To this end let us recall the precondition for legal competition, namely the discrimination of domestic suppliers: If they are going to become outcompeted by foreign suppliers who benefit from advantageous regulations, they cannot but have to relocate their resources; otherwise domestic norms keep on being mandatory for them. For this reason, competition on markets is distorted because regulatory regimes interfere with the efficiency structure of firms and impair the selection quality of markets. Indeed, opponents of legal competition refer to this outcome when they advocate a level playing field.

But as Faure (2000) has pointed out, international trade by no means depends on a level playing field for competitors, but would never start if each firm encountered equal conditions for supply. In this respect, there is no case for exempting legal norms from other supply conditions such as wages or factor endowment. In addition, the demand for equal preconditions concerning rules has suffered from the fact that their advocates have given the quality of these rules second priority; one gets the impression that equal norms, even if they impair welfare, represent a value in itself. Nevertheless, without derogating from the merits of legal competition, the fact of distorted competition remains and thus the possibility of welfare losses caused by domestic discrimination; this prompts the search for welfare improving remedies.

At first glance, suppliers instead of consumers alone should be given free access to legal choice; then, e.g., British suppliers can opt for French or Belgian product norms without crossing the Channel. As a consequence, the power of national rule setters would erode increasingly; they would much more resemble "suppliers for institutions" (Streit and Kiwit 1999) which compete with norm setters of other countries. Reflections on the legitimacy concerning rule setting support such a broadening of the legal choice set, at least if one argues from the angle of Constitutional Political Economy. If a collective decision-maker imposes rules on economic activity, these rules must find justification with respect to the benefits of the constituents, so that rule-following increases welfare; with regard to regulations, consumers should profit from rules guiding economic activity. But if citizens making use of the majority rule impose rules on suppliers in the political sphere and, in their role of economic agents (consumers) ignore these rules by shifting their demand to more-preferred products of other regulatory regimes, the legitimacy of such burdening is questioned. Notably, citizens deciding on rules do not commit themselves to buy a product when they regulate its quality; rather, they take liberties to alter their assessment of rules when they behave as market participants; political and economic decisions are detached from each other. This prompts the question why a polity should have the right to impose costs of its erroneous decisions on specific economic agents, that is to externalize collective errors by making use of majority rule. For this reason, it suggests itself that also suppliers should have the right to choose regulations.

But when we pursue this thought experiment, one important qualification has to be made, since an additional distinction has to be made which hitherto could have been neglected. So far it was argued that cross country externalities must be exempted from legal competition because this invites national regulators to opt for free-riding, that is to lower regulatory costs of their national industry and to externalize the loss of welfare (e.g., in terms of environmental damage) partly to their neighboring countries. But if regulations provide for a *national* collective (say environmental) goods and economic agents have the right to choose regulations of a different country (while staying at home), the national collective good would be subject to erosion now. Economic agents could enjoy the provision of this national collective good (so far it still exists) without contributing to it. As a consequence, our thought experiment concerning equal legal choice for suppliers must be restricted to those cases in which the benefit comes close to a private good – which is the case for many consumer regulations.

But even then legal choice for suppliers would affect the incentive mechanism of regulatory competition. In short, the character of national-rule setting would undergo fundamental change inasmuch as rule-setting itself would turn into a cross-country collective good. If suppliers were given the right to choose regulations of other countries without relocating, domestic regulators could no longer attract investment to their country, that is to appropriate "rents" of setting more preferred rules. On the other hand, the setting of less-preferred rules would escape economic sanctioning because production could still remain in the domestic country.

As a consequence, the introduction of this meta-rule would level the playing field in so far as suppliers could turn to their most preferred rules (something which Walrasian theorists would term "legal equilibrium"); national regulators would have lost their power of imposing rules on domestic industry. But, on the other hand, if suppliers have each attached themselves to one regulatory regime, no incentive mechanism is existent which gives rise to a continuous improvement of regulations. If one government would act accordingly, no "entrepreneurial rent" can be appropriated; as a result there is little chance to escape from this "equilibrium".

Hence, if one sticks to the presumption that regulation should be a matter of governmental activity, domestic discrimination is *functionally needed* in order to fuel legal competition as a permanent process ("discovery procedure"). The market control of governmental rule setting *depends* on disadvantages imposed on regulatees and their reactions to these disadvantages.[24] The only meta-rule which combines legal equality with an incentive mechanism needed here would be transnational commitment: *governments would commit themselves to relieve firms from their relocating cost, i.e., to subsidize firms willing to transfer their resources to a country with more preferred rules.* In this case the incentive mechanisms for legal competition would remain intact, while, at the same time, markets would select firms according to efficiency alone. I will desist from reflecting about the chances for the meta-rule becoming real, but it appears to be the only alternative.[25]

9.6 Conclusions

These sketchy arguments were devoted to structure the problems related to legal competition. Starting from the assumption of "less-than-perfect" rule-setting in reality, cases for regulations have to be sorted out which from the beginning defy exposition to legal competition (cross-border externalities). Unlike these cases, impediments of legal competition exist which competition itself can digest, that is frictions which typically characterize markets at their very beginning. For these reasons, according to my view, many objections to be found in the literature do not really stand up.[26] A "re-emergence of market failure" is far from being a likely outcome. Nevertheless, systematic problems remain which pertain to the cost of legal competition in terms of distortion of competition on markets. With regard to the imperfection of monopolized rule-setting, however, this fact alone does not support supra-national rules as an alternative. But if we pursue the logic of legal competition, we end up with the result that the distortion of economic competition ("unfair norms" in the sense of inequality) emerges as a price for setting legal competition in motion. Hence, a mechanism is needed which, firstly, minimizes the distortion on markets and, secondly, benefits policy-makers if they identify more preferred rules. Such a mechanism would make the evolution of designed institutions more independent of the political sphere in that a feed-back to the economic sphere would be installed. But in view that such a mechanism lacks realisticness, domestic discrimination raises general questions concerning the legitimacy of governmental rule setting. Hence, the alternative of private rule setting should be included in a broader welfare analysis.

Notes

1   We neglect the adjustment of regulations as a result of legal judgments.
2   It must be noted that Sinn's defense of the regulatory nation state (1997) does not take regulatory failure into consideration. Of course, if we presume that the current regulatory regime is optimal, any change cannot but impair economic welfare.
3   Meanwhile a large literature on this issue exists; apart from Bratton *et al.* (1996) see Streit and Wohlgemuth (1999), Gerken (1995), Sinn (2003), Vihanto (1992), Vanberg (2000), van den Bergh (2000), Wegner (2004) and many others; see also Schenk *et al.* (1998).
4   Here I use the terms "rules", "regulations" and "legal norms" synonymously; meta-institutions represent rules of how to apply rules.
5   In the service sector, however, mutual recognition is highly underdeveloped; at present, the European Commission makes a far-reaching proposal to introduce mutual recognition also here.
6   For this reason, firms sometimes prefer to activate their own government in order to prompt the European Commission to start an initiative against a member state; in this case the particular firm has a much better chance to avoid reputation losses.
7   Examples concerning product labeling have also to be mentioned here; for instance, German regulators have prohibited the label "Prosecco" for Italian suppliers and obliged them to use the less attractive label "sparkling wine".
8   The far-reaching Cassis-de-Dijon decision (following the Dassonville-decision) has to be noted here: German regulators have prescribed a minimum (!) rule for alcohol in liqueurs in order to protect (!) human health because otherwise they worried about a starter drug. Compliance of this rule was also mandatory for German producers and did not formally discriminate according to the nationality; effectively, a French supplier of liqueur has been restricted. After the decision by the European Court who banned the regulatory norm, Art. 28 EC was transformed into a non-restriction rule so that member states were obliged to mutual recognition.
9   After the announcement of the Common Market in 1992 the European Commission made further attempts to unify legal norms in the EU but, according to latest reports, has realized that national regulators are most active and unwilling to transfer their legal competence to the EU. At present, however, safeguards have been installed which make national regulations transparent and oblige national regulators in a formal sense (without any Court decision) to accept equivalent regulations from other member states.
10   The interesting FOCI-proposal of Frey and Eichenberger (1995) also applies this idea with regard to public supply.
11   Vihanto (1992), Streit and Kiwit (1999), Wohlgemuth (1999).

12 Equivalent norms realize an identical target of regulation but differ in their concrete requirements as to technical norms.
13 Like Buchanan, I use the term public welfare as an abbreviation for "welfare of the individuals of the society".
14 See Sun and Pelkmans (1995: 72).
15 Tjiong's (2002) objections to legal competition largely point to frictions.
16 This could be observed during the German debate on economic reforms in the second half of 2003 when policy makers announced every 24 hours new future rules concerning taxation, the labor market or public health as well as pension insurance.
17 Let me address the argument pointing to informational deficits below.
18 In Sinn's model this is assumed as well.
19 See, for instance, Long and Siebert (1991), Kerber (1998), Sinn (2003) or Wegner (2004).
20 The other EU member states made use of Art 30 (ex 36) of the EU Treaty which allows the prohibition of imports, e.g., if safety of consumers is endangered. Insofar this article provides a safeguard against *governmental* failure. Although Art 30 defines exemptions from mutual recognition and thus brings regulatory competition temporarily to a halt, consumer protection is only possible *because national regulations still exist*, something which critics of regulatory competition are wanting to abolish.
21 It is conceded that also in case of public authorities revealing information is a costly activity.
22 As, e.g., Vanberg and Kerber (1995) point out, institutional competition requires constraints (rules) as does competition in general; Art 30 EC works as a constraint.
23 See also Wilmoswky (1992).
24 Additionally, transnational benefit from the obligation of firms to follow national rules. In reality they have the right to choose among alternative rules (e.g., pharmaceutical firms choose regulatory agencies of other EU-countries and make use of mutual recognition when they introduce new products in the domestic market). In contrast, small and medium sized firms located in one country depend on their own regulation, so that competition is distorted on behalf of transnational firms.
25 A further alternative would be that regulators demand a price for their acivity, which prompts the question why governments should have exclusive access to the market for regulations.
26 See, for instance, Tjiong's (2002) objections against legal competition.

References

Bratton, W.W., McCahery, J., Piciotto, S. and Scott, C. (1996) 'Introduction: Regulatory Competition and Institutional Evolution', in W.W. Bratton, J. McCahery, S. Picciotto and C. Scott (eds) *International Regulatory Competition and Coordination*, Oxford: Clarendon Press, pp. 1–55.
Buchanan, J.M. (1975) *The Limits of Liberty. Between Anarchy and Leviathan*, Chicago: University of Chicago Press.
Dixit, A.K. (1996) *The Making of Economic Policy: A Transaction-Cost Politics Perspective*, London, Cambridge, MA: MIT Press.
Faure, M.G. (2000) 'Product Liability and Product Safety in Europe: Harmonisation or Differentiation?', *Kyklos*, 53: 467–508.
Frey, B.S. and Eichenberger, R. (1995) 'Competition among Jurisdictions: The Idea of FOCI', in L. Gerken (ed.) *Competition among Institutions*, Houndsmill and London: Macmillan, pp. 209–29.
Galli, G. and Pelkmans, J. (eds) (2000) *Regulatory Reform and Competitiveness in Europe, vol. I: Horizontal Issues*, Cheltenham: E. Elgar.

Gerken, L. (ed.) (1995) *Europa zwischen Ordnungswettbewerb und Harmonisierung*, Berlin: Springer.

Kerber, W. (1998) 'Zum Problem einer Wettbewerbsordnung für den Systemwettbewerb', *Jahrbuch für Neue Politische Ökonomie*, 17: 199–230.

Long, N.V. and Siebert, H. (1991) 'Institutional Competition Versus ex-ante Harmonization: The Case of Environmental Policy', *Journal of Institutional and Theoretical Economics* 147: 296–311.

Porter, M.E. and v.d.Linde, C. (1995) 'Toward a New Conception of the Environment-Competitiveness Relationship', *Journal of Economic Perspectives*, 9: 97–118.

Schenk, K., Schmidtchen, D., Streit, M.E. and Vanberg, V.J. (eds) (1998) *Jahrbuch für Neue Politische Ökonomie*, vol. 17, Tübingen: Mohr.

Sinn, H.-W. (1997) 'Das Selektionsprinzip und der Systemwettbewerb', in A. Oberhauser (ed.) *Fiskalföderalismus in Europa*, Berlin: Duncker & Humblot, pp. 9–60.

Sinn, H.-W. (2003) *The New Systems Competition*, Oxford: Blackwell.

Stigler, G.J. (1971) 'The theory of economic regulation', *Bell Journal of Economics and Management Science*, 2: 3–21.

Streit, M.E. and Kiwit, D. (1999) 'Zur Theorie des Systemwettbewerbs', in M.E. Streit and M. Wohlgemuth (eds) *Systemwettbewerb als Herausforderung an Politik und Theorie*. Baden-Baden: Nomos, pp. 13–48.

Streit, M.E. and Mussler, W. (1994) 'The Economic Constitution of the European Community', 3: 319–53.

Streit, M.E. and Wohlgemuth, M. (eds) (1999) *Systemwettbewerb als Herausforderung an Politik und Theorie*, Baden-Baden: Nomos.

Sun, J.-M. and Pelkmans, J. (1995) 'Regulatory Competition in the Single Market', *Journal of Common Market Studies*, 33: 68–89.

Tjiong, H. (2002) 'Breaking the Spell of Regulatory Competition: Reframing the Problem of Regulatory Exit', *Rabels Zeitschrift für ausländisches und internationales Privatrecht*, 66: 66–96.

Trachtman, J.P. (1993) 'International Regulatory Competition, Externalization, and Jurisdiction', *Harvard International Law Journal*, 34: 47–104.

van den Bergh, R. (2000) 'Regulatory Competition in Europe', *Kyklos*, 53: 453–66.

Vihanto, M. (1992) 'Competition Between Local Governments as a Discovery Procedure', *Journal of Institutional and Theoretical Economics*, 148: 411–36.

Vanberg, V.J. (2000) 'Globalization, Democracy, and Citizens' Sovereignty: Can Competition Among Government Enhance Democracy?', *Constitutional Political Economy*, 11: 87–112.

Vanberg, V. and Kerber, W. (1995) 'Competition among Institutions: Evolution within Constraints', in: L. Gerken (ed.) *Competition among Institutions*, Houndsmill, Basingstoke: Macmillan, pp. 35–64.

Wegner, G. (2004) 'Nationalstaatliche Institutionen im Wettbewerb – Wie funktionsfähig ist der Systemwettbewerb?', Berlin: De Gruyter.

Wilmowsky, P. v. (1992) 'Einführung in das Recht der Europäischen Gemeinschaft', *Juristische Ausbildung*, 337–46.

Winkler, T. (1999) 'Die gegenseitige Anerkennung – Achillesferse des Regulierungswettbewerbs', in M.E. Streit and M. Wohlgemuth (eds) *Systemwettbewerb als Herausforderung an Politik und Theorie*, Baden-Baden: Nomos, pp. 103–21.

Wohlgemuth, M. (1999) 'Systemwettbewerb als Entdeckungsverfahren', in M.E. Streit and M. Wohlgemuth (eds) *Systemwettbewerb als Herausforderung an Politik und Theorie*, Baden-Baden: Nomos, pp. 49–70.

10 Human intentionality and design in cultural evolution

Viktor J. Vanberg

10.1 Introduction[1]

To all we know, today's members of the species homo sapiens are genetically not very different from their ancestors ten or twenty thousand years ago.[2] By contrast, modern human life in advanced societies differs dramatically from the living conditions of our early human ancestors. This reflects, of course, the role that cultural evolution plays within the human species and the much higher speed at which cultural evolution proceeds compared to genetic or natural evolution. That the two kinds of evolutionary processes, natural evolution and cultural evolution, are different from each other in important respects is beyond dispute. Controversy exists, however, about what exactly their essential commonalities and their specific differences are. In dispute is, in particular, the question of what, in this regard, the relevant implications of the fact are that intentional human action and human deliberate design are the essential ingredients of cultural evolution.

The purpose of this chapter is to take a closer look at the relation between human intentionality and design on the one side and the "blind" forces of evolution on the other. I have addressed this issue in a number of earlier papers (Vanberg 1994a, 1994b, 1996, 1997, 2002: 25ff., 2004: 31ff.). My interest in discussing it again in this chapter has been provoked by arguments made by Ulrich Witt in several recent contributions (Witt 1997, 2003a, 2003b, 2003c, 2004). Specifically, I want to take a closer look at two issues that Witt raises, namely, first, the issue of whether the role that human intelligence and intentionality play in man-made or cultural evolution requires us to adopt a *non-Darwinian* concept of evolution, and, second, the issue of what the fact that cultural evolution is *man-made* implies for our capacity to "control" the evolutionary process, and for our "responsibility" with regard to its overall outcomes. I have argued in my previous contributions on this issue, and I argue here again, that a Darwinian outlook at cultural evolution is in no way in conflict with the recognition that human intentionality and deliberate design are constitutive of socio-economic evolution in two regards, namely, first, in the sense that the "inputs" that compete in the socio-economic arena may well be deliberately designed and, second, in the sense that humans may choose to deliberately impose constitutional constraints on socio-economic evolution.

10.2   Darwinian theory and cultural evolution

The principal achievement of Darwin's theory of evolution is that it provides an explanatory account of adaptedness in nature without invoking a "cause" to which the capacity for pre-adaptiveness, i.e., the capacity to bring about adaptedness, is already definitionally ascribed, as is the case, for instance, with creationist accounts that attribute adaptedness in nature to the foresight of an omniscient creator.[3] The principal ambition of theories of cultural evolution – like, in particular, F.A. Hayek's approach (Vanberg 1994a, 1994b) – that apply a Darwinian perspective to processes of socio-economic change is to explain adaptedness in social institutions without invoking a cause to which the capacity for pre-adaptiveness is ascribed, as is the case with "rationalist accounts" that attribute adaptedness in cultural achievements to human design, i.e., to the foresightful intervention of the human mind.

As Hayek has often stressed,[4] the idea of an "evolutionary" explanation of adaptedness was, indeed, applied in studies on cultural and social phenomena long before Charles Darwin used it, in a much more explicit and elaborate manner, in the field of biology. Hayek refers, in particular, to the "Mandeville-Hume-Smith-Ferguson tradition", counting the Scottish Moral Philosophers among the "Darwinians before Darwin", and he cites Adam Ferguson's characterization of social institutions as "the result of human action but not of human design" (Hayek 1967: 96) as a paradigmatic statement of their pre-Darwinian evolutionary thought.[5] The point of Ferguson's statement, and the point that modern proponents of a "Darwinian" theory of cultural evolution argue for, is not at all to deny that the achievements of human culture are "man-made" in the sense that they are "the result of human action," and that humans act intentionally and purposefully. Instead, what is claimed is that the "fruits of civilization" like, in particular, social institutions owe their adaptedness or problem-solving capacity not so much to the ingenuity of human foresightedness but to experimentation and tentative trials in which humans found out *ex post* what works and what does not.[6]

The central tenet of Darwin's theory of evolution that Hayek – as well as other proponents of a generalized Darwinism,[7] like Campbell (1965, 1974, 1987) or Popper (1972)[8] – considers applicable to the evolution of culture no less than to natural evolution is the proposition "that a mechanism of reduplication with transmittable variations and competitive selection of those which prove to have a better chance of survival will in the course of time produce a great variety of structures adapted to continuous adjustment to the environment and to each other" (Hayek 1967: 32). In similar terms Campbell (1974: 42) notes that the core principles of Darwinian evolution, namely "(a) Mechanisms for introducing variation; (b) Consistent selection processes; and (c) Mechanisms for preserving and/or propagating the selected variations", can be generalized beyond the biological realm to all processes which increase the "adaptive fit" of a system relative to its environment. In the same spirit Popper advocates a "Darwinian theory of the growth of knowledge" (Popper 1972: 261) according to which the method of trial and error accounts for genetic evolution as well as for cultural learning and for the growth of scientific knowledge: "new reactions, new forms, new organs, new modes of behavior, new hypotheses, are tentatively put forward and controlled by error-elimination" (ibid.: 242).

It is precisely the notion that the Darwinian principles of variation, selection and retention apply equally to cultural evolution as to natural evolution that Witt takes issue with. He criticizes Campbell and others who regard Darwin's general explanatory perspective as "the prototype of an evolutionary theory" (Witt 2003b: 9), and as universally applicable to all evolutionary processes, for failing to see that their "abstract reduction of the Darwinian principles" does not shed off the "domain specific" nature of Darwin's theory of natural selection (Witt 2003b: 12). An evolutionary economics that applies to socio-economic evolution "a heuristic inspired by neo-Darwinian evolutionary biology" (Witt 2003c: 6), and that analyzes man-made, cultural evolution from "an abstract analogy to the domain-specific model of evolutionary biology" (ibid.: 5) is, in Witt's view, in danger of getting misguided in its research efforts, in similar ways in which neoclassical economics got misguided by adopting the mechanical metaphor (Witt 2003c: 4).

According to Witt, an evolutionary economics that is to avoid the inherent biases of the "still domain-specific" Darwinian analogy must adopt a "general, domain-unspecific conception of evolution" (Witt 2003b: 28), by which he means one that focuses on "the emergence and the dissemination of novelty" as the "characteristic, domain-transcending features of evolution" (Witt 2003c: 7).[9] By contrast to empirically testable conjectures, definitions – including "conceptions of evolution" – cannot be right or wrong. They can only be judged in terms of their usefulness for the analytical purpose they are supposed to serve. Whether one considers Witt's suggested "domain-unspecific conception of evolution" superior to the Darwinian concept will depend on the kinds of questions that one expects a theory of evolution to answer. Witt's own declared interest is in explaining "how novelty is being generated",[10] and for such explanatory interest his "generic" definition of evolution may well be appropriate. Yet, as noted above, the principal ambition of a Darwinian theory of evolution is to explain *adaptedness*, and those who advocate, with such explanatory interest in mind, a Darwinian approach to man-made or cultural evolution cannot ignore the selection-principle, because it is this very principle that plays the critical role in any account of adaptedness that does not presume pre-adaptedness.[11]

Apparently it is the "selection"-part in the "abstract reduction of the Darwinian principles" that Witt finds objectionable, as a "domain-specific" feature, and that he, therefore, excludes from his "generic" definition. This raises the question of what, exactly, he considers to be "domain-specific" about the "selection-metaphor" (Witt 2003b: 29fn.). If his charge were to mean that Darwinian natural selection of genetically coded features is biology-specific one could hardly object. But, as Witt knows, advocates of a Darwinian theory of cultural evolution interpret "selection" in a much more general sense. Apart from his plea for a shift of emphasis from selection to the generation of novelty, the reason why Witt rejects a Darwinian approach to cultural evolution is his view that "the mechanisms and regularities of cultural evolution differ from those of natural evolution" (Witt 2003b: 15f.) and that, therefore, "many facets of cultural evolution require explanatory theories of their own" (Witt 2003c: 8). To this argument, to which I return in Section 10.3 below, Witt adds the charge that, as an account of cultural evolution, "Darwinian theory is not sufficient" (ibid.). If this is meant to say that the general Darwinian principles of variation, selection and retention by themselves are "not sufficient" to explain any particular instances of cultural evolution, Witt is surely right. But this verdict applies no less to biological applications of these principles. There is, in this regard, no categorical difference between a Darwinian approach to natural evolution and a Darwinian approach to cultural evolution. In both realms the Darwinian principles provide no more than a general theoretical perspective that needs to be enriched by specific conjectures whenever it is applied to particular instances. As Hayek has noted, this fact was well recognized by Darwin himself who stated in a letter that "all the labour consists in the application of the theory" (Hayek 1967: 32fn.).[12] This point has been well stated by Hodgson in response to Witt's argument:

> 'Universal Darwinism' upholds that there is a core set of general Darwinian principles that, along with auxiliary explanations specific to each scientific domain, may apply to a wide range of phenomena. Accordingly, even if the detailed mechanisms of change at the social level are quite different from those described in biology, socio-economic evolution is still Darwinian in several important senses. (...) Acceptance of Universal Darwinism does not provide all the necessary causal mechanism and explanations for the social scientist, nor obviate the elaborate additional work of specific investigation and detailed causal explanation in the social sphere (...) Even in biology, Darwinian principles provide a general explanatory framework into which particular explanations have to be placed. Universal Darwinism cannot itself give us a full, detailed explanation of evolutionary processes or outcomes. It is more a meta-theoretical framework than a complete theory.
>
> (Hodgson 2004: 2)[13]

10.3 "Blind" evolution and intentional human action

When Witt asserts that "culture, institutions, technology, and economic activities evolve according to their own regularities" (Witt 2003c: 8) what he primarily appears to have in mind is the role that human intentionality and purposefulness play in "man-made" or cultural evolution by contrast to natural evolution. As he puts it:

> Humans have sufficient intelligence and incentives to anticipate and avoid selection effects. The selection metaphor may therefore divert attention from what seems crucially important for economic evolution – the role played by cognition, learning, and growing knowledge. Adaptations which result from cognitive processes like hypothesis formation and learning from insight follow their own regularities (ibid.: 4f.).[14]

Here, again, one may well agree with Witt's premise, namely that human intentionality plays the crucial role in cultural evolution, without arriving at the same conclusion that he draws, namely that, because it is driven by intentional human actions, cultural evolution cannot be adequately analyzed in Darwinian terms.[15]

It is, in particular, the emphasis that a Darwinian approach puts on the "blindness" of variation (Campbell 1987), i.e., on the absence of pre-adaptedness in the generation of novelty, that Witt finds inappropriately applied to the socio-economic or cultural realm where intelligent human beings act on insight and pre-meditated plans.[16] Because humans respond to the selection forces they face by deliberately designed and intelligently chosen strategies rather than by "blind" random-trials, the "crucial test criterion for Darwin's theory of evolution" (Witt 2003c: 5) is, according to Witt, not met in the case of cultural evolution, namely "the absence of a systematic feedback between selection and variation" (ibid.). As Witt (ibid.) argues: "Such a feedback is characteristic, e.g., for economic evolution where people invent their way out when threatened by 'selection forces'. In the presence of a systematic feedback, the distinction between variation and selection, which is a fundamental premise of the neo-Darwinian theory, is no longer valid."[17]

One cannot properly assess Witt's argument without taking a closer look at the precise meaning in which the notion of "blind variation" is actually used in Darwinian theory. That humans act on the knowledge they possess and that, in this sense, their intentionally chosen strategies are not "blind", but informed by *existing knowledge*, is certainly true. Yet, in the sense of taking advantage of existing "knowledge", variation in natural evolution is not completely "blind" either. As J.H. Holland, advocate of a general Darwinian theory of "adaptive systems" (Holland 1995, 1998), has pointed out, the principal source of innovation in biological evolution, i.e., the source that accounts by far for most of the variation that occurs, is not random mutation but cross-over, i.e., the recombination of genetically coded information (Holland 1995: 65f.). Mutations result from simple errors in the copying of genetic codes and are, as such, a completely "blind" and "undirected", random source of variation and innovation. As Holland (1996: 291) puts it, mutation "is a history-independent operation that does not make use of the system's knowledge or past history". By contrast, cross-over takes advantage of the "background knowledge" of past adaptations. It generates new variants by recombining components of genetic programs that have proven to be successful in the past.

That variation in natural evolution, as far as it results from cross-over, is, in the sense explained, not entirely "blind" does not mean, however, that it cannot be said to be "blind" in another sense. To be sure, the recombination of components of the "knowledge" incorporated in past adaptations is a more likely source of "successful" innovations than pure random mutation, since, by contrast to the haphazard nature of the latter, it uses as its building material what has already proven to be successful. Yet, the use of such building material cannot guarantee, of course, the success of the newly created combination. To the extent that the recombination of components of past adaptations results in genuinely new variants their success cannot be known in advance. In other words, even though such recombination can take advantage of existing knowledge, it is still "blind" in the sense that its products are tentative conjectures the validity of which can only be recognized ex post.

Notwithstanding the much richer sense in which humans can take advantage of existing knowledge in their problem-solving efforts, human intentional, pre-meditated innovations cannot be but "blind" in the same sense, even if they represent, as Witt would probably argue,[18] "*directed* recombinations of already existing elements" by contrast to the *undirected* recombination of genetic cross-over. That we try to make the best use of what we know in designing novel strategies does not mean that we know in advance whether our conjectural trials will work. To be sure, pre-meditation and mental experiments allow us to reject pre-dictably unsuccessful recombinations without trying them out in practice. Yet, to the extent that our new strategies are genuine innovations, in the sense of venturing into unknown territory, they cannot be but "blind". This is the point that Campbell wants to stress when he insists on the "blindness" of all evolutionary processes, including "man-made" evolution. While acquired knowledge of contingencies in the environment can allow an organism to act on "foresight", any *increase* in knowledge, so he argues, can be based on nothing other than "blind variation",[19] in the sense that real gains in knowledge "must have been the product of explo-rations going beyond the limits of foresight or prescience" (Campbell 1987: 92).

Human intelligence and rationality is subject to Darwinian principles not only in the sense explained above but also in the sense that the knowledge on which human intentional action is based is itself the product of evolutionary learning.[20] That all knowledge about the world that assists organisms in coping with the problems they face, including human knowledge, can be viewed as the product of evolutionary processes is, of course, the central tenet of *evolutionary epistemology*, a research paradigm that counts Campbell as well as Hayek and Popper among its principal contributors. The Darwinian method of "learning" by trial and error-elimination is, as Popper suggests, essentially the same at all levels at which adaptive learning takes place, from "the level of the enzyme and the gene ... up to the articulate and critical language of our theories" (Popper 1972: 149), even if its particular manifestations may be quite different at the various levels.[21] One such significant difference is, as Campbell (1987: 93) notes, that "higher evolu-tionary developments shift a part of the locus of adaptation from a trial and error of whole organisms or gene pools, over to processes occurring within the single organism."

As the above arguments suggest, the undisputed fact that human intelligence is the distinctive ingredient of cultural evolution does not require us to abandon the Darwinian paradigm but, instead, requires us carefully to distinguish between dif-ferent processes of variation and selection that operate in an interconnected way in what we may inclusively call the human cultural realm. We need to distinguish, in particular, between processes of variation and selection that operate *within* intelligent human agents and the *external* selection forces they are exposed to in their environment. This point has been made by Geisendorf (2003) in a critical comment on Ulrich Witt's plea for a non-Darwinian theory of socio-economic evolution. As Geisendorf (ibid.: 15) notes, one may well agree with Witt's emphasis on the significance of *internal* selection in the human cultural realm without drawing the conclusion that "Darwinian" *external* selection is no longer a defining characteristic of evolution in this realm.

Intelligent human beings can indeed, so Geisendorf (ibid.: 14) argues, premeditate their responses to problems they face, try out in their thought potential alternative courses of actions, and choose or "select" the alternative that they expect to be most suitable.[22] Yet, all this does not change the fact that their conjectural problem-solutions, however carefully they may have been designed, are subject to the external competitive selection that operates in the realm where they meet other conjectural solutions put forward by other agents. As Geisendorf (ibid.: 11) suggests, instead of looking at internal selection as an alternative to external selection one should look at economic evolution as a multilevel process where, for instance, "external market selection" is preceded by various selection processes that consecutively pre-select what will be passed on to the next level of competitive selection, from the selection among competing ideas in the minds of individual agents involved in production processes to the selection by collective choices, both formal and informal, that take place at various organizational levels within firms. And, as Geisendorf rightly adds, the selection processes at these various levels need not always operate in harmony with each other in the sense of applying consistent criteria for "success".

10.4   Cultural evolution and human purposes

Natural evolution is not only "blind" in the sense explained above, it is purposeless. There is no goal at which it is aiming and against which it could be said to "progress". It is an open-ended process, driven from behind by blindly generated innovations, a process in which the problem-environment to which organisms need to adapt is itself constantly transformed by the new problem-solutions that are discovered. A question that Ulrich Witt raises is whether or not in this regard, too, Darwinian principles or mechanisms are more descriptive of natural evolution than of man-made or cultural evolution. As he notes:

> Although Darwin (...) speculated on evolutionary progress (...) he clearly recognized that there was no final goal served by these mechanisms, as there was no being whose intentions and preferences could be identified with the driving forces of evolution in nature. Socio-economic evolutionary change, by contrast, involves human creativity and cognition. The driving force of recombinatory search for novelty here is human endeavor.
>
> (Witt 1997: 14)

In my understanding of his arguments, what Witt wants to suggest is that, because human intentional action is the "driving force" of socio-economic evolution, "human intelligence" should also in some sense take "responsibility" for the overall results that this man-made evolutionary process produces.[23] Witt's interest in this issue appears to be motivated, in particular, by his concern with harmful unintended consequences of modern industrial production and economic organization that threaten the long-term viability of our ecological as well as our social environment.[24] In his view we ought to be suspicious about an economic policy that takes a too blue-eyed, optimistic attitude towards human innovative experimenting and that is too careless about the risks of innovations with potentially detrimental consequences.[25] And he suggests, in particular, that one should take a second, and more critical, look at the principles of consumer sovereignty and of freedom of contract that belong to the traditional core doctrine of a subjectivist, individualist economics (Witt 2003a: 91, 2004: 40).

Even if his general outlook may appear to some of us overly pessimistic,[26] the issue that Witt raises is, no doubt, an important one. Most of us will readily agree that it would be grossly inappropriate and irresponsible to look at socio-economic evolution simply as a "natural event" that we let run its course without taking steps to prevent it from producing outcomes that are detrimental to human interests. And hardly anybody would be prepared to endorse a "laissez faire regime" that sets no limits to innovative exploration, irrespective of the risks involved. That in this sense we ought to seek to "control" cultural evolution is scarcely controversial. The critical question is how such "control" can be and should be exercised. And to this question, I would like to suggest, there are two principal answers, answers that can be associated with two fundamentally different approaches to policy in general and economic policy in particular, namely *utilitarian welfare economics* on the one side and *contractarian constitutional economics* on the other.

The utilitarian welfarist approach is *outcome-oriented* in the sense that it looks at economic policy as an instrument for *directly* bringing about socio-economic outcomes that are deemed desirable in terms of some measure of "social welfare". Alternative policy measures are compared in terms of their anticipated welfare effects with the aim of identifying the one that promises maximum benefit. By contrast, the contractarian constitutionalist approach is *process-oriented* in the sense that, rather than seeking to control outcomes directly, it seeks to affect outcomes *indirectly*, by subjecting the processes from which outcomes emerge to general rules that promise to generate overall desirable *patterns of outcomes*. Contractarian constitutional economists look at economic policy primarily as a means by which the members-citizens of a polity choose the "rules of the game" under which they want to live, rules that qualify as desirable to the extent that they serve the *common constitutional interests* of, and are therefore agreeable to, the respective constituency. While welfare economics with its maximization-paradigm seeks to identify welfare-maximizing policy measures, constitutional economics with its "gains from joint commitment"-paradigm seeks to identify mutually advantageous rules of the game.

The outcome-oriented approach of utilitarian welfare economics cannot be reconciled with an evolutionary perspective. Its claim to decide in advance which among potential alternative courses of action is "best" is in fundamental conflict with the essential attribute of evolutionary processes, namely their open-endedness. The ambition to control outcomes directly leaves no room for evolutionary exploration. It negates the very role that competition plays as a discovery procedure in any evolutionary process. By contrast, the process-oriented, contractarian constitutionalist approach is perfectly compatible with an evolutionary perspective. It seeks to "control" socio-economic processes in a manner that does not interfere with their evolutionary character. It does not seek to predetermine the outcomes they produce but, instead, seeks to "channel" them by imposing "rules of the game" that are expected to guide their explorative potential in beneficial directions. The constitutional method of "control" defines limits for innovative experimenting by imposing rule-constraints on the permissible choice of strategies, but it leaves room for exploration and discovery.

Witt rightly points out that human innovativeness results not only in "cumulative problem solving and knowledge generation" but also in "a successive creation of new problems" (Witt 2003b: 17) and that, accordingly, the challenge to efforts in political control is to secure an adequate balance between "problem solving and problem generating" (ibid.: 18) or between "favorable and unfavorable consequences of innovations" (Witt 2003a: 90). Yet, his inquiry into potential answers to this challenge and the conclusion he draws suffer, in my view, from a too narrowly focused critique of shortcomings of the utilitarian welfarist perspective and from his failure to consider the contractarian constitutionalist perspective as a potential alternative.[27]

Apart from pointing to the "problems of interpersonal comparisons" (ibid.) and the "epistemological problems" (ibid.) that a utilitarian welfarist approach faces,[28] Witt concentrates his critique specifically on the fact that human desires are largely learned and subject to variable cultural influences, a fact that, as he supposes, gives reason to question an individualist-subjectivist perspective that takes individuals' *present desires* as the relevant criterion for judging policy measures. The "distinction between the inherited parts of the individuals' preferences on the one hand and the culturally determined, and potentially idiosyncratic, learned parts on the other", so Witt (1997: 19) argues, "may raise doubts as to whether a subjectivist interpretation of hedonism is useful at all".[29] And it suggests, as he supposes, that we may have to interpret "the hedonistic core of economic theory in a new, non-subjectivist, way" (ibid.: 21).

Witt is surely right when he argues that we have no reason to expect increased "happiness" from a socio-economic process that provides us with more and more means to satisfy desires that we would not have, had we not learned, by cultural conditioning, to harbor them, and when he suspects that, on the contrary, there is "reason to believe that we may not feel happier after becoming used to the future achievements than we feel right now" (Witt 2003a: 91).[30] He surely is also right when he argues that, because our future preferences may be different from our present preferences, the latter may not be a perfect guide for policy choices that are to shape our future living conditions.[31] But, here again, the critical question is which conclusions we are supposed to draw from such insights. What do they imply for the ways in which we ought to seek to "control" socio-economic evolution? The principal conclusion that Witt draws is that "radical preference subjectivism and its more practical relatives, consumer sovereignty or, for that matter, voter sovereignty, may therefore no longer provide the relevant normative measuring rod" (ibid.). Noting that "a debate on what may instead be a proper frame of orientation for normative judgements about human choices is only just about to begin" (ibid.), he suggests, as potential candidate for an alternative outlook, "a more objective utilitarian approach" (ibid.) in which "possible regulation of innovativeness would not be assessed exclusively according to the current state of our preferences" (ibid.) but in terms of "educated guesses ... about how we would assess the likely outcomes in the light of the probable future state of preferences" (ibid.).

Witt is not very explicit about what a "more objective utilitarian approach" that looks not at "the current state of our preferences" but relies on "educated guesses about the future state of preferences" is meant to imply in terms of practical political decision-making. We can be assured that he does not have in mind the ideal, dating back to Plato's "philosopher king", of an "enlightened avant-garde" that decides what is good for the "people", no matter what they think is good for them in terms of their "current state of preferences", an ideal that could hardly be reconciled with the fundamental democratic ideal that all legitimate political power originates with the people. The challenge that Witt would have to answer is, what his "more objective" approach can mean, in procedural terms, for a democratic polity as a "citizens' cooperative" or, as J. Rawls (1971: 84) has put it, "as a cooperative venture for mutual advantage". The citizens-members of democratic polities are the principals in whose name political power is exercised, and it is difficult to see what other normative standard can be consistently applied in such polities than the preferences of the citizens themselves. And, even though we should wish these preferences not to be *shortsighted*, they cannot be anything other than their "*current*" preferences, i.e., the preferences that determine their decisions at the time they are asked to choose among potential policy options. To be sure, citizens are well advised to critically reflect the preferences they harbor at any point in time in light of the best available knowledge about the "human condition" and about predictable future contingencies, including future desires. But whatever they may prudently do to let their policy choices, as far as this is humanly possible, be guided by enlightened, far-sighted and educated preferences, this cannot change the elementary fact that even their most "educated preferences" cannot be anything other than their current preferences.

The difficulties that Witt rightly identifies with the subjectivist version of a utilitarian welfarist approach, and the apparent difficulties that his own, "more objective" utilitarian approach faces, can, as I would like to suggest, be avoided by adopting a contractarian constitutionalist perspective. As noted above, by contrast to the utilitarian welfarist concern with the direct assessment of outcomes, the contractarian constitutionalist approach directs attention to the *choice of rules* as the principal instrument through which citizens can seek to secure mutual gains from joint commitment. It does not ask, and does not claim to be able to answer, the question of how the welfare effects of specific innovations can be assessed. It asks, instead, the question of what general rules for dealing with the promises and potential risks of innovations citizens may agree upon, because – as judged by the best knowledge available – they promise to bring about a more favorable balance of prospective advantages and disadvantages of innovative exploration than feasible alternative rules. And it alerts us to the fact that the players may well be dissatisfied with particular outcomes that result in the course of playing the "game", but still may have good reasons to agree to its rules because their over-all working properties are more attractive to them than what is to be expected from potential alternative rules of the game.

The important distinction between dissatisfaction with particular outcomes of a game and dissatisfaction with the game as such does not seem to be fully appreciated when Witt (2003a: 90) indiscriminately refers to "devaluations of invest-ments" as well as to the "danger of possible damages and social costs ... which neither the innovator nor society have anticipated" as negative consequences of innovations. It should be noted, though, that there is a categorical difference between the two kinds of "disadvantages" in the sense that the first is an inherent aspect of market competition while the latter is subject to the specific "rules of the market" that people choose as precautions against such "danger". The very productivity of the "game of the market" depends on its openness for the discovery of "superior" products and methods of production. In agreeing to play the market game and in committing to its rules, people accept the risk that their investments may be devalued by such discoveries. The productive advantages of the market game and this risk are two sides of the same coin. One cannot have the one with-out the other, and fairness in playing the "market game" requires all players to accept this risk.[32] By contrast, the "danger of possible damages" from innovations is contingent on the particular "rules of the game" – e.g., the rules of liability – according to which the members of a polity wish to play the "market game". Depending on their attitude to risk they may want to choose more or less restric-tive rules.

To be sure, the constitutional method of "controlling" cultural evolution by sub-mitting it to certain rules cannot provide perfect assurance that human innovative-ness, even if it can be effectively confined to the constitutionally permitted range of exploration,[33] will not produce novelties the detrimental consequences of which become apparent only after the fact. The history of modern technology provides numerous examples of innovations that were originally welcomed as blessings and the downsides of which were only recognized years or decades later. But there is no other feasible alternative method that could provide such perfect protection either. We have certainly not the option to bring evolution to a halt. And whatever other method or procedure we may adopt to "control" evolution, it cannot take advan-tage of any other knowledge than what is available at the time we make our policy choices. The only alternative available to us is, either, to rely on rules that, accord-ing to past experience and to our best knowledge, promise an overall favorable balance of advantages and risks, or to seek to control innovations on the basis of a case-by-case assessment of their specific welfare effects. With its ambition to pro-vide such assessment the welfare economics approach all too easily falls victim to the vice that Hayek (1978) has chastised as "pretence of knowledge".

Recognition of the limits of our knowledge and foresight requires us to admit that there is no other feasible way for us to "control" cultural evolution other than by seeking to secure a favorable balance between the potential advantages and disadvantages of innovations, using our available knowledge in adopting constitutional constraints that "channel" the process of experimental exploration in a manner that promises to protect us from *foreseeable* damages without closing off the prospects of discovering superior solutions to the problems we face. As different groups of people may well have different attitudes towards risks, some may choose to define the constraints on innovations in their respective polities more narrowly than others. And different polities may learn from their alternative constitutional experiments which regimes allow for a socio-economic development that, in terms of its overall attributes, is more serviceable to human needs. As long as we are not dealing with risks of global dimensions, allowing for such alternative constitutional regimes is surely the best way for humans with imperfect knowledge about the consequences of their choices and about their own future preferences to seek deliberate "control" of cultural evolution.

10.5   Conclusion

Explanations from design and evolutionary explanations are commonly contrasted as alternative accounts of observed adaptedness or *Zweckmäßigkeit*. It is not surprising, therefore, that much of the debate on cultural evolution centers around the issue of whether – and if so, how – a recognition of the obvious role that human intentional and intelligent action plays in socio-economic development can be reconciled with the notion of a "blind" evolutionary process that is part of the Darwinian paradigm. In this chapter I have taken issue with arguments that Ulrich Witt has advanced in a number of recent articles in which he suggests that, because human intentionality is the principal driving force of man-made or cultural evolution, the Darwinian paradigm may be misleading rather than enlightening and ought to be replaced by a non-Darwinian concept of evolution. I have sought to defend a Darwinian approach to cultural evolution as it has been advocated by authors like F.A. Hayek, D.T. Campbell and K.R. Popper against Witt's arguments, in particular in two regards. I have argued, firstly, that the fact that humans respond in a deliberate and planned manner to the problems they face is perfectly compatible with a view that emphasizes the conjectural nature of their problem-solutions and the open-endedness of the process in which the validity of their conjectural solutions is tested. And I have argued, secondly, that the notion of an open-ended evolutionary process is equally compatible with the idea that humans may seek to "control" socio-economic development by imposing constitutional constraints that serve to "channel" evolution in ways that are serviceable to human needs.

Notes

1 An anonymous referee's insightful comments are gratefully acknowledged.
2 U. Witt (2003b: 16): "Because natural selection is no longer a source of (rapid) systematic change, the genetic basis can be argued to be much the same as that in early human phylogeny."

3 E. Mayr (1992: 134): "There is adaptedness (Kant's Zweckmässigkeit) in living nature but Darwin showed that its origin can be explained materialistically."

4 For references see Vanberg (1994a: 172f.).

5 The complete sentence in Ferguson's treatise reads: "Every step and every movement of the multitude, even in what are termed enlightened ages, are made with equal blindness to the future; and nations stumble upon establishments, which are indeed the result of human action, but not the execution of any human design" (Ferguson 1980 [1767]: 122).

6 In a paper on the issue of group selection in cultural evolution Witt (2002: 2) approvingly summarizes Hayek's principal conjecture: "Since the complexity of both the price mechanism and systems of rules of conduct make it extremely difficult for the human mind to comprehend both, they cannot be the result of deliberate design and choice."

7 What I call "generalized Darwinism" is a close relative of what is known as "Universal Darwinism", a perspective about which G. Hodgson (2004) notes: "The term 'Universal Darwinism' was coined by Richard Dawkins. It suggests that the core Darwinian principles of variation, replication and selection may apply not only to biological phenomena, but to other open and evolving systems, including human culture or social evolution." – Hodgson (2002: 270): "Universal Darwinism upholds that there is a core set of general Darwinian principles that, *along with auxiliary explanations specific to each scientific domain*, may apply to a wide range of phenomena."

8 For references and a more detailed discussion see Vanberg (1994a: 174ff.; 2002: 19ff., 33ff.; 2004).

9 Witt (2003b: 12): "I submit that the generation of novelty is generic to all cases of evolution." – See also Witt (1997: 10f.): "a generic feature of evolution is the capacity of a system to generate and disseminate novelty within its domain." Witt (ibid.: 11) adds the comment: "Presumably, the way in which novelty is generated is similar in all domains, namely some sort of directed or undirected recombination of already existing elements which creates a variant which was not there before."

10 Witt (2003b: 13) notes that there are "two tasks of any theory of evolution: (i) to explain how ... novelty is being generated (...) and (ii) to explain what happens as a consequence." In his view it is the first task that deserves more attention than it traditionally receives: "The bulk of explanatory efforts usually focuses on the second task. The second task is indeed much less complicated" (ibid.).

11 G. Hodgson (2002: 264) and S. Geisendorf (2003: 6) raise the same objection against Witt's concept.

12 Hayek (1967: 32): "The basic conception of the theory is exceedingly simple and it is only in its application to the concrete circumstances that its extraordinary fertility and the range of phenomena for which it can account manifests itself."

13 See also Hodgson (2002: 272).

14 See also Witt (2004: 36).

15 As S. Geisendorf (2003: 11) rightly notes, one may well acknowledge that there are relevant differences between biological and economic evolution and still insist that the fundamental mechanisms of selection, recombination and imperfect replication do operate in both realms.

16 The Darwinian view with its emphasis on "more or less blind variational mechanisms and natural selection" is in Witt's (1997: 13) view not applicable to the cultural realm where human purposeful action introduces an element of "directional change."

17 See also Witt (2003b: 29fn.)

18 See (fn. 8 above).

19 Campbell (1987: 91): "A blind-variation-and-selective-retention process is fundamental to all inductive achievements, to all genuine increases in knowledge, to all increases in fit of system to environment."

20 For a detailed discussion of this claim see Vanberg (2002, 2004).

21 As Campbell (1974: 413) puts it, the emphasis of evolutionary epistemology is on the argument "that evolution – even in its biological aspects – is a knowledge process, and that the natural-selection paradigm for such knowledge increments can be generalized to other epistemic activities such as learning, thought, and science."

22 As I have noted elsewhere (Vanberg 1996: 691f.): "Human actors seek what they consider success, and they use their accumulated knowledge to come up with strategies that they expect to be successful. In this sense deliberate human problem-solving is, to be sure, always *looking ahead*. But such 'looking ahead' should not be confused with pre-adaptedness. What our 'looking ahead' does is to use our accumulated knowledge of the world for the purpose of a mental trial and error process in which we already eliminate, before acting, those 'errors,' or unsuccessful trials, that we think we can identify without actually trying them out, based on predictions of their likely outcome. If, with regard to human action, the 'blind-variation' assumption of evolutionary theory appears inappropriate, one has to consider two things. First, observed behavior reflects the already 'pre-selected' outcome of a mental selection process, and this mental process, in turn, reflects an 'adaptiveness' that is the result of a *past stream of trials and errors*. Second, the experience-based mental selection process cannot assure success but only serve as a guide. Its usefulness depends on the applicability of past experience to new situations. The 'mentally pre-selected' trials always remain conjectural experiments, and many of the actual experiments that their originators hope to be successful, in fact turn out to be failures. Firms go bankrupt, investments turn into losses, the purposeful design of the decision makers notwithstanding."

23 Since cultural evolution is brought about by human intelligence, Witt (2004: 44) argues, there is the "issue of legitimization", namely whether the same human intelligence must not also face the question of whether the evolution it produces is desirable ("wenn kulturelle Evolution ein von menschlicher Intelligenz hervorgebrachtes Phänomen ist, sollte derselben Intelligenz dann nicht auch die Frage gestellt werden, ob und unter welchen Bedingungen die hervorgebrachten Entwicklung auch wünschenswert ist?").

24 Witt (2004: 40): "Der 'industrielle Metabolismus' ... droht früher oder später die ökologischen Systembedingungen nachhaltig zu stören. ... Eine berechtigte Frage ist daher, ob das gegenwärtige Volumen anthropogener Produktion solche Risiken wert ist ... . Anders gefragt: wer wünscht eigentlich die kulturelle Evolution, die sich eingestellt hat und die den beschriebenen Wandel der Produktion mit allen seinen Effekten bewirkt hat?" – In addition to ecological threats Witt mentions the inequality in the "global distribution of income" as another example of problematic consequences of cultural evolution.

25 As Witt (2003a: 90) states: "In the light of this past experience (i.e., of beneficial consequences of innovations, V.V.), economic policymaking today encourages innovations grosso modo. Yet innovations can also have unpleasant consequences." While acknowledging the "rising standard of living" that socio-economic evolution has produced in the past Witt (ibid.) warns: "But it would be a naive extrapolation to take it for granted as a concomitant of future innovativeness."

26 Witt seems to look at human inventiveness more with distrust than with hope when he notes that "there is always potential danger lurking in everything that has not been previously secured by experience ... danger of possible damages and social costs ... which neither the innovator nor society have anticipated" (Witt 2003a: 90).

27 With this I refer to Witt's contributions that I discuss in this chapter. At the conference for which the chapter was prepared Witt pointed out to me that in Witt (1996) he has explicitly discussed the "innovation issue" from a contractarian perspective.

28 Witt (2003a: 90) points to two principal obstacles that a utilitarian welfarist approach faces: "First, because the future balance of benefits and (social) costs of innovativeness cannot be anticipated. Second, because the personal distribution of any net benefit of innovativeness in the future is indeterminate."

29 Witt (1997: 19f.) continues: "A better understanding of the interaction between genetic endowment and culturally conditioned learning on the basis of a Darwinian world view may well provide criteria for assessing, in a more objectivist way, the needs economic evolution serves, and why (and in which sense) this should be desirable."
30 On this issue see also Witt (2004: 44).
31 Witt (2003a: 91): "Not surprisingly, normative judgements on economic policymaking in the presence of changing individual preferences have not yet been investigated."
32 As the theory of *rent-seeking* emphasizes, players can, of course, lobby governments for special privileges that allow them, at the expense of other players, to enjoy the benefits of the market's productivity while avoiding its accompanying risks. Yet, such rent-seeking behavior is nothing other than cheating on the rules on which the "market-game" is based.
33 Even the best conceivable constitutional system is, of course, not immune against illegal practices. This is true for innovative no less than for conventional activities.

References

Campbell, D.T. (1965) 'Variation and Selective Retention in Socio-Cultural Evolution', in H.R. Barringer, G.I. Blanksten and R.W. Mack (eds) *Social Change in Developing Areas*, Cambridge, MA: Schenkman, pp. 19–49.

Campbell, D.T. (1974) 'Evolutionary Epistemology', in P.A. Schlipp (ed.) *The Philosophy of Karl Popper*, La Salle, IL: Open Court, pp. 313–463.

Campbell, D.T. (1987) 'Blind Variation and Selective Retention in Creative Thought as in Other Knowledge Processes', in G. Radnitzky and W. W. Bartley, III (eds), *Evolutionary Epistemology, Rationality, and the Sociology of Knowledge*, La Salle, IL: Open Court, pp. 91–114.

Ferguson, A. (1980, orig. 1767) *An Essay on the History of Civil Society*, New Brunswick and London: Transaction Books.

Geisendorf, S. 'Der ökonomische Evolutionsbegriff: Biologische Metapher oder endogen bewirkter Wandel?', paper presented at "Workshop zur Evolutorischen Ökonomik", Buchenbach, 14–17 May 2003.

Hayek, F.A. (1967) *Studies in Philosophy, Politics and Economics*, Chicago: The University of Chicago Press.

Hayek, F.A. (1978) *New Studies in Philosophy, Politics, Economics and the History of Ideas*, London: Routledge & Kegan Paul, pp. 23–34.

Hodgson, G.M. (2002) 'Darwinism in economics: from analogy to ontology', *Journal of Evolutionary Economics*, 12: 259–81.

Hodgson, G.M. (2004) 'Generalizing Darwinism to Social Evolution: Genesis and Meaning', *Working Paper*, The Business School, University of Herfordshire.

Holland, J.H. (1995) *Hidden Order: How Adaptation Builds Complexity*, Reading, MA: Helix Books.

Holland, J.H. (1996) 'The Rationality of Adaptive Agents', in K.J. Arrow, E. Colombatto, M. Perlman and C. Schmidt (eds) *The Rational Foundations of Economic Behavior – Proceedings of the IEA Conference held in Turin, Italy*, New York: St. Martin's Press, pp. 281–301.

Holland, J.H. (1998) *Emergence: From Chaos to Order*, Reading, MA: Perseus Books.

Mayr, E. (1992) 'The Idea of Teleology', *Journal of the History of Ideas*, 53: 117–35.

Popper, K.R. (1972) *Objective Knowledge – An Evolutionary Approach*, Oxford: Clarendon Press.

Rawls, J. (1971) *A Theory of Justice*, Cambridge, MA: Harvard University Press.

Vanberg, V.J. (1994a) 'Cultural Evolution, Collective Learning, and Constitutional Design', in D. Reisman (ed.) *Economic Thought and Political Theory*, Dordrecht, Boston, London: Kluwer Academic Publishers, pp. 171–204.

Vanberg, V.J. (1994b) 'Hayek's Legacy and the Future of Liberal Thought: Rational Liberalism vs. Evolutionary Agnosticism', *Journal des Economistes et des Etudes Humaines* 5, pp. 451–481; reprinted in V.J. Vanberg (ed.)(2004) *The Constitution of Markets – Essays in Political Economy*, London and New York: Routledge.

Vanberg, V.J. (1996) 'Institutional Evolution Within Constraints', *Journal of Institutional and Theoretical Economics*, 152: 690–6.

Vanberg, V.J. (1997) 'Institutional Evolution Through Purposeful Selection: The Constitutional Economics of John R. Commons', *Constitutional Political Economy*, 8: 105–22.

Vanberg, V.J. (2002) 'Rational Choice vs. Program-Based Behavior. Alternative Theoretical Approaches and their Relevance for the Study of Institutions', *Rationality and Society*, 14, 7–54.

Vanberg, V.J. (2004) 'The Rationality Postulate in Economics: Its Ambiguity, its Deficiency and its Evolutionary Alternative', *Journal of Economic Methodology*, 11: 19–47.

Witt, U. (1996) 'Innovations, externalities and the problem of economic progress', *Public Choice*, 89: 113–30.

Witt, U. (1997) 'Economics and Darwinism', *Papers on Economics & Evolution* # 9705, Jena: Max-Planck-Institute of Economics.

Witt, U. (2002) 'Social Cognitive Learning and Group Selection – A Hayekian Model of Societal Evolution', *Papers on Economics & Evolution* # 0110, Jena: Max-Planck-Institute of Economics.

Witt, U. (2003a) 'Economic policy making in evolutionary perspective', *Journal of Evolutionary Economics*, 13, 77–94.

Witt, U. (2003b) 'Evolutionary economics and the extension of evolution to the economy', in U. Witt (ed.) *The Evolving Economy – Essays in the Evolutionary Approach to Economics*, Cheltenham: Edward Elgar, pp. 3–34.

Witt, U. (2003c) 'On the Proper Interpretation of "Evolution" in Economics and its Implications, e.g. for Production Theory', *Papers on Economics & Evolution* # 0305, Jena: Max-Planck-Institute of Economics.

Witt, U. (2004) 'Beharrung und Wandel – ist wirtschaftliche Evolution theoriefähig?', *Erwägen, Wissen, Ethik*, 15, 33 45.

Index

For Product Safety Concerns and Information please contact our EU
representative GPSR@taylorandfrancis.com
Taylor & Francis Verlag GmbH, Kaufingerstraße 24, 80331 München, Germany